T0295713

Social Sector Development and Inclusive Growth in India

DIVERSE PERSPECTIVES ON CREATING A FAIRER SOCIETY

A fair society is one that is just, inclusive and embracing of all without any barriers to participation based on sex, sexual orientation, religion or belief, ethnicity, age, class, ability or any other social difference. One where there is access to healthcare and education, technology, justice, strong institutions, peace and security, social protection, decent work and housing. But how can research truly contribute to creating global equity and diversity without showcasing diverse voices that are underrepresented in academia or paying specific attention to the Global South?

Including books addressing key challenges and issues within the social sciences which are essential to creating a fairer society for all with specific reference to the Global South, *Diverse Perspectives on Creating a Fairer Society* amplifies underrepresented voices – showcasing Black, Asian and minority ethnic voices, authorship from the Global South and academics who work to amplify diverse voices.

With the primary aim of showcasing authorship and voices from beyond the Global North, the series welcomes submissions from established and junior authors on cutting-edge and high-level research on key topics that feature in global news and public debate, specifically from and about the Global South in national and international contexts. Harnessing research across a range of diversities of people and places to generate previously unheard insights, the series offers a truly global perspective on the current societal debates of the twenty-first century – bringing contemporary debate in the social sciences from diverse voices to light.

Previous Titles

Disaster, Displacement and Resilient Livelihoods: Perspectives from South Asia
Edited by M. Rezaul Islam

Pandemic, Politics, and a Fairer Society in Southeast Asia: A Malaysian Perspective
Edited by Syaza Shukri

Empowering Female Climate Change Activists in the Global South: The Path Toward Environmental Social Justice
Edited by Peggy Ann Spitzer

Gendered Perspectives of Restorative Justice, Violence and Resilience: An International Framework
Edited by Bev Orton

Forthcoming Titles

Youth Development in South Africa: Harnessing the Demographic Dividend
Edited by Botshabelo Maja and Busani Ngcaweni

The Socially Constructed and Reproduced Youth Delinquency in Southeast Asia: Advancing Positive Youth Involvement in Sustainable Futures
Edited by Jason Hung

Debt Crisis and Popular Social Protest in Sri Lanka: Investigating Citizenship, Development and Democracy Within Global North-South Dynamics
Edited by S. Janaka Biyanwila

Critical Reflections on the Internationalisation of Higher Education in the Global South
Edited by Emnet Tadesse Woldegiorgis and Cheryl Qiumei Yu

Social Sector Development and Inclusive Growth in India

BY

ISHU CHADDA

Amritsar Group of Colleges, India

United Kingdom – North America – Japan – India – Malaysia – China

Emerald Publishing Limited
Howard House, Wagon Lane, Bingley BD16 1WA, UK

First edition 2023

Reprints and permissions service
Contact: permissions@emeraldinsight.com

British Library Cataloguing in Publication Data
A catalogue record for this book is available from the British Library

ISBN: 978-1-83753-187-5 (Print)
ISBN: 978-1-83753-186-8 (Online)
ISBN: 978-1-83753-188-2 (Epub)

ISOQAR certified
Management System,
awarded to Emerald
for adherence to
Environmental
standard
ISO 14001:2004.

Certificate Number 1985
ISO 14001

INVESTOR IN PEOPLE

Dedicated to
my dear husband
Mr Gaurav Khanna
and my beloved son
Hiren Khanna

Contents

List of Figures and Tables

About the Author

Dr Ishu Chadda is presently working as an Assistant Professor in the Department of Management Studies at Amritsar Group of Colleges, Amritsar. She received her Master's & PhD from Guru Nanak Dev University, Amritsar. The title of her thesis is 'Impact of Social Sector Development and Inclusive Growth in India since Economic Reforms: Challenges and Prospects with Special Reference to Punjab'. She teaches a range of UG and PG courses in the management area. Her research articles have appeared in reputed international and national journals published by Emerald, Springer, Sage, etc. Her areas of interest are public financial management, inclusive growth, sustainable development, social sector development, research methodology, and econometrics. She has been involved with reputed journals as a peer-reviewer and guest editor.

Acknowledgements

I would like to acknowledge those, whose assistance and contribution have been instrumental in the realisation of this book, which otherwise would not have been possible. I feel fortunate that a large number of people have contributed to and inspired me during my research work but all cannot be mentioned, however, none is forgotten.

First and foremost, I bow my head with folded hands in reverence to the Almighty God for granting me the wisdom, health, strength, and energy to work on this research task and enabling me to reach far beyond my restricted ambit of thoughts and actions.

I wish to acknowledge, with a great sense of gratitude, the guidance, inspiration, and encouragement, which I received from my mentor and supervisor Dr Vikram Chadha, Professor, Punjab School of Economics, Guru Nanak Dev University, Amritsar, in accomplishing this work. Despite his additional academic commitments and other responsibilities, he spared his valuable time to solve my difficulties. This work is the reward of his blessings.

I would always be indebted to my parents, Mr Parveen Chadda and Mrs Anu Chadda, for their endless and unconditional sacrifices for the better lives of their children. Words cannot express the gratitude that I owe to them. They have always been a guiding light and an ideal for me and my life would have been on a different plane, had they not cared to provide me with the best educational facilities right from my childhood.

My profound thanks go to my mother-in-law Mrs Prabha Khanna for her constant support. I am thankful to my father-in-law Late Mr Vinod Khanna for showering his blessings from heaven.

I am grateful to my friends Dr Deepika Kumari, Dr Niharika Mahajan, Ms Dilpreet Kaur, and Ms Simranpreet Kaur as they were always there to motivate me whenever I went through emotional ups and downs during my research work.

I want to express my thanks to Sage and Springer Publishing House for publishing my work in their respective journals namely *The Indian Economic Journal* and *Journal of Social and Economic Development*.

I am thankful to Emerald Publishing House for providing me with this opportunity and guiding me at every stage of this publication.

Dr Ishu Chadda

Introduction

Brief summary: The basic research question lurking in the study is whether the growth strategies based on the human development approach, that is, social sector development would render growth inclusive. The present work is very comprehensive considering all components of the social sector in aggregate and also covering both financial and physical aspects of the social sector.

Full book description: Two broad approaches to economic development had been experimented within India, viz. trickle-down approach and human development approach. After independence, India, till the Fourth Five Year Plan, experimented with the first approach which was advocated by Pt Jawahar Lal Nehru, P. C. Mahalanobis, and Jagdish Bhagwati. Even when India based its development policy on the Nehruvian approach involving high investment, heavy industrialisation, import substitution, and indigenisation of goods and services, even then employment generation and income growth and redistribution were not kept at the bay. India intended to involve people in its strategic approach to development. Elimination of monopolies, prevention of concentration of economic power, socio-economic justice, and participative growth has all veered around the poorest of the poor. The failures of the trickle-down approach further strengthened India's resolution to reinforce the inclusiveness of growth.

Dr Amartya Sen, Jean Dreze, and Brahmachanda, on the other hand, continued to profess the human development approach to economic development by reinforcing the social sector development; which India started emphasising since Fifth Five Year Plan. The stress had been laid on strengthening and expanding the social sectors with the premise that it would boost the inclusive growth agenda by directly increasing the income and productivity of the people even at the lowest rung, manifesting in equal access to employment and economic opportunities, and equal participation in decision-making and reduction in poverty and inequality. The earlier studies focussed on the development of the social sector and its components in India. Only partial-level studies on the social sector have been done and these have been limited to one or two components majorly.

Both social sector development and inclusive growth are synergetic. Social sector development stimulates the achievement of inclusive growth, while the realisation of inclusive growth manifests in social sector development. Government programmes and policies are framed for bringing the weaker sections into the mainstream. Social sector development in concomitance with inclusive growth came into the limelight because of the concern of policymakers towards abject poverty and deprivation of masses and to promote democratic-based economic growth.

India emphasised high economic growth, spontaneously eventuating in inclusiveness. Earlier it was realised that literacy, education, health, and maternal and infant mortality rates had shown improvement, but at a marginal pace. The sustained development of India was considered imperative so that growth could be equitable and inclusive.

Subject/topic description: This study considers the various World Bank reports and various views of scholars on this subject to quantify the inclusiveness in India. The study further intends to highlight the major dimensions of inclusive development like poverty alleviation, employment generation, and access to equal participation.

The majority of earlier studies consider the relationship between economic growth and government spending in India. But none of the studies look at the relationship between social sector development and inclusive growth in India at a macro-level. This type of study has been conducted to scrutinise the long- and short-run association between the social sector and inclusive growth in India using the autoregressive distributed lag approach.

Chapter 1

Introduction: The Theoretical Framework

Human Development Dimensions of Growth

Economic development can be perceived as a multidimensional process that involves the reorganisation and reorientation of the whole economy as well as the social system, and it is much more than just the increase in income and output. Throughout this process of accelerating economic growth, it is vital to include the ones who have benefitted the least from economic development (Todaro & Smith, 2003). Economic growth is the progression of a community, along with the evolution of new and better methods of production and the rising of the level of output through the development of human skills and energy, better organisation, and acquisition of capital resources (Singh, 1966). There are three main categories of capital resources comprising physical capital, human capital, and technology, which determine long-run differences in income per capita.

Economic growth which encompasses the welfare of the citizens of a country has been the major thrust for a modern capitalist economic system. The introduction of the concept of escalating returns from the division of labour in the field of economics was Adam Smith's most important contribution to the discipline. He stressed the role of parsimony, expansion of markets, and promotion of interests of farmers, traders, and manufacturers by the liberal government (Taneja & Myers, 2000). Investment and capital accumulation are essential for the development of economy and wealth distribution. Savings from industrial and agricultural profits, as well as the extent of labour specialisation, impact further investment (Thirlwall, 2006).

The neoclassical theory concentrated on short-run economic processes. According to neoclassical economics, profit is determined by the marginal productivity of capital, and the wage of workers is determined similarly by the marginal productivity of labour (Rynn, 2001). The major source of growth in developing countries is increased factor inputs, supported by enhancements in the quality of labour through health improvement and education. In the long-run steady state, the growth of output is determined by the rate of growth of the labour force in terms of efficiency. A higher investment ratio is counterbalanced by a higher capital–output ratio or lower productivity of capital due to the

Social Sector Development and Inclusive Growth in India, 1–22
Copyright © 2023 by Ishu Chadda
Published under exclusive license by Emerald Publishing Limited
doi:10.1108/978-1-83753-186-820231002

neoclassical supposition of diminishing returns to capital. The level of per capita income varies optimistically with the savings–investment ratio and pessimistically with the rate of growth of the population (Thirwall, 2006).

The vital proposition of growth theory is to facilitate the positive growth rate of output per capita in the long run and it should be achieved only with the adoption of continual modifications in technological knowledge in the form of new goods, new markets, and new processes. The neoclassical growth model developed by Solow (1956) and Swan (1956) exhibited that the effects of diminishing returns would eventually cause economic growth to hamper and stymie technological progress (Aghion & Howitt, 1998). The theory states that by changing the magnitude of labour and capital in the production function, a state of equilibrium can be achieved. With the availability of new technology, the labour and capital have to be modified to maintain the growth equilibrium. Meade (1961) explained the effect of population growth, capital accumulation, and technological progress on economic development. He also examined the conditions for steady growth and assumed that the population grows at a constant proportional rate rather than remaining at a constant level (Taneja & Myers, 2000).

Both the classical and the neoclassical growth models put physical capital accumulation as an epitome of growth and long-run income. Extensions of the neoclassical growth model revealed the role of human capital ahead of physical capital (Thirlwall, 2006). Intangible assets like human capital or human health did not play important role in the growth of the economy as premised in the classical and neoclassical growth models.

Schumpeterian growth theory goes beyond this viewpoint. As per Schumpeterian theory, the concept of innovations, human capital accumulation, and physical capital accumulation acts as the sources of economic growth (Howitt, 2005). The theory believes that the fundamental impulse which sets and maintains a capitalist economy in motion; comes from the introduction of new combinations through innovation fostered by the entrepreneur (Dinopoulos, 2006). In the *Theory of Economic Development*, Schumpeter (1934) stressed the importance of the role of the entrepreneur, who plays a vital role in his analysis of capitalist evolution (Acs & Audretsch, 1988). The rate of accumulation of physical capital and human capital can be considered as the outcomes determined by more fundamental factors. Human capital accumulates similarly to physical capital. The savings and the rate of investment in education and health, simultaneously, determine the steady-state income differences both in physical as well as in human capital (Schumpeter, 1942). As per Schumpeter's perception of research, the process of economic development would take place by an amalgamation of entrepreneurship and innovation, which further acts as an internal mechanism of change along with the cyclical fluctuations characterising the development process (Ebner, 2000).

Endogenous growth theory is distinguished from neoclassical economics as it emphasised a combination of technological progression and other physical and qualitative factors as the main sources of economic growth. Robert Lucas (1988) and Paul Romer (1986) pioneered endogenous growth models and they stated that the association of human capital formation and research and development would prevent the marginal product of capital from falling and the capital–output ratio from rising (Todaro & Smith, 2003). Romer (1986) developed the model of expanding returns with the endogenous accumulation of knowledge when there was a steady positive equilibrium growth rate. It was imperative to break off from the existing literature, in which technological progress had been largely treated as totally exogenous.

Lucas (1988) mentioned a two-sector model of growth in which the physical capital is produced as the consumption good with the same technology, but human capital is created with different technology. Human capital is an essential factor of production as the core constituent of growth is human capital. The combination of labour, capital, and technology will be more efficiently manifest if the firm invests in educated, skilled, and healthy workers (Hasan, 2001). The process of development takes place if physical capital accumulation is substituted by human capital accumulation (Galor, 2011). This theory stated that efficient and effective means of production and the use of new forms of technology will result in the growth of a nation's human capital (Todaro & Smith, 2003).

Accumulation involves behavioural outcomes to amend composite conditions. As soon as accumulation is achieved, it alters the endowments from which existing and potential outputs and revenues are generated. This elevates the prospects for further growth and the progression of the country goes on. The idea of accumulation is general and does not confine to technology and physical capital but is also applicable to the cluster of factors including education, on-the-job training, health, nutrition, water, and sanitation (Yotopoulos & Nugent, 1976).

Social Welfare: Human Development Versus Human Capital

Human welfare is the central theme of economic development. That is why, since independence, the social welfare of the masses has been the objective of economic policy in India. However, there are two-way linkages between human development and overall economic progress. Strengthening the social sector would be served as a foundation for economic growth and contributes to human development by focussing on human welfare and equity which leads to economic development (Government of India, 2002). Pigou (1920) introduced the concept of economic welfare as that part of social welfare that can be brought directly or indirectly into a relation with the measuring rod of money. Lange (1942) explained

> the concept of welfare economics as the norm of behaviour for optimum allocation of resources with equal distribution of inputs among society. Welfare Economics refers to all economic and non-economic goods and services that provide utilities or satisfaction to individuals living in a community and therefore guarantee social welfare. (Ahuja, 2007)

Economic growth is a significant mechanism to expand social welfare and enhance social welfare through improved health outcomes, food intake, and access to other basic needs which is a rational objective of society and government (Clarke, 2003).

A welfare state is one where the state participates in the protection and promotion of the economic and social well-being of its citizens. The basic notion is to provide equality of opportunity and equitable distribution of wealth along with the responsibility for those who were not able to avail the basic facilities for a good life (Rastogi, 2011). All the welfare states grant assistance to the poor in form of social protection programmes and provide the vulnerable sections with social insurance against certain risks (Gale, 2008). Social welfare provides social protection by improving the employability of poor people which would contribute to social cohesion and permanence. It improves participation in the labour market, manages risks, encourages investment and entrepreneurship, and empowers human resources through community development, education, health, and sanitation (Organization for Economic Cooperation and Development (OECD), 2009).

The term human development indicates both the process of expanding people's choices and the level of people's achieved well-being. It also facilitates two concepts of human development. One is the creation of human capabilities and the other is to utilise the acquired capabilities by the people (United Nations Development Programme (UNDP), 1990). The human development paradigm of economic development emerged in the late 1980s and was conceived, articulated, and advocated around the world by Dr Mahbub ul Haq and Dr Amartya Sen.

> The goals of development must be defined in terms of progressive attenuation and eventually lead to the eradication of malnutrition, disease, illiteracy, unemployment, and inequalities. The concept of equitable distribution along with more products should be promoted together to define the development. (Haq, 2011)

Human development concentrated on a more equitable distribution of income and assets which create a closer linkage between economic growth and human development. As a result, human development goes ahead of programmes of social development or social welfare (Haq, 2011). A human-centric approach to development has been built which identifies the three most critical choices, that is, a long life and healthy life, education, and decent standard of living, and also additional choices which include political freedom, guaranteed human rights, and self-respect (UNDP, 1990). During the 1980s, numerous policies had been implemented for employment-intensive growth, which further generated opportunities for poor households by raising the demand for labour, thus, increasing employment, wage rate, and the political power of the community. Social welfare policies should endow the community with adequate human capital, to exploit these new opportunities and create a safety net for vulnerable and needy sections (Lipton & Gaag, 1993).

The concept of human capital for economic growth was promoted by Theodore Schultz and Gary Becker during the 1960s. Human capital refers to the productive capacities of human beings as income-generating agents in the economy and may be defined as the collection of skills and product knowledge personified in people (Rosen, 1989). Schultz (1961) invented the term human capital explaining that humans could be endowed with education, training, and augmented benefits that would lead to an enhancement in the quality and level of production. The investment in human capital builds capabilities such as investment in preschool activities, schooling and higher education, post-school training and learning, migration, health, information, and investment in children. These sub-classifications of investment have different relative effects on earnings and consumption. But by and large, all these different classifications improve the physical and mental abilities of people and thereby raise real income prospects (Becker, 1962).

Human capital includes the enhancement of acquired cognitive skills and discrete knowledge. The investment in human capital builds capabilities that include various non-cognitive skills and other attributes that equally contribute to well-being. The formation of personal, social, and economic well-being will accompany the formation of human capital by personifying the knowledge, skills, competencies, and attributes. Human capital is strengthened with experience, employment, and informal and formal learning (OECD, 2001).

Government of India (2011b) mentioned in the Indian Human Development Report (IHDR) about the enhancement of basic capabilities and involvement of human development as the core ingredients for economic growth which will successfully eliminate poverty and facilitate the adaptation of social and economic policies. Though human development connotes human welfare, while human capital extends human capital through education, skill formation, and R&D, still human development eventually manifests in human capital. Human development is a much wider notion than human capital. The rationale of the growth strategy is to eliminate poverty via deploying the model for human development. This being the main endeavour, it would result in equal access to development-centric amenities such as good health and nutrition, potable drinking water, accessibility of sanitation, and educated and employed personnel (Mehrotra, 2005).

Measures that Enhanced Human Development

Economic development is linked with human welfare and human development which makes growth inclusive. Although human development is enhanced by the strengthening of the social sectors, providing a basis for developing human capital, which further builds human capabilities. The UNDP, in both developing and developed nations, analysed the comparative status of socio-economic development in its annual series of Human Development Reports (HDRs). The First HDR, brought out by Mahbub ul Haq in 1990, was an elementary, yet refreshing mode of measuring development to form a composite human development index (HDI) by combining three indicators, that is, life expectancy, educational attainment, and income. To measure the standard of living of a country, HDI is utilised. HDI is calculated based on four criteria; 'Life expectancy at birth, mean years of schooling, expected years of schooling, and gross national income per capita' (Haq, 1990). It ranges from zero to one. The HDRs rank all countries according to HDI and group them as low human development countries (HDI < 0.54), medium human development countries (HDI 0.55–0.69), high human development countries (0.7–0.79), and very high human development countries (0.8–1) (UNDP, 1990).

Human development, thus, is viewed as the process of broadening a person's capacities to function with the comprehensive things that a person could incorporate in his life and articulated as expanding choices in the HDRs (Sen, 1989). Table 1 elucidates the human development status of some selected countries for the year 2018. Among the 170 countries listed in the HDR, Norway occupies the topmost position and Cote d Ivoire is the last. It has been observed that in the year 2018, 59 countries have an HDI value between 0.8 and 1 and were categorised as countries with high human development. High development countries, with HDI values between 0.7 and 0.79, rank from 60 to 112. Medium development countries rank between 113 and 151 and India ranks 130 on among the 170 countries in terms of HDI. On the positive side, India's HDI value has gone

Table 1.   HDI and its Components.

HDI Rank	Country	HDI 2018	Life Expectancy 2018	Mean Years of Schooling	Expected Years of Schooling	Gross National Income Per capita
Very High HDI						
1	Norway	0.953	82.3	12.6	17.9	68,012
5	Germany	0.936	81.2	14.1	17.0	46,136
9	Singapore	0.932	83.2	11.5	16.2	82,503
47	Argentina	0.825	76.7	9.9	17.4	18,641
57	Malaysia	0.802	75.5	10.2	13.7	26,107
High HDI						
76	Sri Lanka	0.770	75.5	10.9	13.9	11,326
79	Brazil	0.759	75.7	7.8	15.4	13,755
86	China	0.752	76.4	7.8	13.8	15,270
94	Dominican Republic	0.736	74.0	7.8	13.7	13,921
Medium HDI						
113	South Africa	0.699	63.4	10.1	13.3	11,923
130	India	0.640	68.8	6.4	12.3	6,353
136	Bangladesh	0.608	72.8	5.8	11.4	3,677
149	Nepal	0.574	70.6	4.9	12.2	2,471
150	Pakistan	0.562	66.6	5.2	8.6	5,311
Low HDI						
156	Zimbabwe	0.535	61.7	7.2	8.1	1,683
168	Afghanistan	0.498	64.0	3.8	10.4	1,824
170	Cote d Ivoire	0.492	54.1	5.2	9.0	3,481

Source: Chadha and Chadda (2020a).

up from 0.345 to 0.640 between 1980 and 2018, an increase of 85 per cent. Life expectancy at birth has increased to 68.8 years, mean years of schooling to 6.4 years, and expected years of schooling to 12.3 years. The countries from 152 to 170 belong to the low development group (UNDP, 2018).

Welfare and well-being can be measured in three different methods and these include 'economic welfare, social well-being, and subjective well-being' (OECD, 2011). Earlier economic welfare measured and referred to monetary concepts only by using gross domestic product (GDP). The second measurement is based on socio-economic well-being and development. HDI is one of the most important concepts to measure socio-economic well-being, which is used and followed globally (UNDP, 1990). Later on, GDP and HDI failed to accurately reflect the level of well-being and welfare in society. Both are not comprehensive enough to explain the concept of human well-being, welfare, and quality of life (Sagar & Najam, 1998). So, to overcome these, a new index was developed by deploying a unique methodology called the Quality of Life Index (QLI) to give a broader picture of human welfare. To determine QLI, nine indicators were represented, viz.

> material wellbeing; health; political stability and security; family life; community life, climate and geography, job security, political freedom, and gender equality. India is yet to make any marked leaps on the quality of living index scale. (Morris, 1996)

India introduced economic reforms aimed at liberalising the economy through several proposals with a direct focus on human development. Therefore, beginning with the Eighth Five-year Plan (FYP), the subsequent FYPs have also continued to be firmly set within the human development paradigm. This focus on human development led to a greater emphasis on addressing inequalities amidst accelerated growth in the 2000s (Government of India, 1991). The links between development and social opportunity had been feeble in Indian states. India has diversity among its states, there were some states which achieved high levels of human development like Kerala and Tamil Nadu; some states like Punjab and Haryana had a high level of per capita income, whereas Bihar, Madhya Pradesh, Orissa, and Rajasthan were neither economically nor socially sound (Prabhu, 2005).

Human development can be attained in several ways. Initially, the process of this development commenced with education and health particularly, for the weaker and marginalised sections of society. Later, the role of improved schooling has been an essential part of the development strategies in most countries and shows significant improvements in school attainment across the developing world in recent decades (Hanushek, 2013). Schooling also has a role in human capital formation. The impact of human capital becomes strong and vital when the role of quality schooling was emphasised. The cognitive skills of the population are connected to individual earnings followed by equal distribution of income and subsequently to economic growth (Hanushek, 2013).

After theoretical education, the most effective mode of human development is on-the-job training which transforms educational skills and training. It can be systematic or informal (Harbison & Myers, 1964). The inclusive approach to development highlights the importance of education as a basic human need (knowledge, attitudes, values, and skills), as a means of meeting other basic needs (adequate nutrition, safe drinking water, health services, and shelter), and as an activity that enhances the overall development (Kumari & Yadav, 2008). The imbalanced access to education would result in information asymmetries, and disparate conditions of job opportunities which further trigger poverty and health hazards, inability, and human deprivation (Biradar, 2008).

Health is another aspect of human development that is equally important. Improved health generates economic growth in the long run. Kaushik et al. (2008) stated that health generate both higher income and individual well-being as only a physically and medically fit individual or group or society at large, could make better use of their resources (Harbison & Myers, 1964). The World Health Organization emphasised the three specific dimensions of health, the physical, the mental, and the social. The factors which influenced health are inherited problems, environmental issues, lifestyle, adequate housing facilities, good hygiene, and potable water, basic sanitation and sewerage facilities, income earned, education, availability, and equality of health infrastructure (Park, 1994).

Nutrition is a component of health, and malnutrition is part of the disease that results in poverty. Human nutrition is not concerned with merely the availability and intake of food. Good nutrition is the result of many interconnecting factors which function jointly and concurrently on the person in the physical, ecological, and cultural environment of the society (Rani, 2008). Nutrition is related to general health which ensures better physical and mental health required for human development. Nutritious and good food is the core ingredient of good health (Antony & Laxmaiah, 2007).

There seems to be a close connection between education and health. Education, health, and poverty are closely related. If education and health are elevated, it means poverty is eliminated. Education nurtures character; health guarantees efficient work, and jointly these contribute to effective human development. Enhancement of human development requires more investments in the social sector that ultimately lead to higher growth of a nation. It means strengthening the spread effects by including vulnerable sections for accelerated economic development (Naidu et al., 2008).

The definitive objective of a planned economy is to facilitate the well-being of the masses, particularly the poor and the needy sections of society. Social infrastructure and the social sector are two sides of the same coin and both are associated and correlated (Harnawala & Iyer, 2012).

> Social Sector includes departmental and actuation concerning human development (elementary education, secondary and higher education, adult education, development of women and children), health (public health facilities, disease prevention, and control, drug administration, medical education, training, and research), family welfare (population policy, family welfare programme), social justice (development of weaker sections), labour and employment, social security schemes, housing, road connectivity, water supply, sanitation, rural-urban development, and food storage and warehousing. (Sarma, 2005)

Social Sector and Human Development

Social sector development has been recognised as an important factor of economic development. People moved from rural to urban areas as a result of the absence of adequate living conditions, modern facilities, and services in rural areas. As a result, in order for India to experience true progress, the social sector needs to be developed (Maheswari, 2012). The social sector comprises sub-sectors like housing, education, water supply, public health, and medical care, hygiene and sanitation, conservation and pollution control, epidemic control environment, labour and employment, and welfare of weaker sections which contribute to human capital formation and human development (Mooij & Dev, 2004).

Components of the Social Sector

> Social Sector consists of Social Services and Economic Services. Social Services include education, art & culture, medical & public health, family welfare, water supply and sanitation, housing & urban development, the welfare of underprivileged classes, labour & employment, social security & welfare, and other social services. On the other hand, Economic Services relate to rural development and food storage and food warehousing. (Chadha & Chadda, 2020b)

The expenditure incurred for the development of the social sector has a wider perspective of escalating the social indicators and opportunities like better health services, increase in educational rate, clear water supply, and other basic needs of society. There are several social sector development programmes that are mostly intended to eradicate poverty but apart from employment programmes, there are specific health and nutritional programmes for women and children that aim at the poorer segments of society (Dev & Mooij, 2004).

- *Social services:*
    - Education, sports, art, and culture,
    - Medical and public health,
    - Family welfare,
    - Water supply and sanitation,
    - Housing and urban development,
    - The welfare of under privileged classes,
    - Labour and employment,
    - Social security and welfare, and
    - Others social services.

Other social services include information and publicity, broadcasting, and nutrition.

- *Economic services:*
    - Rural development and
    - Food storage and warehousing.

Prabhu (2001) viewed social sector development as better access to education, health, and nutrition sectors. Apart from these, it also includes poverty alleviation programmes including asset generation, employment generation, and social protection measures.

> In addition to these, the term social sector may allude to the value system of the economy like values of freedom, promoting gender equity, decentralization, democratic federalism, inter-regional balances, nationalism, the value of prudence, thrift habit and control on utilization, long-term perspective of implementation of policies, etc. (Panchamukhi, 2000)

The components of the social sector should add to the progression of such qualities both at the micro- and macro-level. Thus, there is no particular definition of the social sector, yet it tends to be broadly defined as comprising those sectors of the economy which frequently deal with human welfare orientation. As it is not a branch of pure economics or economic considerations; so no specific returns in monetary terms are expected from it (Aggarwal, 2011).

Social sector expenditure has been characterised as the aggregate of all expenditures incurred by the central and state governments on promotional and protective measures. The promotional measures include medium- and long-term impacts while the protective measures are extemporised or temporary in nature. Promotional measures consist of social and community services like education, medical, public health, family welfare, water supply and sanitation, expenditure on rural development, and food subsidy. Protective measures include natural calamities (Joshi, 2006). Out of the overall expenditures in India, the central government spent one-fifth on the development of the social sector, with the states bearing the remaining 80 per cent. The Constitution established the allocation of duties between the states and the centre. State government deals with the health-related and most rural development issues, while issues related to education, welfare, and employment come under the responsibility of the centre as well as the states (Mooij & Dev, 2004).

Social Sector Development Scenario in India

India acquired a burgeoning population, food deficiency, widespread poverty, illiteracy, and ignorance, as well as the overall lopsided and degenerate socio-economic roots of eastern society at independence. Nonetheless, the planners were aware of the fact that development and welfare would not be possible until the benefits of economic growth trickled down to the neediest rungs of society (Chadha & Chadda, 2020b). Nehru, Mahalanobis, and Jagdish Bhagwati propounded and advocated the trickle-down approach to development in India. The Nehruvian/Mahalanobis model continued till the Fourth FYP and followed the trickle-down approach, that is, to surge the momentum of growth with big monolithic investment and capital formation and achieve high-income growth such that the high income will spontaneously trickle down to lower strata.

Nehruvian Approach to Development

The prime and principal concern of India's First Prime Minister Pt. Jawaharlal Nehru was issues like a vicious cycle of poverty, ignorance, and inequality of opportunity. All these issues had created havoc for the already stagnant Indian society and economy. From the perspective of these concerns, the Planning Commission of India was set up to formulate the Nation's FYPs for assessing all the available and limited resources along with the methods for augmenting deficient resources, and also determining priorities for development. The First FYP was launched, without meeting much specific planning strategy connecting sectoral investment proposals to accomplish the targets of the plan. Nevertheless, in the Second FYP, the objective of India's development strategy was of setting up the socialistic pattern of society through economic growth with self-sufficiency, social equity, and eradication of poverty. These objectives were ensured to be achieved in the frame of a mixed economy. The medium for this was the Nehru–Mahalanobis strategy. The foundation of the approach was to assemble machines as capital goods as soon as it could and these must be used as a basic input of production. This was expected to generate employment opportunities and reduce inequalities in society by trickling down benefits to the less fortunate sections of society (Balkrishnan, 2013).

Trickle-down implied a vertical flow from rich to poor that took place on its momentum. That is how Nehru wanted to use it once the growth process gets established; the institutional changes would guarantee that gains of development trickle down to the poor people (Arndt, 1983). Although, Aghion and Bolton (1997) contended that wealth does trickle down from the rich to the poor and would lead to a unique and steady distribution of wealth under sufficiently high returns to capital acquired. Despite this, there was still room for wealth redistribution policies to enroot the process of long-run efficiency for the economy. Hence, the trickle-down approach was not enough to ultimately achieve an equitable distribution of resources. The redistribution improved production efficiency and consequently, the incentives to maximise profits would be more apparent. With redistribution, equality of opportunity would be achieved which ultimately improves the efficiency of the economy as it strengthens the process of trickle-down process. In the 1950s and 1960s, development had been considered an economic phenomenon as the continuous returns would consequently bring prolific benefits, that is, trickle down to the masses with more employment opportunities (Arndt, 1983). Once, development commenced, it would trickle down and automatically benefit the poor from the policies benefitting the rich (Nugent & Yotopoulos, 1979).

While in reality, the trickle-down approach had proved insufficient and inconsistent with a vision of overall economic growth because unemployment and inequality had exacerbated and the development process had gone astray (Arndt, 1983). Thus, it was paradoxical to claim that the country would result in an inimitable steady state with sufficient high rates of capital accumulation. The wealth redistribution policies along with growth adjustment policies required to improve the long-run efficiency of the economy (Aghion & Bolton, 1997). The Indian economy grew at a comparatively low rate of growth of 3.5 per cent from 1950 to 1980. In the absence of high economic growth, resources to invest in human development were limited, and with a poor standard of living, and limited access to education and nutrition, economic development became a distant dream. Thus, since the 1980s, India has been suffering from the problem of 'lopsided development' with slow human development (Akhtar, 2008).

Sen's Social Sector Development Approach

A consensus emerged that the development policy needed to pursue a high growth rate or per capita income along with more equality of distribution till social objectives are achieved, that is, employment generation and alleviation of poverty (Arndt, 1983). This explains the model of growth, that is, growth preceding equity and redistribution of income through wage-oriented and employment-generating programmes and hence, the focus was shifted to employment for masses through social sector development via inclusive growth. Sen and Derze's model of growth hinges on the development of the social sector, a strategy that integrates the capability approach and, as a result, involves growth inclusiveness. It advocates creating employment opportunities and engagement of the deprived and marginal segments. This approach to development is imperative for directly eliminating poverty and making growth inclusive (Chadha & Chadda, 2020b).

Dr Amartya Sen contributed towards the human development approach by ameliorating the socio-economic conditions of the deprived sections, by advocating gender equality (UNDP, 1995), poverty eradication (UNDP, 1997), consumption and sustainable development (UNDP, 1998), human rights (UNDP, 2000), and democracy (Fukuda-Parr, 2003; UNDP, 2002). The concept of human development is complex and multidimensional. Prof. Amartya Sen called this concept of human development 'Eastern strategy'. This Eastern strategy propagated the enhancement of quality of life like more literacy, life expectancy, and broadening of basic facilities like education, and healthcare which is are essential for human development (Naidu et al., 2008).

The social sector is essential for promoting economic development and social equity. It had been witnessed from the experience of different nations in the world that the countries that had overlooked the development of the social sector had adversely influenced economic growth and social equity. It is essentially perceived that social sector development is the most essential requisite for the growth of a nation (Trivedi, 2005). Nevertheless, it has been observed that for the social sector in India, more cautious steps have to be taken to remove the problems related to inequality. If the inequalities continue to persist, they will not only hamper human development but also economic growth in the long run. However, along with the increase in social sector spending, due care should be focussed on the efficient allocation of resources; so the gains would percolate down to the lower rungs (Banerjee, 2008).

Social Sector Development Programmes in India

India experienced acute poverty, gnawing deprivation, and exclusivity among the lowest rung of the society since independence. Ever since the government has been persuaded to consider development policies with the prime purpose of promoting growth in a manner that fosters equity. Subsequently, the policies are framed to manifest more participation and involvement in decision-making, access to employment opportunities, and eradication of inequality and poverty. In light of this, the planners emphasised strengthening and developing the social sector which further supports the agenda of inclusive and sustainable growth (Chadha & Chadda, 2020a).

The Planning Commission was set up 60 years ago and central planning for centralised allocations of resources was advocated (Government of India, 2012a). Balkrishnan (2013) also emphasised about the fundamental objective of Indian development policy that continues to be eradicating poverty and creating more employment opportunities. India's inclusive growth spectrum would involve the eradication of inequalities, hunger, and deprivation which further enable people participation, broad-based, and pro-poor growth. Employment creation and participation were not affected even when India anchored its development policy on Nehruvian principles comprising indigenisation of goods and services, trade liberalisation, substantial investment, and intensive industrialisation. India wanted to build a development strategy that involved people (Chadha & Chadda, 2020a). However, exclusion persisted in terms of dwindling growth in agriculture, deteriorating quality job growth, low human development, regional imbalances and disparities, gender inequities and social discrimination, etc. A pragmatic approach should be followed to make growth inclusive so that poverty would be alleviated and other disparities would be removed (Dev, 2010).

From the commencement of the planning process in 1950, till the Fourth FYP, India experimented with the trickle-down approach and failed. The earlier FYPs did not devote the required attention to social sector development, but the Fifth FYP reinforcing social sector development proceeded (Ahmad & Bhakta, 2008). Even otherwise, since independence, the expansion of the social sector has been given top priority in order to support democratic inclusive growth owing to the persistent deprivation and poverty of the populace. Community development was given high priority as India has the largest population of poor and needy people. Initially, these programmes targeted the rural poor and covered agriculture growth, animal rearing, road construction, better access to education and health, employment generation, housing development, and social and cultural activities (Hegde, 2000).

During the First FYP, the Community Development Programme (CDP) was introduced in 1952. The main motives behind this programme were the development of rural regions and promoting people's participation. This programme was designed to follow an administrative regulatory structure so that the government could reach the district, tehsil/taluka, and village levels. Each region was separated into development blocks and these blocks were administered by block development officer (BDO). BDO was made responsible for each block. Workers were appointed by BDO called village level workers (VLW). VLW were made in charge of 10–12 villages. In this way, across the nation, a well-structured framework was rooted. The training was provided to several BDOs and VLW to enhance their skills for the proper execution of government programmes. The main job of BDO and VLW was to ensure that the benefits of programmes reached grass root levels. Community development organisation was the main authority and a community development research centre was established to make this programme successful (Government of India, 1952).

The CDP later turned out to be redundant and a necessitated specific focus on agriculture. To specifically cater to agriculture and rural development, the Intensive Agriculture Development Programme (IADP) was launched in 1960–1961. Numerous services were offered in these programmes and it was also known as a package programme. This programme was executed in seven states by taking one district at that time by providing loans to farmers for seeds and fertilisers on a pilot basis. The IADP was extended to the rest of the country and later a new Intensive Agriculture Area Programme (IAAP) was initiated to extend the special harvest in the agriculture area which had production prospects (Chandra, 2008). The fundamental goal of India's development should essentially provide the masses of India the opportunity to lead a decent life. The basic goals were set under 'The Directive Principles of State Policy' during the Third FYP in the Constitution to envisage a welfare state. The directive principles framed the policies and laws based on the code of conduct symbolised in the preamble 'Equity, Social, Economic, Political; liberty, equality, and fraternity' (Government of India, 1961).

The period duration between the Third FYP and the Fourth FYP was of critical importance for Indian agriculture. Under the Fourth FYP, High Yielding Varieties Programme and Multiple Cropping Programme (1966–1967) launched because the key to the new agricultural strategy, which went on to achieve self-sustenance in food by the end of the year 1970–1971 (Chandra, 2008). Among the different programmes and schemes introduced for rural development, a new scheme was introduced, known as, Accelerated Rural Water Supply Programme (ARWSP) in 1972–1973. This scheme maximised the flow of rural water supply and also assuring the regular supply of potable water throughout the country (Government of India, 2010).

The Drought Prone Areas Programme (DPAP) was the area development programme implemented by the central government in 1973–1974 to handle the problems related to severe drought conditions and depletion faced by fragile regions. The main target of the programme was to minimise the severe impact of drought on the production of crops and livestock. The efforts were to enhance the productivity of land, water, and human resources which eventually resulted in making the affected areas drought resistant. Furthermore, the programme intended to improve the socio-economic conditions of the destitute and disadvantaged sections inhabiting those areas and promote overall economic development (Government of India, 2007).

The Minimum Needs Programme (MNP) was launched during the Fifth FYP. The core philosophy of the programme was to set up a well-structured, specified time-framed panel of primary services and facilities of social consumption in India. The programme intended to help in elevating the living standards and in decreasing regional disparities. The basic requirements for this programme are elementary education and adult education including training, rural health, rural roads connectivity, rural electrification, rural housing, environmental improvement for urban slums, and better nutrition (Government of India, 1974).

The Integrated Child Development Services (ICDS) Scheme was executed in 1975 and envisaged the holistic growth of children below six years of age to deliver the amalgamated package of early childhood facilities like proper nutrition and access to health education for pregnant and lactating mothers. It initiated 33 projects and 4,891 Anganwadi Centres (AWCs). The scheme focussed on improving the nutritional and health status of preschool children, pregnant women, and nursing mothers. The basic services comprised supplementary nutrition, preschool education for children, provide vaccination services, regular health check-ups, referral facilities, and availability of health education (United Nations International Children's Education Fund, 2011a).

The Sixth FYP implemented a strategy that centred on reinforcing the framework for both agriculture and industry to have faster growth in investments, and more exports, and amplified the employment opportunities for employment mainly in the rural areas and the unorganised sector, to meet the minimum basic needs of people. So, keeping this vision in mind, the government introduced the flagship programme called Integrated Rural Development Programme (IRDP) in 1980. This programme was proposed to support the rural people especially the poor beneficiaries to raise their incomes above the poverty line. Poor beneficiaries could apply for loans to purchase assets from banks and also subsidise the cost of assets by 25–50 per cent (Gangopadhyay et al., 2009).

Indira Awaas Yojana (IAY) 1985, a lead plan of the Ministry of Rural Development, was executed for assisting Below Poverty Line (BPL) families who did not have a house or no insufficient housing funds for building safe and durable accommodation. The genesis of this programme was the wage employment programmes, viz. the National Rural Employment Programme (NREP) (1980) and the Rural Landless Employment Guarantee Programme (RLEGP) (1983). With the motive of rendering acute poverty, the construction of houses was granted under these programmes, so, the poor people must have an address to access different rural development programmes (Government of India, 2013).

The Seventh FYP focussed on social equity, utilisation of modern technology, agricultural development, poverty removal programmes, sufficient food, clothing, and shelter, increasing the productivity of small and medium farmers; hence making India a progressive self-sufficient economy. National Drinking Water Mission (NDWM) was implemented by the Government of India in 1986, and later in the year 1991, this mission was renamed Rajiv Gandhi National Drinking Water Mission (RGNDWM). The states which were not covered earlier under any water supply programme would be an integral part of this programme including drought prone, rock regions, and desert areas (Government of India, 2010).

The National Policy on Education (1986) perceived that with the participation of girls and women in the educational process, the empowerment of women is potentially possible. The Mahila Samakhya Programme was executed in 1988 to seek the aims of the above-mentioned programme. The main focus of this programme was to empower women by providing them with education in rural areas, especially women of socially and economically marginalised groups (Government of India, 2013).

The Eighth FYP focussed on the reorientation of the development policy. The prime agenda of this programme was to provide the poor the basic needs, specifically, generation of employment opportunities, access to sufficient means of livelihood, availability of food, better education, health, and child care services, and other necessities. Accordingly, Prime Minister Rozgar Yojana was implemented in 1993 with a motive to provide around ten lakh employment opportunities by setting up seven lakh tiny units in industry, service, and trade areas. Swarna Jayanti Shahari Rozgar Yojana (1997) was launched with a vision to provide gainful employment opportunities in urban areas. To achieve this objective, self-employment ventures were set up by providing training to individuals including women. Mid-day Meal Scheme (1995) was implemented to augment the school enrolment ratio, decrease the dropout rate, improve the retention rate, more participation of children in school activities, and also improve the nutritional status of children (Government of India, 2001).

The objectives of the Ninth FYP emerging from the Common Minimum Programme of the Government aimed at providing Basic Minimum Services. These services included the four important dimensions, viz. good quality of life of the citizens, generation of productive employment opportunities, removal of regional disparities, and self-sufficiency. Nirmal Bharat Abhiyan (1999) was executed to make individuals aware at household levels of the need of using sanitation practices in rural areas. Pradhan Mantri Gram Sadak Yojana (PMGSY) became operational in the year 2000 to construct pucca roads to provide connectivity to all unconnected habitations in rural areas. Swarna Jayanti Gram Swarozgar Yojana (1999) was launched with the vision to remove the grave problems in India like poverty and unemployment. Sarva Shiksha Abhiyan (SSA) (2000) and Shiksha Sahyog Yojana (2001) came into existence to endow all children of age group 6–14 years with relevant elementary education. Annapurna Yojana (1999) and Antyodaya Anna Yojana (2000) were to provide food security to destitute senior citizens who were not receiving a pension under National Old Age Pension Scheme, and for the families who were below the poverty line (Government of India, 2002).

The millennium development goals (MDGs) comprised eight goals to address health and its related concerns. The MDGs were approved by the United Nations in the year 2000 with the motive to achieve the goals by 2015. These eight goals were classified into eighteen numerical objectives which were further classified into forty quantifiable indicators. The eight MDG goals included the factors that significantly influenced health. The main intentions were to eliminate acute poverty and hunger; accomplish universal basic education; encourage gender equality and empower women; decrease child mortality; encourage good maternal health; eradicate diseases like HIV/AIDS, malaria, and others; and guarantee environmental sustainability and build up a worldwide partnership for development (Nath, 2011).

The Tenth FYP proposed to accomplish the specific targets related to economic, social, and environmental elements of human development. These targets focussed on, decreased poverty ratio, access to pre-primary and primary education, increasing literacy rate, a decline in infant mortality rate and maternal mortality rate, escalating employment growth rate, more coverage of villages for accessibility to potable drinking water, falling gender gaps in literacy and wage rates, cleaning of major contaminated rivers, more coverage of forest and diminishing the decadal population growth rate. Bharat Nirman Programme (2005) was implemented for the development of rural infrastructure and framework including six components: irrigation, water supply, housing, road, electricity, and network connectivity. Mahatma Gandhi National Rural Employment Guarantee Act (MGNREGA) was started in 2005 for wage employment, to reinforce natural resources management, and support sustainable development. National Rural Health Mission (NRHM) (2005) was executed to increase accessibility, affordability, and accountability for quality health services to the least fortunate in the remotest rural areas also (Government of India, 2000).

The central vision of the Eleventh FYP was to make growth more inclusive by significantly increasing the outlays for priority sector programmes. This plan incorporated several interrelated components, like eradicating poverty, generating employment opportunities, and access to participatory benefits. To achieve this well-structured framework of inclusive growth, access to basic services in health and education especially for poor people, equality of opportunities, strengthened the marginalised sections through education and skill development, environment sustainability, recognition of women's role in participation, and good governance must be provided. This plan intended to provide an exclusive identification number, named Aadhaar, to every Indian (Government of India, 2006).

The overall goal of the government was to improve the way of living of the people. For that, the Twelfth FYP concentrated on faster, more sustainable, and more inclusiveness of the country's growth (Government of India, 2011a). The Ministry for Housing and Urban Poverty Alleviation implemented a new scheme 'Rajiv Awas Yojana (RAY)' (2013–2022) envisaged to make India free from slums. Inclusive and equitable cities for every citizen and access to basic infrastructure, social facilities, and decent shelter would meet this goal (Government of India, 2013).

On evaluating the planning process, three distinct stages appeared that were interspersed with growth and social equity objective. During the first stage, the major emphasis was on Mahalanobis' strategy based on heavy and substantial industrialisation. In the next stage, it was realised that the growth had failed to percolate to the needy sections. So, since the Fifth FYP, focus was on fulfilling the objective of equality and special programmes were framed for this objective. In the next and present stage, the emphasis has been on strategies based on equity and poverty alleviation. The concept of equity imbibes that everyone must have equal access to basic requirements of life such as education, safe drinking water, sanitation, and health services (Bhat, 2005). To alleviate poverty, the focus in development planning shifted to employment generation and its implementation. Expanding productive employment is essential for chronic poverty reduction. Thus, economic growth is required to create more resources and also generate opportunities in the form of productive employment for needy people. Hence, there is a need to raise the level of income of the poor along with growth-promoting policies and direct poverty alleviation programmes (Dev, 2006).

Inclusive Growth in India

The criterion of equity and justice calls for the incorporation of the ones who remained bereft of the fruits of economic development, in the virtual process of economic growth. The priority must be on disseminating the benefits to under-privileged populations, particularly minorities, disabled people, and scheduled castes and tribes (Government of India, 2007). India has not recently acquired the concept of inclusive growth. India had been following the strategies oriented with the socialistic pattern of society with the prime goal of self-reliance, social justice, and the reduction of poverty. But later on, India veered to the growth model of high investment and high growth, premising spontaneous effectuation of inclu-siveness. Earlier, it was realised that though the rates of maternal and infant mor-tality had decreased, progress in literacy, education, health, and other areas had been observed; nonetheless, the progress was still slothful. India's growth has to be equal and inclusive, keeping in mind its colonial history. So, the notion of inclusiveness growth emitting both the pace and pattern of growth must aim for attaining the two main objectives, that is, elevated sustainable growth, as well as eradicating poverty. So, inclusive growth alludes to both the pace and pattern of growth that necessitate being addressed collectively (World Bank, 2008).

In keeping with this goal, the Eleventh FYP established new goals for reviving agri-cultural dynamism and developing adequate infrastructure facilities in remote areas. It also placed a strong emphasis on implementing programmes to enhance the social standard of the weaker sections and to increase their access to economic prospects for socio-economic empowerment of masses. The eradication of severe poverty, illiteracy, diseases, and discrimination is also possible only by improved access to healthcare and education. Even though multifaceted inclusive growth may be challenging to attain in a diverse country like India, it is nevertheless a required objective of the country's economic policy (Chadha & Chadda, 2020a).

Inclusive growth by very definition infers an equal distribution of resources, along with its benefits percolating to the lowest segments of society. It is a com-prehensive approach, based both on a micro- or macro-level, to generate pro-ductive employment instead of income redistribution facilitating a good life that eventually leads to rapid and sustained poverty reduction. The definition of inclusive growth includes both an absolute definition and a relative definition of pro-poor growth. The absolute definition of pro-poor growth reduced absolute poverty, while the relative definition of pro-poor growth signifies removing ine-qualities and disparities (World Bank, 2008). The focus of the government should be on growth-enhancing policies for an effective poverty alleviation strategy that would benefit the poorest in the country. The results of distribution strategies of the policies suggested that the increase in average incomes tends to advantage the poor and everyone in the society (Dollar & Kraay, 2001).

Dimensions of Inclusive Growth

The inclusive growth approach entails a decrease in poverty and disparity as well as fair opportunities for everyone related to social and economic prospects. Thus, both at the micro-village level and the macro-level of the entire economy, inclusive growth will be reflected in fair distribution, the creation of more employment opportunities, and equitable participation (Chadha & Chadda, 2020a). Three broad dimensions of inclusive growth, as proposed by the Asian Development Bank (2011), comprise economic, social, and institutional dimensions. The economic dimension incorporates the reduction of poverty achieved through high, efficient, and sustained growth; social safety nets include social protection and social inclusion that ensures equal access to opportunities to protect the most vulnerable and deprived sections of society. These are the three critical policy pillars that aim at high economic growth, along with ensuring that all members of the society would share the fruits of growth equitably.

(i) *Economic growth via productive employment:* High, perpetual, and economic growth could be a key to generating productive and decent job opportunities. It is essential to not only reduce poverty but also create ample resources; so, it would enable better access to education, health, physical infrastructure, and resources that facilitate equal opportunity.

(ii) *Social safety nets:* Social safety nets ensure the provision of basic needs to the chronically poor and vulnerable sections of society, who could not assert to attain the benefits of growth, viz. unemployment correction, rehabilitation, retraining, and reorienting displaced labour due to rationalisation of programmes. This includes the programmes related to labour policies and programmes for child protection, social insurance protection, and welfare schemes.

(iii) *Institutional dimensions:* Basic schooling and good health are essential to expanding human capacities, especially of the poor and marginalised sections including women. This is important to increase equality in accessing economic opportunities that lead to enhanced social and economic justice.

The multifaceted concept of inclusive growth alludes to the equitable allocation of resources, with benefits dispersed to every section of society. It would make growth participative, leading to a decline in perpetual poverty, substantial improvement in health, universal education to children, and skill development that creates better and more productive employment opportunities. Furthermore, it would improve access to basic facilities like water, sanitation, electricity, housing, and road connectivity. Adequate livelihood opportunities, productive employment generation, and equal distribution of resources, in conjunction with reducing poverty, would be critical for an inclusive growth strategy (Government of India, 2007).

Interfaces Between Social Sector Development and Growth Inclusiveness

The growth that is inclusive and focussed on the social sector is mutually reinforcing and complementary. While the accomplishment of inclusive growth expresses in social sector development, social sector development drives the attainment of inclusive growth (Chadha & Chadda, 2020b). Government programmes and policies are framed for bringing the weaker sections into the mainstream. It might result in increased incomes, which might have further implications including better access to school and housing as well as more availability of food, affordable healthcare, and basic sanitation. The best way to achieve inclusive growth is through the strengthening of human capacities and improved delivery of social services and economic services (Government of India, 2012a). Due to the growing concern of policymakers towards gnawing poverty and escalating unemployment, social sector development in concomitant with inclusive growth assumed importance. That's why the policies and programmes of the government aimed at employment generation and poverty eradication to make growth more inclusive while formulating the Eleventh FYP (Burange et al., 2012).

The important objectives of development planning in India have been, increasing employment opportunities, bringing self-sufficiency, economic stability, social welfare, reduction in economic inequalities, and removal of regional disparities, social protection, and social justice to justify equity conjectures. India experienced the menace of social inequalities, economic imbalances, regional disparities, and caste-based discrimination since independence and these perils of inequality and discrimination would be removed only if more employment opportunities are created and participation of the weaker sections ensured. The vision of this broad-based growth strategy is to accelerate inclusiveness by encompassing equality of opportunities as well as the removal of economic and social imbalances for all sections of society. The key to achieving inclusive and sustainable growth is indeed the prime agenda of inclusive growth. The capability approach to human development and the social sector development necessitated through this inclusive growth model ensures swift and steady growth (Chadha & Chadda, 2020b).

The government has made various attempts to improve the welfare of disadvantaged groups, yet they still experience societal and economic discrimination. Along with important components like the abolition of poverty, the creation of productive employment, improved health, access to education, social safety nets, and welfare program, inclusive development also encompasses social inclusion as well as financial inclusion of the destitute and marginalised populace (Government of India, 2012a). Central government expenditure, as well as state government expenditure, incurred on social services and economic services had augmented in the last decade; yet India's social sector accomplishments have not been satisfactory and could have been improved (Varma, 2012).

To provide basic amenities to the people, there is a need to increase the people's participation, decentralisation of planning, the extension of irrigation facilities, and better equipment and technologies in rural areas to lift the standards of living in villages. Several efforts have been made by the Government of India through programmes and projects for this purpose. Numerous steps have been taken to improve the standard of living of the least benefitted people by empowering the rural poor, skill and knowledge development, empowering women and children, developing community-based programmes, more productive employment generation opportunities, eradicating chronic poverty, improving literacy and health services, and access to safe and potable water. The main focus of these schemes and programmes has been to improve the quality of life of vulnerable and poor people in society. India aimed for inclusivity in its growth process so that the benefits trickled down to everyone and hunger, disease, and inequity would all be eliminated as a result of this development process. All facets of society should profit from the growth.

However, despite the fact that the level of chronic poverty has been steadily and slowly declining, a substantial proportion of the population continues to live below the national and international poverty levels. India intended to involve people in a people-centric approach to development. The poorest of the poor have been receiving the benefits of economic policies such as the dismantling of monopolies, minimising the accumulation of power, encouraging equality, and democratic inclusive growth. India's determination to strengthen the inclusiveness of the growth agenda was further bolstered by the inadequacies of the trickle-down approach (Chadha & Chadda, 2020a). There is a need to eliminate regional, social and economic disparities, along with the assurance of a higher standard of living and development opportunities for every section of society. Making the entire process of social sector growth more inclusive would mean the empowerment of the underprivileged and marginalised classes (Government of India, 2012a).

The present study is designed to look into and explore the nature, extent, and pattern of social sector development priorities, expenditure, and allocations, and how much India's government is committed to alleviating social inequality and affecting the redistribution of wealth. The study's primary objective is to examine how India's policy for inclusive growth and the expansion of the social sector corroborate one another.

Need and Importance of the Study

The study's significance can be found in both its theoretical and practical applications. Regarding the theoretical side, the study is anticipated to examine the significance of social sector growth in India for ensuring inclusive development. On the practical side, policymakers may choose to concentrate on those components of social sectors that would hasten inclusive growth depending on the analysis. The strand of development strategy, oriented with the prior development of social sectors justifies equity with development. It reinforces capacities and capabilities in the human assets of the country through equitable access to assets and opportunities and thus, percolates the path of a trickle-down approach to growth.

Human development is fundamental for promoting national development and the appropriate approach is through social sector development. Social sector development follows the people-centred approach by expanding the capabilities and capacities of people. Besides reviewing the progress of important government programmes related to social sector development, the study endeavours to explore the role of social sector development in tackling and mitigating the perpetuated poverty and the generation of productive employment. The study also aims to highlight the key components of inclusive development, such as the creation of more employment opportunities, access to equal participation, and the reduction of poverty. This study seeks to examine some of the issues concerning the linkages between inclusivity and social sector growth in India. This study aims to evaluate the implications of India's social sector development and its sub-sectors on inclusiveness of growth.

Objectives of the Study

In light of the above theoretical and practical manifestations, the study attempts to evaluate the nature, extent, and pattern of social sector spending and allocations in India since the economic reforms. This study also intends to gauge the effect and contribution of different components of social sector development in India, on the inclusiveness of growth. The present study focusses on the following objectives:

- To assess the physical and financial performance of various programmes and schemes related to social sector development.
- Developing and measuring the composite inclusivity index of India's economic growth.
- To observe how India's inclusive growth will be impacted by the expansion of the social sector.
- To elucidate the relationship between inclusive growth and various sub-sectors of social sector development in India.

Hypothesis

The present study dwells upon the hypothesis that social sector development is fundamental to making economic growth inclusive.

Chapter Scheme

1. Introduction: The Theoretical Framework.
2. Review of Literature.
3. Data, Scope, and Research Methodology.
4. Social Sector Development: Programmes and Policies in India.
5. Growth and Development of the Social Sector in India.
6. Construction of India's Index of Growth Inclusivity.
7. Social Sector Development and Inclusive Growth in India: A Quantitative Approach.
8. Problems, Government Measures, and Policy Implications.

Chapter 2

Review of Literature

In this chapter, a review of literature about the development of social sectors for nurturing human development for promoting inclusive growth has been carried out. Both human development and social sector are synergetic which scaffold national development. The social sector comprises those sectors of the economy, viz. education, health, potable water supply and basic sanitation, housing development, the welfare of disadvantaged classes, and rural development, which promote human welfare. Because policymakers are concerned about rising unemployment and poverty, social sector development has recently gained attention in tandem with inclusive growth (Chadha & Chadda, 2020b). This chapter consists of studies relating to human development dimensions of growth, social welfare and human development, social sector development and inclusive growth, and their interrelationship.

Human Development Dimension of Growth

Development is defined in a national framework that requires the enhancement of basic human needs to increase the masses' standard of living. The theories stated by Smith (1776) and Malthus (1798) stressed land, labour, and capital as the three main economic model elements. Classical economists emphasised shifting the dynamic state to a constant state of the economy; so, there must be full employment. Being followers of Laissez-faire economy, the classical economists opposed government interventions in the economy and favoured the concept of the free market and free economic competition.

Subsequently, Marx (1867) focussed on the importance of technological progression. The idea of introducing technological progress was the result of competition among capitalists. These technological changes, hence, foster production relations in the country. Classical development economics underestimated the significant role of technical progress and international trade in the development process.

Neoclassical economists Solow (1956), Swan (1956), Meade (1961), and Aghion and Howitt (1998) advocated the concept of technology along with labour and capital for the long-run economic growth process. Solow–Swan focussed on explaining the significant role of technological change in economic growth. Their model assumed that technological change interaction progresses exogenously and

Social Sector Development and Inclusive Growth in India, 23–40
Copyright © 2023 by Ishu Chadda
Published under exclusive license by Emerald Publishing Limited
doi:10.1108/978-1-83753-186-820231003

postulated that by incorporating the mechanism of linking labour and capital with a continuous production function, the output would generate steady progress in the economy.

In the classical and neoclassical growth models, non-economic variables like human capital or human development did not play any significant role in economic growth. On the other hand, Schumpeterian growth theory focussed on the importance of the role of an entrepreneur by emphasising three determinants, viz. physical capital, technology, and human capital for growth. Schumpeter (1934, 1942) propagated the notion of innovation and stated that the essential requirements for development related to cash, credit, and innovative returns. As a protagonist of entrepreneurial profit, Schumpeter insisted that in a developing economy, innovation would encourage new business ventures to restore the old business. Booms and depressions are, actually, unavoidable and may not be excluded or rectified to avoid upsetting the creation of new wealth via innovation.

Acs and Audretsch (1988) tested the Schumpeterian hypothesis and stressed that Schumpeter had conceptualised the two approaches for economic development, that is, innovation approach and a contemporary approach. The first approach to innovation established that innovation is directly and significantly affected by industry market structure. The level of concentration, the size, and distribution of firms, the extent of entry barriers, and the technological progress in the industry largely affected the economic growth process. While the contemporary approach emphasised the new firms utilising innovation as a strategy that focussed on decentralising the markets and in addition to this, creating a competitive environment between small and large firms in the huge corporate sector.

Development is concerned with human beings and includes improvements in incomes and outputs; and also, it involves changes in institutional, social, and administrative structures. Romer (1986) and Lucas (1988) stated the development process of an economy required investment in human capital, innovation, and knowledge. Their endogenous growth theory highlighted the process of economic growth using new forms of technology with efficient and effective means of production and human involvement. It was perceived that the notion of economic growth happened when people rearrange the resources in a manner of usefulness. The emphasis was laid on learning by the means of the process where employees of the firm would be trained to manufacture superior and qualified products and would be amplified in the production by firms.

Hasan (2001), Galor and Moav (2004), and Galor (2011) elucidated the substitution of physical capital accumulation for human capital accumulation. Human capital accumulation was considered the primary ingredient of economic growth which changed the subjective impact of imbalances on the process of economic development. In the initial phases of industrialisation, physical capital accumulation was a leading foundation of economic growth, and disparities occurred in the process of development by diverting the resources towards individuals whose marginal propensity to save was high. However, in later phases of development, as human capital becomes the foremost source of economic growth, an approach towards the equal distribution of income facilitates the process of economic growth. The combination of labour, capital, and technology will be more efficiently utilised, if the firm invests in educated, skilled, and healthy workers. It implied that the labour workforce would be more productive and capital, as well as technology, would be used efficiently by investing in human capital.

Social Welfare and Human Development

Human capital and economic welfare are closely related, which in turn impact human development and human welfare. The development process will become substantial with investment in education and health particularly, for the weaker and marginalised sections of society. Starting to Schultz (1961), education has been viewed as an investment in human capital, instead of being a consumption good according to Keynes. In a number of studies, Blaung et al. (1969), Tilak (1987a), and Psacharopoulos (1994) explained that investment in education capitulates in a higher rate of return than investment in physical capital. Initially, education includes formal education at the primary level, then the secondary level, and subsequently higher education which includes colleges, universities, and higher technical institutes. After formal theoretical education, the most effective mode of human capital formation is on-the-job training, which transforms educational skills and training into practical vocation (Harbison & Myers, 1964).

While politically, human development is concerned with equal participation of people in the political process, and being a good citizen, would strengthen democracy. From social and cultural points of view, human development would take place with proper schooling, good health, and all basic needs. These basic needs are the basic objectives of development and these are the most important ends in themselves. Srinivasan and Verma (1993) have given the four dimensions of development associated with economic, political, socio-psychological, and spiritual characteristics. These characteristics crystallised in a pattern to achieve human development. The flow initiates with the economic facet, followed by the socio-psychological aspect, political characteristics, and lastly the spiritual phase. These stages of human development cannot be achieved in isolation and must follow the whole sequence to achieve economic development.

Economic growth is concerned with the general welfare of the downtrodden. Human development eventually translates into the economic growth of the nation. It aims at improving the quality of life, thus, enhancing the capabilities and capacities of the people. The think tanks should not only concentrate on the consumption of goods and services but, also consider the basic amenities needed to have a good life (Morris & Alpin, 1982). Sen (1997) and Alkire (2002) explained that human development has two dimensions, viz. acquiring of human capabilities and utilisation of acquired capabilities as these capabilities have an economic value for employers and the economy as a whole.

Hicks and Streeten (1979) and Hicks (1987) stated that the countries with more literacy rates and good life expectancy are considered to be growing countries. It was also mentioned that there existed a strong association between growth and literacy levels in the growing countries. The reason could be, that as the growing countries have more resources to be spent on education and health, the latter could have a strong connection between literacy, life expectancy, and growth.

United Nations Development Programme (1990) introduced the concept of human development as 'the process of enlarging people's choice'. This included the concept of cooperation, equality, security, empowerment, and sustainability for human development via education, a long and healthy life, and productive employment for a decent standard of living. Haq (1995) and Sen (2000) stated that the concept of human development is broader than GDP growth, income and wealth, production of commodities, and accumulation of capital. Society's welfare should be evaluated based on people's capabilities like knowledge, health, education, and active participation in social life. Thus, expanding human capabilities, guarding the freedom of the people, and the people of the country become the actual wealth of the country.

Sen (1992) contributed to the human development approach by extending and enlarging the fundamental ideas and measurement tools. There existed new areas of policy challenges, ranging from sustainable development to gender equality; poverty eradication; consumption and sustainable development; human rights; and democracy (Fukuda-Parr, 2003). The concept of human development is complex and multidimensional and often called 'Eastern strategy'. This Eastern strategy propagated the enhancement of quality of life like more literacy, life expectancy, and broadening of basic facilities like education, and healthcare which are essential for human development (Naidu et al., 2008). The development policies and programmes should be related to education. Healthcare and other social welfare activities should be dynamic and pragmatically linked with policy innovations that have long-term implications for human development (United Nations Development Programme, 2013).

Kumar and Sharma (2008) and Naidu et al. (2008) explained that more access to higher education, decent healthcare, and productive work leads to human development. Human development is a fundamental facet of economic growth, and investment in the social sector would have positive results for the higher growth of the nation. The focus should be on empowering the lowest rung of the society to minimise backwash effects and maximise spread effects to accelerate economic development. Hence, it can be said that the prompt objective of human development is to ultimately lead to higher economic growth.

Anand and Sen (2000), Antony and Laxmaiah (2008), and Akhtar (2008) expressed their views on the relationship between human development and economic growth. Their concept of sustainable human development is connected to human development with environmental aspects. Sustainability is linked with healthcare directly. Proper diet, health awareness, cleanliness, proper sanitation, provision of sewages green environment, and health awareness are substantial for the development transition. The increase or decrease of national income is allied with the quality of life of human beings and the accessibility of social basic needs. Pal and Pant (1993) added new measures and modified the human development index (HDI). The measures already included are education, healthcare, and accessibility to basic needs, but the concept of equality and equity is missing. So, the new concept included poverty eradication and equal distribution of growth benefits in measuring the HDI.

Some researchers studied the association between economic growth and human development. Sharma and Kumar (1993) analysed the relationship between these two by taking 16 major states of India from the period 1960–1987. This study concluded that the gaps that existed between human development are contracting now, and more the human development, more will be the economic growth. Similarly, Ranis et al. (2000) measured the relationship between human development and economic growth using 76 developing countries' data by deploying regression for the time reference of 1960–1992. The country that favoured human development resulted in benign human development and further accelerates economic development and vice versa.

Ranis and Stewart (2000) stated that a two-way relationship exists between this economic growth and human development. The study employed the regression analysis to a cross-country sample and highlighted that expenditure incurred on education, healthcare, and especially for women's development showed a substantial relationship between the two. Mazumdar (2001) and Prabhu and Kamdar (2002) also investigated the causal relationship between economic growth and social development. The study analysed that human development should be given primary focus. Human development would be reinforced and contribute to social attainments with more productivity, consequently leading to economic growth. Hari (2003) investigated the relationship between public expenditure, human development, and economic growth from 1970 to 2000 among 14 major states of India. The study stated that public expenditure incurred on education and health positively contributed towards human development, and attaining human development is undeniably essential to have sustainable economic growth.

Social Sector Development

Social sector development encompasses the activities which contribute to human development.

> This sector includes unorganized sector and informal sector, economically vulnerable or backward classes and other categories of persons, both in rural and urban areas (*The Economic Times*, 2016), and services catering to these categories, including education, health, and medical care, water supply, and sanitation, equality of employment opportunities, housing conditions, are the factors contributing to human development. (Naidu et al., 2008)

Prabhu (2001) defined the social sector

> as those providing social security, which as defined by the International Labour Office (ILO) includes, protection which society provides for its members, through a series of measures against the economic and social distress that otherwise would be caused by the stoppage or substantial reduction of earnings resulting from sickness, maternity, employment, injury, unemployment, invalidity, old age, death, the provision of medical care and the provision of subsidies for families with children.

However, Dreze and Sen (2013) insisted that the social sector should not confine to these strategies, as in developing countries since the unemployment rate is more. So, productive employment opportunities along with social security benefits would indicate the wider aspect of the social sector. Thus, the study proposed two approaches to the social sector, that is, income-led approach and the social expenditure-led approach. The approach of the income-led social sector included productive employment opportunities via providing strategies for rural areas' development and poverty eradication programmes. The social expenditure-led approach highlighted the services provided to the masses related to education, healthcare, and nutrition also. So, the combined development of these two approaches would contribute to social sector development. Aghion and Bolton (1997) also emphasised the inclusion of numerous policies and programmes related to poverty eradication and employment generation. These programmes were necessary to remove the problems like inequalities, endemic deprivation, unemployment, poverty, and discrimination in India.

Guhun (1995), Prabhu (1997), and Sen (1997) stated that the social welfare of the masses has been the objective of India's economic policy for strengthening the social sector. Central and state governments spent a vast amount on both social and economic services. The pattern of social sector expenditure was analysed in these studies, highlighting that the expenditure was mostly incurred on education followed by health, housing, urban development, broadcasting, labour and employment, social security and welfare, and relief for natural calamities by the government.

Many studies like Rao (1964), Panchamukhi (2000), and Tilak (1987b) stated that before the human development approach to development, the expenditure incurred on education and health was very low. After the introduction of the HDI, the expenditure increased. Prabhu and Chatterjee (1993) mentioned the low social spending of India, as the social allocation ratio (SAR) of India was lesser than recommended ratio of United Nations Development Programme. Some states like Madhya Pradesh, Bihar, Orissa, Uttar Pradesh, and Rajasthan apparent were with low HDI and more population. So, to achieve the desired results, India should concentrate on collective efforts by both the centre and the states for improving HDI.

Chakraborthy (2002) analysed the country-wise impact of social sector spending on HDI for three years from 1993 to 1995. Countries were selected based on high and low HDI for the study using pooled least squares method. These were Bangladesh, Pakistan, India, Sri Lanka, Australia, Sweden, the United States, Canada, the United Kingdom, Norway, Indonesia, South Korea, China, and Malaysia. The study revealed the significant and positive relationship between HDI and per capita expenditure related to education and health. Kaur and Misra (2003) studied the relationship between HDI and social sector expenditure. States were ranked as per HDI by deploying rank correlation first. A positive association had been seen between HDI and social sector development at an aggregated level. In addition to it, the association between education and health, and HDI was also observed at disaggregated levels. The result revealed that government spending on education showed a more important role compared with health expenditure.

Panchamukhi (2000), Basu (2005), Sarma (2005), and Dev (2010) emphasised the components of the social sector that contributed to the promotion of human development. Social sector programmes are intended for human development, particularly the upliftment of the people at the grass root level. So, it becomes incumbent upon the central government to carefully monitor the transfer of funds and resources to avoid any misappropriation of funds. Thus, the state governments should have a significant role in the distribution and allocation of funds among different segments of social sector spending, so that component allocations were utilised efficiently. This division of responsibility would be the main factor for the proper allocation of social sector spending across India.

Many studies also investigated the impact of economic reforms on the social sector in India. Prabhu (1996) studied the three ratios namely 'Social Allocation Ratio (SAR), Social Priority Ratio (SPR), and Public Allocation Ratio (PAR) among Indian states for four years since 1991. The SAR indicated the proportion of total revenue expenditure of state government for social services. The SPR referred to the proportion of revenue expenditure on social services and the PAR signified the ratio of revenue expenditure on social sectors to total revenue expenditure. The study revealed that SAR decreased in the majority of Indian states, and SPR did not make any significant change in the distribution of components of social services. PAR also indicated the diminishing drift in 9 states out of 15 states. The states which have high SAR and SPR also indicated low PAR. This indicated that economic reforms did not have a positive impact on social sector development.

Panchamukhi (2000) investigated the state and central expenditure on social sector development using the time of 1987–1998. The study stated that economic reforms brought more disparity and more inequalities across the states in India. Pathak (2005) and Ahmad (2005) examined the association between social sector outlays and economic growth during different plans. These studies revealed that the government undertook several efforts to eradicate poverty by expanding social services in India. The plan outlays for the same registered a rising trend from First Five Year Plan to the Ninth Five Year Plan period. However, despite such efforts, India had not achieved 100 per cent literacy.

Dev and Mooij (2002) examined the allocations and expenditure on components of social services at the centre level, at the state level, and at the central and state levels combined. The study investigated the trends of plan and non-plan expenditure of various components of social services as a percentage of gross domestic product (GDP), as a proportion of average budgetary expenditure, and also as a share of real per capita expenditure. During the 1980s, the expenditure incurred on social services as a proportion of GDP showed an increasing trend since the mid-1990s. Per capita real expenditure also indicated a rising trend for the same period. Although, state government expenditure incurred on social services and economic services registered a declining trend. Then, in 1996, the government shifted the focus to rural infrastructure and rural employment schemes.

Shariff et al. (2002a) elaborated on the number of schemes and strategies adopted by the government for the development of the nation. The programmes were, Wage and Employment Programmes, Housing and Urban Development

Programmes, Social Security Programmes, Education and Health-related Programmes like Sampoorna Gramin Yojana, Food for Work Programme, Public Distribution System, National Old Age Pension Scheme, Integrated Rural Development Programme, National Family Benefit Scheme, Operation Black Board, Mid-day Meal, Integrated Child Development Programmes, etc., for poverty eradication and to ameliorate the weaker section of the society. The policymakers should make plans and policies with more focus on inclusive growth in the planning process.

Shariff et al. (2002b) revealed that the funds were distributed by the central government for employment generation as well as rural development. The provision of providing basic services to the rural people was the main focus, like basic education, healthcare, maternal benefits, potable water, sewerage provision, sanitation practices, nutrition, and road construction. One major benefit of road construction was that many unemployed became employed because of this labour-intensive activity.

Tilak (2007a) stated that government should follow the recommendations of Kothari's commission about spending at least 6 per cent of GDP on education, against the present 3.5 per cent. Different trends were registered in education spending in the 1960s; the increasing trends in the spending on education were followed by a sudden decrease in the 1970s, and in the 1980s marginal increase, followed by again decreasing trends in the 1990s were registered.

Sudhakar and Mose (2005) revealed that the percentage share of social sector spending in India had been growing but at a marginal pace at the central level and state level combined, from the pre-reform to the post-reform period. In the case of states, the combined expenditure of all 26 states showed a decreasing trend. In the case of the centre, the expenditure incurred on social services as well as economic services out of total budgetary expenditure indicated a rising trend.

The study by Dev and Mooij (2004) pointed out that the core aim of the Indian government is to reduce the rampant poverty and development of the most vulnerable and destitute population. The policies and programmes designed by the government should focus on social mobilisation, inclusiveness, and poverty alleviation. The study revealed that expenditure on the social sector was much more in the 1980s as compared to the 1990s, and the annual growth rates of the central government are higher than the states.

Mooij and Dev (2004) elaborated on the priorities given to different social sector components, based on actual expenditure incurred, in different budget speeches between 1990 and 2002. The study stated that budget speeches made by finance ministers focussed on the poor and all decisions were related to the poor only. But in reality, no work was done on the removal of social inequality, redistribution of income policies, and employment generation programmes.

Prabhu (2005) observed the adverse impact on social sector development and poverty generation programmes because of economic reforms. This problem was more associated with countries where problems of poverty, illiteracy, malnutrition, and unemployment existed along with the massive population. The central theme of economic reforms was to shift the focus of state government on social sector development, from economic activities but it failed. Gaur (2006) investigated the relationship between education and healthcare by deploying regression analysis on Indian states for the period 1980–2002. Pre-economic reform period, as well as the post-reform period, showed a low amount of spending on education and healthcare. States like Haryana, Bihar, Orissa, Gujarat, Madhya Pradesh, Maharashtra, and Rajasthan, except Punjab registered a low SAR. The study suggested increasing the social sector spending urgently.

Bhat (2005), Tulsidhar and Sarma (1993), and Adi (2004) studied that the combined expenditure in absolute terms incurred on social sector development increased since economic reforms, but at a marginal pace. Some studies also examined the components of social sector development separately. Kadekodi and Kulkarni (2006) explained the impact of economic reforms on public expenditure incurred on health. The study developed a model taking revenue deficit, health sector performance, and reforms as the dummy. A positive relationship had been observed in the post-reform period between the variables. The deficits in public spending at the central level indicated the expected incidence of unemployed and scale economies in public sector health facilities.

Joshi (2006) studied the combined expenditure of centres and states on education and health from the period 1986 to 2003. Since 1991, central government expenditure incurred on social sector spending increased while in the case of states, it showed a declining trend. Central plan and non-plan outlay on promotional and protective social sector, and on its components during the pre-reform (1986–1991) and post-reform periods (1991—2003) revealed the growth from 6.58 per cent in the pre-reform period to 8.59 per cent of plan outlay in the post-reform period. It was pointed out that the increase in central government expenditure was partly attained by dropping the distributions by the centre and state plans. In the case of education and health, the central share registered a rising trend, and the state's share decreased.

Rawat et al. (2008) analysed the components of health and family welfare for the period 1986–2003. The study highlighted the revenue and capital outlay of the centre, states, and union territories of India. It revealed that despite numerous efforts to improve the health of the public since independence, yet failed to achieve the desired results. Government should increase the quality of services with the rising amount of expenditure incurred. It has been observed that there is a lack of human resources like teachers, doctors, and well-trained specialists in the health and education sectors. So, there is a need to have adequate human resources to strengthen infrastructural development. India has enlarged a better health infrastructure framework and manpower for primary, secondary, and tertiary care in government, voluntary, and private sectors throughout the last five decades.

Ahmad and Bhakta (2008) analysed the problems and prospects of education and health in India. The expenditure incurred on education and health had been varying. There had been the presence of constraints like resources and limited participation of the community. So, it emphasised that effective implementation of the programme played an important role to have satisfactory and good performance in social sector development. The expenditure incurred on social sector development by the central and state governments was generally not enough to have higher outcomes.

Maheshwari (2012) explained different components of the social sector like education, health, medical care, housing, and water supply that helped to uplift the living standard of poor masses and are essential for the economic development of any state. The study explained that since economic reforms up to the year 2010, social sector spending was stagnant. It is necessary to have an effectual monitoring system to check the outcomes of the implementation of social sector development programmes to achieve the desired targets set in the plans and to streamline expenditures.

Wadhwa (2013) studied the trends and structure of the outlay incurred by the union government since 1980. Since independence, the government increased the pace of expenditure because of increased economic activity. The economic crisis in 1991 was the reason to reduce the expenditure and it also led to a decline in development and capital expenditures. A rise in government expenditure simultaneously escalated the deficits of the government. The social services expenditure ratio remained stagnant since the economic reforms, that is, from 1991 to the year 2000–2001, and from 2002 to 2003 onwards this ratio had constantly levitated.

Nayak and Mishra (2014) stated that the social sector leads to the reduction of regional disparities and poverty alleviation through employment generation. Thus, the social sector has emerged as an important sector. Earlier, human development incorporated health and education as the major components, but recently, with an ever-rising concern of the government and policymakers, the development of infrastructure and other components of the social sector are also considered imperative ingredients for economic development. That is why, this sector of development claims a large public expenditure and it would remove the imbalances in the Indian economy as the social sector expands.

Basantaray and Barik (2015) analysed the trends and patterns of social sector spending of centre, state, and centre states combined since 1991. At the centre level, the majority of the share was spent on education, health, and rural development while per capita expenditure was raised for all states. Despite such an increase in outlays, India lagged in comparison to other countries. Fiscal capacity was the key for social sector expenditure to increase the efficiency in the performance of the social sector.

Barik (2015) examined the growth effects of spending on education, health, and rural development in India from the period 1990 to 2011. The study used Johansen and Jeselius multivariate cointegration analysis to investigate the impact of the above-stated three components of the social sector on economic growth. A positive and significant relationship was observed both in the long and short run for education, health, and rural development on economic growth.

Purohit (2015) carried out a state-level analysis of health and education by taking major states of India. The study used both parametric and non-parametric methods and also employed the free disposable hull (FDH) analysis and stochastic frontier model for evaluating the performance of the social sector in India. State-level inequalities were observed as different outlays were provided across states. Education and health showed increasing trends in outcomes and could improve more via reallocations of strategies, effectively using more resources, and indulging more participation of the private sector.

Inclusive Growth

In recent years, social sector development in concomitance with inclusive growth taking precedence due to the rapid increase in rampant poverty and grave unemployment problems. Kakwani and Pernia (2000) and Ali (2007) argued that tackling merely pro-poor growth policies is inadequate to address concerns like extreme poverty, widespread unemployment, and blatant inequality; however, strengthening the social sector must be given the highest priority; consequently, that policy for pro-poor and rapid growth was reoriented to encourage democratic inclusive and sustainable growth (Chadha & Chadda, 2020b).

Both absolute pro-poor growth and relative pro-poor growth have been used to describe the concept of inclusive growth. The relative definition of the pro-poor growth strategy emphasises declining inequalities meanwhile the absolute pro-poor growth reflects a drop in the actual number of poor people. Ravallion and Chen (2003) favoured the absolute pro-poor growth-oriented strategy because a decline in the total number of poor people could be a spontaneous outcome of implementing income redistribution schemes. Increased productivity and more employment opportunities would augment the pace of growth which makes it more inclusive.

Ali and Son (2007) and Bhalla (2011) contended that inclusive growth implied an equitable allocation of resources. But the allocation of resources must be taken into account the intended short- and long-term benefits of the society such as the availability of consumer goods, people's access, the standard of living, and employment, etc. A strategy of inclusiveness also calls for a renewed emphasis on education, health, and other basic public facilities along with sectoral policies which aim at improving livelihood support and increasing employment.

Organization for Economic Cooperation and Development (2006) associated inclusive growth with the absolute pro-poor growth strategy. The study observed that the basic aim of alleviating poverty was to increase the contribution, participation, and distribution of growth outcomes among poor people. Poverty and economic growth have significant and positive relations. Pro-poor growth-oriented strategy based upon equal opportunities to participate in the growth process and reduction in inequalities also signifies inclusiveness of growth.

Ali and Zhuang (2007) and Zhuang and Ali (2009) dilated upon the concept of inclusive growth as promotion and access to more equal opportunities that would lead to higher economic growth. More productive employment opportunities would ensure high and sustainable growth, and make the nation's growth inclusive. The focus of this inclusive growth definition was only on the promotion of equal opportunities. Generating more jobs may be presumed to be vital for a sustainable growth strategy which is a proper approach to the alleviation of poverty. Both income and non-income dimensions must be used to have an inclusive growth strategy (World Bank, 2008).

Commission on Growth and Development (2008) reported in the *Growth Report: Strategies for Sustained Growth and Inclusive Development* that inclusive growth incorporates the concept of equity, equal opportunity, security in the market, and more employment opportunities in the progress of economic development. Economic development could be impeded if rampant poverty and inequalities still persisted.

Ianchovichina and Lundstrom (2009) identified the concept of inclusive growth with productive employment opportunities. Inclusive growth is understood from two perspectives, that is, long run and short run. In the case study of Zambia, lack of proper education and health, poor accessibility of capital in the market for the poor, and inadequate infrastructure and basic facilities in rural areas acted as obstacles to inclusive growth. The direct redistribution of income policy did not work well. So, policies should be implemented in the short run to have productive employment for the poor people to make growth inclusive.

Klasen (2010) defined inclusive growth from two angles, that is, absolute definition and relative definition of inclusive growth. The absolute definition linked growth with the increase in income of poor people, while the relative definition propagated pro-poor growth with the proportionate rise in income among the poor, that is, lowering the inequality. If inclusive growth is related to absolute poverty reduction only, it purely diminished the abject poverty, but simultaneously it may increase the disparities. Consequently, there would be no inclusive growth. Nonetheless, inclusive growth is related to the relative pro-poor growth, which professed fair and equitable distribution of benefits to all societal segments whether more fortunate or less fortunate. This type of growth reflects the development of weaker, poor, and destitute sections.

In order to develop a composite inclusive growth index, McKinley (2010) considers four dimensions of 'growth, productive employment, and economic infrastructure; income poverty and equity; human capabilities, and social protection' and assign weights to each of them. The generated index has a range of 1–10 and it is also further put to the test countries like Indonesia, India, Philippines, Cambodia, Bangladesh, and Uzbekistan. A score of 1–3 falls under the category of unsatisfactory progress, a score of 4–7 indicates satisfactory progress, and an 8–10 score specifies superior progress. India, Bangladesh, Uzbekistan, Indonesia, and Cambodia have a score that hovers in the range of 4–7 which highlighted satisfactory progress. Only Philippines has a score below 4, indicating unsatisfactory progress (Chadha & Chadda, 2020b).

Nayak et al. (2010) advocated the concept of equity, equal opportunity, security in the market, and more employment opportunities, as fundamental for inclusive economic growth. The growth-oriented policies need to be linked with participative development that ultimately results in the equal dispersion of benefits to all sections of society. The actual growth should include everyone who participated in the growth process both in terms of decision-making as well as contributing to the growth process. Thus, inclusive growth has been related to broad-based or people-oriented growth that consisted of even-handed participation.

Rauniyar and Kanbur (2010) stated that there is no particular definition of inclusive growth. The study highlighted inclusive growth with the decreasing disparities and inequalities through the approach of income dimension as well as non-income dimension that included social, economic, and institutional dimensions. Hence, inclusiveness, by using non-income dimensions like education and health, will have the outcome of benefitting the most disadvantaged section.

Three broad dimensions of inclusive growth, as proposed by Asian Development Bank (2011), comprise economic, social, and institutional dimensions. The economic dimension incorporates the reduction of poverty achieved through high, efficient, and sustained growth; social safety nets include social protection and social inclusion ensuring equal access to opportunities, and the institutional dimension facilitates protecting the most vulnerable and deprived sections of society. These are the three critical policy pillars that aim at high economic growth, along with ensuring that all members of the society would share the fruits of growth equitably.

Hirway (2011) emphasised that the broad-based growth process of a nation would indicate inclusive growth; if it includes the eradication of poverty, new job prospects, and reduction of urban-rural inequalities among different socio-economic groups. The increase in opportunities for the destitute and deprived groups would indicate inclusive growth if these groups participate as contributors, not as beneficiaries.

Palanivel (2011) explained that to bring inclusiveness to the country, efforts should be put into improving the sectors like education and healthcare. More employment opportunities must be generated to empower the meagre group through equal access and opportunities. Thus, the concept of inclusive growth is defined as that growth that ensures equitable distribution among all the members of society who participated and contributed to the economy. The most direct way to achieve inclusive growth is to bring the objective of full employment to the top of the policy agenda (Felipe, 2012).

Palanivel and Unal (2010) mentioned that the inclusivity of growth would be strengthened and expanded when poverty will be abolished. This theory states that when markets where the poor work is more accessible, with improved living conditions for the poor, including better housing and related amenities, as well as lower costs for items that the poor must pay, then growth becomes inclusive. Since independence, there have not been any explicitly pro-poor and broad-based policies because the concentration has been on pro-growth policies and initiatives to address and eliminate poverty by trickling down. Though, this path of economic growth resulted in significant and rising inequalities, which made it difficult to eradicate poverty and, in turn, slowed the process of economic development. Therefore, the benefits of growth policies must result in additional opportunities for productive employment and increased earnings for the poor. As a result, the development strategy needs to be more broad-based, sustainable, democratic, equitable, and people-centric. Since the majority of people consumed public goods more frequently, increasing social spending might elevate their standard of living. Consequently, social sector expenditure assures that the socio-economically disadvantaged groups in the country have access to essential requirements like quality healthcare and education, increased employment opportunities, and improved infrastructure, all of which will eventually result in sustainable inclusive development (Chadha & Chadda, 2020b).

The three dimensions of inclusive growth identified by Ramos et al. (2013) are reducing poverty and inequality, fair opportunities for employment opportunities, and economic and social involvement in the developmental process.

This study investigated two points in time, namely 1996 and 2006, in 43 developing countries using cross-country data analysis. A scale from 0 to 1 was used to create the inclusivity index. If the index's value was more mainly geared to the lower side, it meant that performance had been better. As a result, a country was deemed to be more inclusive the nearer the index value was to 0. A high level of inclusion was represented by the low index score. The index was categorised as having a very high level of inclusivity if it falls between 0 and 0.2, a high level if it falls between 0.2 and 0.4, a medium level if it falls between 0.4 and 0.6, a low level if it falls between 0.6 and 0.8, and an extremely low level if it falls between 0.8 and 1 (Chadha & Chadda, 2020b).

Suryanarayana (2013) explained the concept of inclusive growth via conventional and current approaches. The conventional approach measured the economic performance of a country by quantifying the outcome of economic activity in terms of percentage changes. But this approach neglected the concept of distribution among poor masses. On the other hand, the current approach focussed on the welfare approach, which emphasised on overall reduction of poverty and food insecurity. This approach also ignored the measure of relative consumption and poverty after income growth.

Social Sector Development and Inclusive Growth in India

The growth that is inclusive and focussed on the social sector is mutually reinforcing and complementary. The social sector promotes inclusive growth, and inclusive growth necessitates social sector development. Bolt (2004) highlighted the role of agriculture and the rural economy, in making growth more inclusive. One-third of the population lived in rural areas and depends upon rural-based activities for earnings. That is why the study laid stress on the acceleration of agriculture and rural development. Improving technology, the right incentives, well-functioning markets, non-farm goods and services, employment, incomes, high-value commodities, and infrastructure connectivity would provide the base for value addition in the farm sector.

Mukhopadhaya and Saha (2005) and Shukla and Mishra (2013) viewed that while framing the policies for the poor and the vulnerable sections, there is a need to increase the investment in social sectors, health, and education. However, there is a considerable gap between policy-making and its implementation that impinges upon distributive justice and equity.

A new strategy of achieving quicker growth while being inclusive was adopted by the Indian government, refocussing its traditional policy of substantial investment and economic growth. Improved economic conditions for the populace were the goal of India's adherence to intended economic development. Widespread expansion is necessary for the destitute and downtrodden segments of society to partake in it, especially income and employment. In keeping with this goal, the Eleventh Five Year Plan established new goals for reviving agricultural dynamism and developing adequate infrastructure facilities in remote areas. It also placed a strong emphasis on implementing programmes to enhance the social standard of the weaker sections and to increase their access to economic prospects for the socio-economic empowerment of the masses. The eradication of severe poverty, illiteracy, diseases, and discrimination is also possible only by improved access to healthcare and education (Chadha & Chadda, 2020a).

However, Kannan (2007) in his study, opposed the advocacy of inclusive growth in India, as enunciated by Planning Commission in the Eleventh Five Year Plan. Regardless of the rhetoric of inclusive growth, there had been an over-bearing emphasis on raising GDP growth, to more than 9 per cent; establishing Special Economic Zones (SEZs), continuing to increase incentives for investment from abroad (FDI), expelling the urban land ceiling, lenient labour laws, the inadequate obligation to provide welfare benefits, pertaining protective measures at the workplace in the unorganised sector, and has no clearly defined strategy for agriculture. Employment generation was the core ingredient of the plan but was poorly adjusted to the macro-economic framework of the Eleventh Five Year Plan as there had been a lack of well-structured planning, articulation, and the presence of inconclusiveness.

Femando (2008) explained how the up-gradation of the rural infrastructure will help in the easy accessibility of markets, which improves the basic services to rural people. In addition, it influenced the rural economic growth and more income opportunities for the rural people. The physical infrastructure deficiencies present in rural areas need to be improved so that better access could be provided for the basic services to make life better. Kuroda (2006) stated that policies and strategies must be framed to improve the quality of infrastructure, especially in rural areas. The creation of farm and non-farm employment opportunities and equitable redistribution policy in rural and urban areas must ensure the development process is more inclusive of the nation.

By generating composite economic growth indexes that included economic, social, and basic amenities components, Kundu and Varghese (2010) explored the pattern and trends of inequality among Indian states. These parameters subsequently narrowed down to a group of sub-indicators and revealed that the level of poverty eradication is less in low-developed states. It was found that designed measures of economic growth showed a significant positive link with social development and access to basic requirements (Chadha & Chadda, 2020b).

However, despite the fact that the level of chronic poverty has been steadily and slowly declining, a substantial proportion of the population continues to live below the national and international poverty levels. A substantial portion of the population was working in the informal sector, which often offered occupations with low pay and productivity. India had minimal access to basic services. However, a strong macro-economic strategy and successful economic reform execution can provide fair access to growth opportunities, demonstrating growth's inclusivity. All levels of government would need to participate in the initiatives for the successful implementation of the strategies and policies. In order for policies to be effective, these must reach the poorest people, since rising income inequality and increasing unemployment cannot be addressed by social spending alone (OECD, 2012).

Anand et al. (2013) built a model that included indices of economic growth performance in order to measure inclusive growth. In that approach, indicators of economic growth were treated as independent factors and inclusive growth was treated as a dependent variable by considering the log differences of both independent and dependent variables. This study examined the unbalanced five-year panel data of 143 countries from 1970 to 2010. Variables like trade openness, lower initial incomes, fixed investment, and total capital stock did not affect economic growth, while the variables like financial openness, FDI, and infrastructure quality have a significant relationship with economic growth.

A composite measure of inclusive growth from 2004 to 2010 was also created by Tripathi (2013). The study conducted an examination of urban India by choosing factors such as poverty, inequality, economic development, education, employment, unemployment, and standard of living. Sub-components also exist for these components. Using the Baroda ranking, the overall inclusive growth of 52 cities was calculated. Urban inequality has increased and urban poverty has decreased in correlation with higher urban growth. According to the study, urban development lacks inclusivity because it has a lower level of inclusivity (Chadha & Chadda, 2020b).

The objective of inclusiveness is the reduction of poverty by promoting productive employment and the upliftment of deprived sections. Inclusiveness has been defined as poverty reduction, socio-economic participation of marginal classes, regional balance, reducing inequality, and empowerment. Thus, inclusiveness is not only concerned with ensuring a broad-based flow of benefits or economic opportunities but also included empowerment and participation. The participatory democratic system allows people actively demand benefits and opportunities (Government of India, 2013).

Anand et al. (2014) studied the role of growth and distribution in eradicating poverty and inequalities. For this purpose, the study examined the state-level panel data of India and used the four National Sample Survey Office (NSSO) surveys of 1993–1994, 1999–2000, 2004–2005, and 2009–2010 to gauge the impact of social sector spending and financial and macro-economic conditions on inclusive growth. The study concluded that GDP growth would provide a larger base for total income and production, which ultimately leads to higher living standards for the Indian population by providing them with employment and other income-enhancing activities. Government expenditure for social sector development is associated with promoting inclusive growth and eradicating poverty. Hence, the increase in expenditure on the social sector by 1 per cent of GDP is directly linked with decreasing in the poverty rate by 0.5 per cent.

Gupta (2014) and Sharma (2014) pointed out the interdependence of the social sector and economic development in India. These studies explained that earlier India focussed on socialism which was the dominant social structure, and its inalienable objectives were economic justice, self-reliance, and the alleviation of poverty. But later on, India reoriented the strategy to high economic growth, to have a spontaneous trickle-down for inclusiveness. According to the study, there has been a slight improvement in maternal, baby, and infant death rates as well as in literacy and schooling. Numerous initiatives are carried out by the Indian government to diminish poverty and at the macro-level, these steps would be significant and beneficial for the Indian economy to make growth inclusive.

Presumptively, economic growth should promote equality in income redistribution but the slowdown of the Indian economy portrays no such evidence.

Ponmuthusaravanan and Ravi (2014) analysed the linkages between India's social sector, poverty, and inclusive growth. The condition of the vulnerable and neglected groups of society needed more attention from planners and policymakers. In order to increase inclusivity in growth, it is important to pay attention to all disadvantaged groups, not only the underprivileged classes. The underprivileged populations, such as the semi-peripatetic tribes, de-notified tribal groups, primitive tribal classes, differently-abled individuals, widows, senior citizens, internally displaced people, those suffering from HIV/AIDS, and those taking drugs, needed additional attention. The process of inclusive growth will likely be strengthened by narrowing this yawning gap.

Naqvi (2015) argued for a comprehensive vision of inclusive growth through the elimination of poverty and distributive justice. The strategy of inclusive growth is aimed at growth, distribution, and poverty reduction simultaneously. With the eradication of perpetuated poverty, distributive policies justify equity on both economic and moral grounds. So, the policies that promote equality of opportunities will lead to rapid long-run growth. The impact of the major social sector programmes in achieving inclusiveness is possible if there is wider coverage of the schemes, more evaluation of existing beneficiaries, monitoring of every scheme, and transparency. This strategy must combine dynamic efficiency, growth, and social justice as criteria for the creation of a well-ordered society, that is, free and equal opportunities, so benefits are equally shared with the least privileged members of society.

Kolawole (2016) used the auto-regressive distributed lag (ARDL) bound testing technique to examine the relationship between government expenditure and inclusive growth in Nigeria from 1995 to 2014. The study showed a long-term relationship between real GDP growth rate, inclusive growth, public resources, health, and economic freedom. Only real GDP had positive and significant relation with inclusive growth.

Pattayat and Rani (2017) investigated the relationship between social sector development and economic growth in Haryana. The study applied the Johansen cointegration test and Granger causality test using time series data from 1985 to 2016. A high degree of association was found between social sector spending and economic growth in Haryana. Granger causality signified the short-run relationships between growth and components of the social sector and suggested translating them into the long-run relationship of these variables.

According to Thorat (2011), the marginalised groups were not included in the benefit-sharing or redistribution process. There was a prevailing bias against the underprivileged group. This hindered both the improvement of inclusion and the capabilities of the marginalised sector to participate in the economy. Mukhopadhaya and Saha (2005), Thorat and Dubey (2013), and Shukla and Mishra (2013) also stated that the government has made various attempts to improve the welfare of the disadvantaged groups, yet they still face social and economic deprivation. Since the deprived classes were denied access to jobs and income-generating prospects, the disparities had indeed started to negatively impact the attempt to eradicate poverty. The advantages of growth have not been shared equally. Social and financial inclusion are both essential components of inclusive development. Major components of a democratic welfare society must be provided equally across all demographic groups, including the elimination of poverty, creation of productive jobs, improved healthcare services, and opportunities for education, social safety nets, and welfare programs.

Research Gaps Filled

The above literature review focussed on the development of the social sector and its components in India. Only partial-level studies on the social sector have been done and these have been limited to one or two components majorly. The present work is comprehensive considering all components of the social sector in aggregate and covering both financial and physical aspects of the social sector.

The study considers the various World Bank reports and various views of scholars on this subject to quantify the inclusiveness in India. The study also aims to highlight the key components of inclusive development, such as the creation of jobs, access to equal participation, and the reduction of poverty.

The majority of past studies have examined the association between Indian government spending and economic growth. However, none of the studies examines the relationship between India's inclusive growth and the development of the social sector including its components.

This type of study has been conducted to scrutinise the long- and short-run associations between the social sector and inclusive growth in India using the ARDL approach.

Chapter 3

Data, Scope, and Research Methodology

Strengthening the social sector contributes to human development, which is concerned with the equality and well-being of people as the foundation of economic growth. Economic growth is the progression of a community along with the evolution of new and better methods of production and expanding of the level of output through the development of human skills (Singh, 1966). However, welfare nations like India use the maxim 'development with justice' as the cornerstone of their socio-economic policies. To accomplish this, poverty must be abolished and income must be redistributed to benefit the majority. To ensure inclusive growth, the government must make investments in the social sector.

The study's principal research question is whether growth plans based on the human development approach, that is, social sector development, will make growth inclusive. In order to achieve the goals of economic redistribution and social fairness, India did try a trickle-down method of development, but by the end of the Fourth Plan, it had collapsed. Human welfare and development strategies have since been in the spotlight. Therefore, the purpose of the present study was to investigate the relationship between the expansion of the social sector and the inclusivity of the growth plan. The best way to achieve inclusive growth is through providing better health services, potable water, sanitation practices, access to education and housing, skill development, better opportunities for both wage employment and livelihood, electricity, and road connectivity that speed up the growth.

The main research purpose of the study is to investigate whether social sector development in India has catalysed inclusiveness of growth, and also to find out the component of the social sector that contributed to inclusiveness of growth in India. Designing of suitable methodology and selecting analytical tools are important for the significant analysis of any research problem. This chapter explains the secondary sources of data, procedure, and sampling design along with the statistical/quantitative tools which are deployed to analyse the results of the study.

The study's significance resides in both theoretical and practical dimensions. The study's theoretical component is anticipated to examine the significance of

Social Sector Development and Inclusive Growth in India, 41–66
Copyright © 2023 by Ishu Chadda
Published under exclusive license by Emerald Publishing Limited
doi:10.1108/978-1-83753-186-820231004

India's social sector growth for ensuring equitable development. On the practical side, policymakers can use the analysis of the relative importance of the various social sector components in affecting change in inclusive growth as a guide to focus on the social sector that would achieve the inclusivity goal (Chadha & Chadda, 2020a). As elaborated in the introductory chapter, the major focus of the present study is to investigate how India's inclusive growth has been affected by the expansion of the social sector.

Data Sources and Time Reference of Study

As per the nature of the study, it covers secondary data. The World Bank, Ministry of Statistics and Programme Implementation, Ministry of Human Development, various Government websites, Economic Surveys, Annual Budgets, Statistical Abstracts, and other sources provided the data for the current study. The research spans the years from 1985–1986 to 2015–2016. For the purpose of gathering information to investigate the association between the social sector and inclusive economic growth, both published and unpublished sources have been used. The information was gathered from numerous sources.

Table 2 lists the data series and sources used in the research. All financial values have been stated in 2004–2005 constant prices, and all financial values have been deflated using the proper GNP deflators.

$$\text{GNP Deflator} = \left(\frac{\text{Nominal Value of GNP}}{\text{Real Value of GNP}} \right) \times 100$$

Quantitative Tools to Analyse Data

The data were tabulated for further processing. The tables were prepared according to the objective of the study. The data were analysed with the help of percentage, mean, standard deviation, coefficient of variation, compound growth rates, principal component analysis (PCA), stepwise multiple linear regression, unit root testing, and autoregressive distributed lag (ARDL) model. Results were analysed using software IBM SPSS Statistics Version 21 and EVIEWS 10. Various quantitative techniques adopted to analyse secondary data are discussed below:

1. Coefficient of Variation

A relative measure of dispersion based on the standard deviation is the coefficient of variation. It was used to check the data consistency. There exists an inverse relationship between the coefficient of variation and consistency. The distribution with more coefficient of variation depicted that the series is more variable or more heterogeneous and with less coefficient of variation explained the less variability or more homogeneous than the other (Gupta, 2013). It was computed using the following equation:

$$CV = \frac{\sigma}{\overline{X}} * 100$$

Table 2.   Variables with Respective Data Sources.

S. No.	Variables	Data Source
1	Absolute poverty	Government of India (2009), World Bank (Datt & Ravillion, 2010), and Planning Commission
2	Income inequalities	World Bank (Datt, 1999) and United Nation Development Programme (Radhakrishna & Panda, 2006)
3	Female to male ratio in labour	Government of India (2015); World Bank Open Data (2016), (Government of India, (various rounds-a)) of Employment Exchange Statistics in India and various rounds of NSSO quinquennial data on employment and unemployment situation in India
4	Universal employment generation (MGNREGA)	Report on MGNREGA, Ministry of Rural Development (2016)
5	Share of employment of SC and ST classes	Various series of NSSO quinquennial data on employment and unemployment situation among social groups in India, various reports of Employment Exchange Statistics in India, and Handbook on Social Welfare Statistics (Government of India, (various rounds-b))
6	GPI	Various reports of Education Statistics at a Glance, Ministry of Human Resource Development
7	Female to male ratio in Parliament	Human Development Reports (HDRs) by UNDP and Electoral Statistics Pocketbook of Elections Commission of India (Government of India, (various reports-a))
8	Gross enrolment of SC/ST classes	Various reports of Handbook on Social Welfare Statistics (Government of India, (various reports-b))
9	Political participation of reserved category	Elections Commission of India issued the data (Government of India. (various reports-a)) about political participation of SCs and STs in Electoral Statistics Pocketbook

(Continued)

Table 2.   *(Continued)*

S. No.	Variables	Data Source
10	Various expenditure on components of social sector development	Annual Reports of Planning Commission (Government of India, (various issues-a)), Economic Surveys (Government of India, (various issues-b)), and Outlays Budget (Government of India, (various issues-c))
11	Gross enrolment ratio	Various reports of Education Statistics at a Glance, Ministry of Human Resource Development
12	Pupil teacher ratio	Various reports of Education Statistics at a Glance, Ministry of Human Resource Development
13	Number of hospital beds available per 1,000 population	Data from 1985 to 2008 from Indisstat.com, various reports of National Health Profile, Ministry of Health and Family Welfare
14	Number of doctors available per 1,000 population	Various reports of National Health Profile, Ministry of Health and Family Welfare
15	Number of health centres available per 1,000 population	Various reports of National Health Profile, Ministry of Health & Family Welfare and Report of Rural Health Statistics, 2014–2015 (Government of India, (various issues-f))
16	Percentage of patients recovered under epidemiological diseases out of total population	Various reports of National Health Profile, Ministry of Health & Family Welfare (Government of India, (various issues-f))
17	Percentage of child immunised out of total child population	Reports of National Family Health Survey (Burton et al., 2009; WHO, 2017)
18	Percentage of population access to potable water	Various reports of National Health Profile, Ministry of Health and Family Welfare
19	Percentage of population who have availability of toilets	Various annual reports of Ministry of Drinking Water & Sanitation

20	Percentage of population served by sewage treatment	Various annual reports of Ministry of Drinking Water & Sanitation
21	Percentage of population covered under EWS and LIG housing scheme	Various annual reports of Ministry of Housing and Urban Poverty Alleviation and Report of the Technical Group on Urban Housing Shortage
22	Number of beneficiaries covered under different welfare schemes	Various reports of Handbook on Social Welfare Statistics, India Exclusion Reports, and various annual reports (Government of India, (various reports-b)) of National Scheduled Castes Finance and Development
23	Number of construction workers employed	Construction Workers' Federation of India (Government of India, (various rounds-a))
24	Number of beneficiaries covered under social security benefits	Reports on Social Security, Development Commissioner, Ministry of Micro, Small and Medium Enterprises and various annual reports of Ministry of Labour and Employment
25	Number of beneficiaries insured under Employees State Insurance Scheme	Various annual reports of Employees State Insurance Scheme, Financial Estimates, and Performance Budget of ESIS (Government of India, (various rounds-b))
26	Percentage of population access to electricity in rural areas	World Bank Open Data (2016)
27	Road constructed in rural areas out of total roads constructed	Various reports of Basic Road Statistics in India and Ministry of Rural Development/ National Rural Road Development Agency (NRRDA)
28	Rural food consumption	Various series of NSSO report on Consumption Expenditure
29	Rural literacy rate	Various reports of Education Statistics at a Glance; Selected Socio-Economic Indicators, 2011, Ministry of Human Resource Development
30	Rural poverty	Planning Commission Data and World Bank Open Data
31	Food grains procured by FCI (lakhs tons)/production	Various reports of Ministry of Consumer Affairs, Food and Public Distribution Department of Food and Public Distribution; Handbook of Statistics on the Indian Economy (2002–2003), Reserve Bank of India

Source: Author's own configuration.

where CV is the coefficient of variation and σ is the standard deviation and it measures the absolute dispersion for the variability of the distribution. It was calculated using the following formulae:

$$\sigma = \sqrt{\frac{\sum fx^2}{N}}$$

$\overline{X}$ mean is the single value selected within the range of data which is used to represent the whole series. It was calculated using the following formulae:

$$\overline{X} = \frac{\sum X}{N}$$

In the present study, we used the coefficient of variation to look into the variation in allocations and outlays incurred on different components of the social sector. Pathak (2005) also used the coefficient of variation to observe the variation among the outlays of social sector development.

2. Compound Growth Rates

The compound annual growth rate is an effective measure to investigate growth over different periods. It is generally (Compound Annual Growth Rate (CAGR)) used to compare growth rates from different data sets. Compound growth rates have been estimated to investigate the pattern. To accomplish this, the exponential relationship has been assessed:

$$Y_t = ab^t e^{ut}$$

A linear transformation of the equation is:

$$\log Y_t = \log a + t \log b + u_t$$

where a dependent variable's value for which the growth rate needs to be calculated is $\log Y_t$. The stochastic disturbance terms a and b are constant, while t is a trend/time variable. The compound growth rate was determined using the estimated value of the regression coefficient 'b' as follows:

$$r = \text{antilog}\,(b-1)\,*100$$

where b is the projected value of the ordinary least square (OLS) and r is the compound growth rate.

In the present study, CAGR was deployed to interpret the growth of expenditure incurred on different components of the social sector. Dev and Mooij (2004), Mercy (2007), and Aggarwal (2011) examined the trends of the social sector in India during the pre-reform and post-reforms periods.

3. Principal Component Analysis

Krishnan (2010) stated that using a set of correlated variables, PCA extracts the largest volume of information represented by all the variables, which is then utilised as the index, to help pinpoint the fundamental factors in which the data move. It entails calculating a dataset's covariance matrix to reduce redundancy and increase variance (Chadha & Chadda, 2020b). Antony and Rao (2007) mentioned that a useful method for condensing a huge number of variables into a more comprehensible subset of uncorrelated factors is the PCA. It makes an effort to pinpoint the underlying factors or elements responsible for the correlation pattern among a group of variables that have been observed (Chadha & Chadda, 2020a). The basic terms relating to PCA are explained as follows:

(i) *Kaiser–Meyer–Olkin (KMO):* The KMO test tells whether or not enough items are predicted by each factor. Field (2009) mentioned that KMO score values above 0.5 are considered acceptable, values between 0.5 and 0.7 are considered medium, values between 0.7 and 0.8 are considered acceptable, values between 0.8 and 0.9 are considered excellent, and values above 0.9 are considered fantastic.

(ii) *Bartlett's test of sphericity:* The variables should be sufficiently correlated by Bartlett's test of sphericity to serve as a sound foundation to run PCA. The population correlation matrix's variables are tested for their lack of correlation using Bartlett's test of sphericity. Factor analysis should be used because Bartlett's test is immensely important ($p < 0.001$) (Malhotra et al., 2006).

(iii) *Principal component:* A principal component is a linear combination of weighted observed variables. An observed variable can be measured directly, called a measurable variable or indicator. Principal components are uncorrelated and orthogonal. The linear combination of the variables x_1, x_2, ..., x_p results in the first main component (y_1):

$$y_1 = a_{11}x_1 + a_{12}x_2 + \cdots + a_{1p}x_p$$

By selecting large values for the weights a_{11}, a_{12}, ..., a_{1p}, it is feasible to avoid the weights from being calculated with the constant that their sum of squares is 1, which would result in the first main component accounting for the least amount of variation in the data set. Underneath the condition that it is uncorrelated with the first principal component and accounts for the majority proportion of the residual variances, the second principal component is determined in an identical manner (Leech et al., 2014).

(iv) *Component loadings:* Component loadings refer to the coefficients of correlation between the variables and the principal components. The proportion of the square loading that can be attributed to the major component. It implies that loadings are the component that explains variance in each variable (OECD, 2008).

(v) *Eigenvalue:* Eigenvalue, which must decrease from the first principal component to the last, represents the percentage of variation explained by each principal component or factor. The sum of squared values of component loadings relating to the component is called Eigenvalue or latent root. It represents the association between the components and the original variables (Malhotra et al., 2006).

(vi) *Scree Plot:* The Scree Plot displays the subsequent Eigenvalues' rapid drops and subsequent levels. In the severe decline before the first one on the line where they begin to level out, it is suggested that all Eigenvalues be kept. The relationship between the Eigenvalues from the major components is depicted graphically (OECD, 2008).

Total variance: The observed variables in PCA are standardised, which implies that each variable is modified to have a mean and variance of zero and one, respectively. The sum of the variances for all of these observed variables constitutes the data set's total variance, which will always be the same as the number of observed variables under consideration for analysis. Once all of the data set's variations have been taken into consideration, the analysis keeps going in this manner (Malhotra et al., 2006).

With the help of PCA, the current study aims to create a composite measure of India's growing inclusivity. A scoring system and a weighted system are used to establish a composite indicator of inclusive growth. The statistics and analysis use the years from 1985 to 2016 as their frame of reference.

Ramos et al. (2013) mentioned that the elimination of poverty, fair opportunities for job prospects, and economic and social involvement in the developmental process are the three elements that make up the notion of inclusive growth. An additional set of variables that represent these three aspects of inclusive growth is used to create the inclusive growth index (Chadha & Chadda, 2020a).

(a) The elimination of destitution and poverty, exemplified by (i) absolute and abject poverty and (ii) disparities in income.

(b) Fair opportunities for employment options are suggested by (i) the proportion of men and women who participate in the labour force; (ii) MGN-REGA's employment creation programme; and (iii) the percentage of the workforce that belongs to the Scheduled Caste (SC) and Scheduled Tribe (ST) classifications.

(c) Evidence of increasing economic and social inclusion is shown by (i) the index of gender parity, (ii) the gender balance in Parliament, (iii) the overall enrolment for the reserved group; and (iv) political representation by reserved classes.

The discussion of these variables has been explained later in the chapter.

Construction of inclusive growth index: The objective of the current research was to build the index of inclusive growth, therefore it applied PCA to the nine variables indicated above. The starting variables are combined in a linear weighted manner to express each component in the present research. Factors $F_1, F_2, ..., F_K$ and the variables $X_1, X_2, ..., X_K$ are exponentially associated with each other.

Each X variable is linearly related to the two factors, as follows:

$$X_1 = \beta_{10} + \beta_{11} F_1 + \beta_{12} F_2 + e_1$$

$$X_2 = \beta_{20} + \beta_{21} F_1 + \beta_{22} F_2 + e_2$$

$$X_3 = \beta_{30} + \beta_{31} F_1 + \beta_{32} F_2 + e_3$$

The error terms e_1, e_2, and e_3 present to indicate that the hypothesised relationships are incorrect. The terms 'loadings' relate to the variables β_{ij}.

In the existing research,

$$X_1 = \beta_{10} + \beta_{11} F_1 + \beta_{12} F_2 + e_1$$

$$X_2 = \beta_{20} + \beta_{21} F_1 + \beta_{22} F_2 + e_2$$

$$X_9 = \beta_{90} + \beta_{91} F_1 + \beta_{92} F_2 + e_9$$

$X_1, X_2, X_3, \ldots$, and X_9 are the nine variables representing the three components of inclusiveness as detailed above.

The two retrieved components are F_1 and F_2.

The factor F_2 is loaded with variable X_1 and is expressed by β_{12}.

Since the variables in the data collection could have different measurement units, normalisation is essential before any further data processing. It has been checked to see the presence of outliers in the data set. The set of original variables is normalised first and then standardised to convert indicators to a common scale with a mean of zero and a standard deviation of one (Chadha & Chadha, 2020a, 2020b; OECD, 2008).

The weights, referred to as component loadings, are used to further consolidate the range of data into the compound variables. When there is just one common component, component loadings are the same as the correlation between components and variables. The interpretation of factors is given by high loadings. Principal components, which are then employed to build the index, can be produced by conducting PCA. The set of standard indicators' first principal component represents the substantial percentage of the variance, whereas the second component describes the significant proportion of the residual variables, the variation that the primary principal component does not account for, and so forth. Despite not being associated with the first component, the second factor accounts for the majority of the residual variance. There are different methods for the number of factors to be extracted. In most cases, the first principal component or sum of the first two to three principal components is normally used as a composite index (Chadha & Chadha, 2020a; Pradhan & Puttuswamaiah, 2005).

The current investigation has made use of the total percentage of variation that the factors have extracted. With this approach, the number of variables retrieved is selected to ensure that the total amount of variation obtained by the factors is acceptable. The extracted components should account for at least 60 per cent of the variance, according to criteria (Malhotra et al., 2006).

Sekhar et al. (1991) suggested that the proportions of these percentages were used as weights on principal component score coefficients to generate a cumulative adjusted inclusive growth index (Chadha & Chadda, 2020a, 2020b).

The following formula was used to create it:

Non-standardised inclusive development index = (percentage of variance of component 1/sum of percentage of variance of components entered) * (PC1 score) + (percentage of variance of component 2/sum of percentage of variance of components entered) * (PC2 score)

Antony and Rao (2007) also explained that as the values of the index so produced are either positive or negative, a standardised index with values varying from 0 to 1 was developed, using the following formula:

Standardised inclusive growth index

$$= \frac{\text{Non} - \text{standardised Inclusive growth index} \ - \ \text{Minimum value non} - \text{standardized inclusive growth index}}{\text{Maximum non} - \text{standardised inclusive growth index} \ - \ \text{Minimum non} - \text{standardised inclusive growth index}}$$

Following the literature, the methodology adopted by OECD (2008), Anthony and Rao (2007), Sekhar et al. (1991), and Krishnan (2010) constructed a composite index using PCA.

4. The Stepwise Multiple Linear Regression

After the construction of the index of inclusive growth, stepwise multiple regression analysis is applied. As a predictive analysis, this method is usually preferable. This method is used to explain the relationship between one continuous dependent variable with two or more other independent variables. The model deployed a backward elimination method of stepwise multiple regression analysis. The stepwise method of regression gradually eliminates variables that don't contribute as much to the model. It is a methodical way of systematically deleting multi-linear variables from the model based on the statistical significance of their regression results. When no variable significantly enhances the model, this approach finishes (Gujarati, 2003).

Smith (2018) stated that it is difficult to perform backward stepwise multiple regression when there are many candidate variables, and it is impractical if there are more candidate variables than observations (Chadha & Chadda, 2020a).

(i)   *Constant or intercept:* The intercept or constant in a multiple regression model is considered to be the expected mean value of the explained variable which will be less than zero and all the explanatory variables tend to be zero. A negative sign of constant should not be because of concern.

(ii) *Regression coefficient or slope:* The dependent variable changes when the related independent variables change, which is represented by the slope or regression coefficient of the regression model.

(iii) *t-Statistics:* The t-statistics are a coefficient calculated by dividing the coefficient by standard error. The measure of the standard error is by estimating the standard deviation of the coefficient. It is the measure of accuracy through which the coefficient of regression is measured. The negative and positive signs of t-statistics indicate the direction in the normal distribution. The negative sign shows that the sample mean is skewed to the left side and the positive sign explains that it moves towards the right side of the distribution (Gujarati, 2003).

(iv) *Durbin–Watson statistics:* The residuals (prediction errors) do not contain autocorrelation, which is one of the presumptions of regression; the Durbin–Watson test should be between 1.5 and 2.5 (Gujarati, 2003).

(v) *F-test:* The F ratio represents the change in the prediction that occurs as a result of the model being fitting. The value of F will be bigger than 1, which is exceedingly unlikely to occur by coincidence if the improvement brought about by estimating the regression is significantly more than the model's inaccuracy.

(vi) *Variance inflation factors (VIF) and tolerance level:* To check multicollinearity in the data, certain measures have to be followed. These measures are VIF and tolerance level. The tolerance level is $1 - R^2$. Some measures related to VIF and tolerance levels are explained as follows:

(a) Tolerance less than 0.10 indicates multicollinearity (O'Brien, 2007).

(b) If the value of VIF is less than 5, then multicollinearity is not serious, and if beyond 5, then it is substantial, and more than 10 is quite serious (O'Brien, 2007).

In the present study, two models have been studied by regressing the different components of the social sector as the explanatory variables as well as the inclusive development score as the experimental variable. The construction of the first model takes into account expenditure incurred on various components of social sectors, and the second model is constructed by selecting physical achievements of the components of social sectors. Both models were deployed by taking log differences of independent and dependent variables. The problem of heteroscedasticity and redundancy while designing the model is addressed through using natural log modifications of the components. According to Gujarati (2003), this change reduces the scale's tenfold range of possible values to a scale of two (Chadha & Chadda, 2020a).

Anand et al. (2013) developed a framework that also included parameters of economic growth outcomes in order to gauge inclusive and sustainable growth. By comparing the natural logarithm of the independent and dependent variables, the model used inclusive growth as an experimental variable and economic growth indicators as explanatory variables (Chadha & Chadda, 2020a). The two models of this study have been explained as follows:

(a) Model 1. For the purpose of fostering economic growth, it is necessary to implement both economic and social changes concurrently. By producing employment and eradicating economic disparities while simultaneously delivering social security benefits and boosting economic activity, significant improvement secures the achievement of the ultimate goal. Exploring the relationship between government spending on various social sector components and the inclusivity index of India's growth was the key objective of the present research.

The first model explores how spending on various social sector elements affects the composite indicator of inclusive growth in India (LDIIG). Log differences of both the explanatory and response variables are used to create the model in this case.

Parameters of social sector as explanatory variables for the first model: The following social sector elements have been selected to act as regressors in the regression model and to imply their relative importance in promoting inclusive growth in India:

(a)   The percentage of total government spending that goes on education, sports, the arts, and culture (LDED).
(b)   The proportion of total government spending that goes towards healthcare, public health, and family welfare (LDHFW).
(c)   The amount spent on water supply and sanitation relative to total government spending (LDWSS).
(d)   The proportion of total government spending that goes towards housing and urban development (LDHUD).
(e)   The percentage of total government spending allocated to spending on the welfare of underprivileged groups (LDWPC).
(f)   The proportion of labour and employment spending to total government spending (LDLE).
(g)   The amount spent on social security and welfare relative to total government spending (LDSSW).
(h)   Rural development expenditures as a percentage of overall government spending (LDRD).
(i)   The amount spent on food storage and warehousing relative to total government spending (LDFSW).

Here, total government expenditure includes expenditure incurred by state and central government collectively.

SPSS has been used to run the regression estimations. The developed model is displayed below:

$$\text{LDY}^* = a + b_1 \, \text{LD}(X^*) + U_t$$

Here, $\text{LDY}^* = \text{LD}\,(Y_{i,t} - Y_{i,t-1})$
a is a constant and b_1, the regression coefficient.

$$\text{LD}(X)^* = \text{LD}(X_{i,t} - X_{i,t-1})$$

LD, the natural logarithm with differences and

U_t, the white noise disturbance term.

Y^* is the composite index of inclusive growth constructed as shown in the previous section. X^* are the independent variables as elaborated above, used in the lagged form.

(b) Model 2.   The second model has been studied by regressing the *physical achievements* of the different components of the social sector as the exploratory variables, on the inclusive growth index in India as a dependent variable. Anand et al. (2013, 2014) and Deb (2017) also investigated the association between economic growth as well as social sector development. All the mentioned parameters have been identified based on a review of the vast literature available and due care has been taken to consider the relevant variables for the present model. The variables that have been chosen to fulfil the objectives of the study are as follows:

Indicators selected as regressors for Model 2: In order to determine the significance of each in promoting inclusive growth in India, the following physical components of the social sector have been selected to act as explanatory variables in the regression model:

- ➤ *Education, sports, art, and culture:*
  - Gross enrolment ratio (LDGER).
  - Pupil teacher ratio (LDPTR).
- ➤ *Medical and public health and family welfare:*
  - The number of beds available per 1,000 people (LDBED).
  - The number of doctors available per 1,000people (LDDR).
  - The number of health centres available per 1,000people (LDHC).
  - The percentage of people who recovered from an illness under the category of epidemiology out of the general population (LDPRE).
  - The proportion of vaccinated children in the target child population (LDCI).
- ➤ *Water supply and sanitation:*
  - Percentage of the population access to potable water (LDPPW).
  - Percentage of the population who have availability of toilets (LDPAT).
  - Percentage of the population served by sewage treatment (LDPST).
- ➤ *Housing and urban development:*
  - Percentage of population covered under economic weaker sections (EWS) and lower income groups (LIG) housing scheme out of a targeted population (LDBH).
- ➤ *The welfare of underprivileged classes:*
  - Number of beneficiaries covered under different welfare schemes (LDBWS).
- ➤ *Labour and employment:*
  - Number of construction workers employed (LDCW).
- ➤ *Social security and welfare:*
  - Number of beneficiaries insured under Employee State Insurance Scheme (LDBEN).
  - Number of beneficiaries covered under social security benefits (LDBSS).

➤ *Rural development:*
- Percentage of the population's access to electricity in rural areas (LDPER).
- Road constructed in rural areas out of total roads constructed (LDR).
- Rural food consumption expenditure out of total expenditure (LDRF)
- Rural literacy rate (LDRL).
- Rural poverty (LDRP).

➤ *Food storage and warehousing:*
- Food grains procured by Food Corporation of India (FCI) (lakhs tons) (LDPFG).

A detailed discussion of the above-mentioned variables has been carried out later in the chapter.

5. Unit Root Testing

In the estimation procedure for testing the long-run relationship between the components of the social sector and the inclusive growth index of India, there is a need to examine the stationary (free from unit root) of the individual time series to have unbiased and reliable results. For this purpose, two models are framed here to check the long-run relation between independent and dependent variables.

These models are based on the model constructed by Kolawole (2016). From 1995 to 2016, this study investigated the association between public expenditure and equitable development in Nigeria. Each of these series has been converted into a log form. Heteroscedasticity can be minimised by using log transformation.

According to Gujarati (2003), the Augmented Dickey–Fuller (ADF) test and the Phillips–Perron (PP) test were used in the current study to determine if the data were stationary. The order of integration of each time series may be found out using the ADF and PP tests, and the best method for further analysis can also be found. Both tests used the null hypothesis that the series is non-stationary, that is, that it has a unit root, and the alternate hypothesis that the series is stationary.

(i) *ADF unit root test statistic:* ADF test is based on the assumption that the error term (μ_t) is uncorrelated and has constant variance. ADF test statistic performs the regression of the first difference of the variables against the series which lagged once, have lagged differences, and a time trend (Gujarati, 2003). This can be expressed as follows:

$$\Delta Y_t = \alpha\, Y_{t-1} + X_t\, \delta + \beta_1\, \Delta Y_{t-1} + \beta_2\, \Delta Y_{t-2} + \cdots + \beta_p\, \Delta Y_{t-p} + \mu_t$$

where μ_t represents pure white noise error term,

$$\Delta Y_{t-1} = (Y_{t-1} - Y_{t-2}),\ \Delta Y_{t-2} = (Y_{t-2} - Y_{t-3}),\ \text{etc.}$$

$\alpha = p - 1$ and p is the parameter to be estimated, X_t is an optional exogenous regressor and may contain either a constant or a constant and trend, β_1 is the intercept, δ is the coefficient, and T is the time variable.

In order to ensure that the error term is statistically independent, the number of lagged difference items to include is usually determined analytically (EViews 10, 2017).

(ii) *PP unit root test statistic:* PP test is a more comprehensive theory of unit root test. The same asymptotic distribution of the ADF test is followed in the PP test too; hence, the same critical values can be used. Phillips and Perron used an alternate method to control serial correlation and proposed a nonparametric statistical method. Without including the lagged difference terms, the PP test statistic handles serial correlation and heteroskedasticity in the error terms. For autocorrelated residuals, the Dickey–Fuller procedure is automatically corrected (Brooks, 2008). According to the following statistics, the PP test is conducted:

$$\tilde{t}_\alpha = t_\alpha \left(\frac{y_0}{f_0} \right)^{1/2} - \frac{T\ (f_0 - y_0)(Se(\hat{a}))}{2f_0^{1/2} s}$$

where $\hat{a}$ is the estimate, $\tilde{t}_\alpha$ is the t-ratio of α, $Se\ (\hat{a})$ is the coefficient standard error, s represents standard error of the test regression, y_0 is a consistent estimate of the error variance, and f_0 represents an estimator of the residual spectrum at frequency zero (EViews 10, 2017).

The data need to examine the stationary (free from unit root) of the individual time series. The time series data may not be stationary at the level and the outcome of non-stationary variables may cause spurious results. To avoid this, stationary tests of all variables have been conducted to have reliable and unbiased results (Granger & Newbold, 1974).

6. ARDL Model

There is an alternative cointegration test in the literature which is better suitable if the variables are integrated at different orders. This test is called the bounds cointegration test or ARDL model. The ARDL has been found to be the most effective in creating long-term relationships between independent and dependent variables when the variables are not integrated in the same order (Chadha & Chadda, 2020b).

The next stage is to examine the long-term association between the expenditure related to different social sector components and the composite inclusive growth in India of the Model 1 index. In Model 2, India's inclusiveness growth has been studied in conjunction with the physical variables that significantly contributed, as determined by stepwise regression. Because of annual frequency, only short lags might be plausible, so, for the robustness of the model, the indicators which significantly contributed to inclusiveness have been used to run ARDL (Kolawole, 2016). These indicators are:

- ➢ Gross enrolment ratio (LDGER).
- ➢ The number of beds available per 1,000 people (LDBED).
- ➢ Percentage of the population access to potable water (LDPPW).
- ➢ Number of beneficiaries covered under the housing scheme of Economically Weaker Section (EWS) and Low Income Group (LIG) (LDBH).
- ➢ Number of beneficiaries covered under different welfare schemes of marginalised classes (LDBWS).
- ➢ Number of beneficiaries insured under different Insurance Schemes (LDBEN).
- ➢ Rural food consumption expenditure (LDRF).
- ➢ Rural poverty (LDRP).
- ➢ Food grains procured by FCI (lakhs tons) (LDPFG).

Pesaran and Shin (1999) and Pesaran et al. (2001) proposed the ARDL cointegration method. Using the ARDL technique, it is feasible to calculate unbiased estimates of the short-run and long-run models simultaneously. Prior to using ARDL, diagnostic tests such as the Breusch–Godfrey serial correlation LM test, Jarque–Bera (JB) normality test, Breusch–Pagan–Godfrey heteroskedasticity test, Wald test, and Ramsey RESET test must be performed. Lag length selection criteria must also be specified by the VAR (Kolawole, 2016).

(i)   *VAR lag order selection criteria*: The model must be devoid of autocorrelation, non-normality, and heteroskedasticity in order to run ARDL as Gaussian error terms, which means standard normal error terms are recommended. Therefore, the best lag length must be determined by applying VAR lag length order selection criteria in order to choose the right model for the long run (Nkoro & Uko, 2016).

(ii) *Wald test:* The cointegration procedure follows ARDL bound testing approach. The ARDL bound test depends on the Wald test (F-statistic) with a non-standard asymptotic distribution and a null hypothesis of no cointegration between the variables, as illustrated below:

Null hypothesis: $H_0 = C(1){=}C(2){=}C(3){=}C(4){=}C(5){=}C(6){=}C(7){=}C(9)$
$= C(10){=}0$ (no long-run relationship)

Alternate hypothesis: $H_1 = C(1) \neq C(2) \neq C(3) \neq C(4) \neq C(5) \neq C(6) \neq C(7) \neq C(9)$
$\neq C(10) \neq 0$ (long-run relationship)

The cointegration test requires two ranges of critical bounds. There was no cointegration implied by the lower critical bound's assumption that all the model's variables were $I(0)$, and there was cointegration implied by the higher critical bound's assumption that all the variables were $I(1)$ (Chadha & Chadda, 2020b).

The range 2.365–3.513 was the pertinent critical value for the upper bound at the 95 per cent confidence level. Accordingly, if the *F* statistic is between these levels, there is no long-term association between the model's independent variables and the dependent variable (Pesaran et al., 1996).

(iii) *Breusch–Godfrey serial correlation LM test:* The following diagnostic procedure determines whether a serial correlation exists in the residual or not. There is no serial correlation up to the defined order of lag, according to the model's null hypothesis. This means that there is no autocorrelation if the model is unable to reject the null hypothesis up to the lag value (Kolawole, 2016).

(iv) *Breusch–Pagan–Godfrey heteroskedasticity test:* The model's heteroskedasticity was investigated by Breusch, Pagan, and Godfrey. This test assumes that homoscedasticity exists in the series, which is the null hypothesis. As a result, the model's residuals do not exhibit heteroskedasticity if this test fails to reject the null hypothesis (Kolawole, 2016).

(v) *Ramsey RESET test:* To test the presence of specification errors, Ramsey RESET is being used. The test is applicable if any of these specification errors are there like the omission of an important variable, the model is transformed in incorrect functional form, and if there exists a correlation between *X* and the error term. To test the presence of specification errors, Ramsey RESET is being used. Furthermore, this test provided evidence that the model is well-specified. This test's null hypothesis is that the model's specification is accurate. It is necessary to reject the null hypothesis since the RESET *F* statistic is higher than the threshold value. If we are unable to reject the null hypothesis then the equation passes the Ramsey RESET test. Hence, in light of this, the theoretical model is appropriately defined (EViews 10, 2017).

(vi) *JB normality test of model:* According to the JB test, the residuals' non-normality distribution would be the null hypothesis. The JB normality test should not be significant if the residuals are normally distributed, and the histogram should be bell-shaped (EViews 10, 2017).

The specification of ARDL of the empirical model for estimation is as follows:

$$\psi\,(L) = a_0 + a_1 t + \sum_{j=1}^{k} \beta_2\,(L) x_{j,t} + \varepsilon_t$$

where L denotes the usual lag operator, α_0 is a constant term, α_1, β_j, t, and ψ are the coefficients related with linear trends, lags of k regressors $x_{j,t}$ for $j = 1,...,k$, and lags of y_t respectively, $\psi(L)$ and $\beta(L)$ are the lag polynomials, and ε_t is the white noise residual (EViews 10, 2017).

The present study deployed ARDL to study the long- and short-run relationship among the constructed inclusivity index of India and the diverse ingredients of the social sector. Kolawole (2016) and Pattayat and Rani (2017) investigated the association exist between economic growth and social sector development.

Elaboration and Discussion on the Selection of Dependent and Independent Variables of Models

A discussion on the selection of dependent as well as independent variables is as follows:

Composite Index of Inclusive Growth as Dependent Variable

Inclusive growth is associated with the pro-poor growth strategy. The basic aim of inclusive growth is alleviating poverty, and increasing contribution, participation, and distribution of growth outcomes among poor people. Most of the time, poverty and economic growth have significant and positive relation, but a pro-poor growth-oriented strategy, based upon equal opportunities to participate in the growth process and reduction in inequalities makes growth inclusive (OECD, 2006).

Components and indicators: As elaborated in the previous section, *the elimination of poverty, fair opportunities for job prospects, and economic and social involvement in the developmental process are the three elements that make up the notion of inclusive growth.* Each of these components is represented by indicators as a dependent variable and an elaborate discussion on each of these is as follows:

The Elimination of Destitution and Poverty. Eradication of poverty is the first pillar of inclusive growth. The source of poverty is diverse and multifaceted. Multiple deprivations, such as a lack of access to resources for skill development, education, healthcare, and other amenities, are indicators of poverty (Government of India, 2008a). A third of the world's poor, according to estimates, reside in India. Indian poverty is primarily rural, with landless labourers and casual employees being the most economically disadvantaged category, according to official figures from the Indian government, even though just one in four Indians are considered to be poor. Female children, elderly persons, members of SCs and STs, women, and families headed by women experience greater deprivation than other groups (Saxena & Farrington, 2003).

In absolute terms, the poverty eradication rate in rural and urban areas between 1985–1986 and 2015–2016 decreased from 43.88 per cent to 22.4 per cent, however the decline is not very substantial (Venkat, 2016). Therefore, pro-poor/inclusive economic growth will occur when the needs of the poorest of the poor are addressed in a growth policy and the benefits of growth are divvied up across all socio-economic segments (Chadha & Chadda, 2020b).

The indicators of poverty reduction used to create the inclusive growth index from 1985 to 2016 are mentioned below:

Absolute and Abject Poverty. Lack of essential necessities like food, healthcare, potable water, basic sanitation, and schooling are characteristics of poverty. It depicts challenges to the populace for their progress and consequently, their capacity for growth through participation. Various techniques have been used to gauge poverty (United Nations, 1995).

The World Bank (Datt & Ravillion, 2010) and the Planning Commission provided official estimates for the head count ratio of India, which were employed in the present research. In accordance with the approach outlined by an Expert Group, the Planning Commission assesses the official level of poverty in India using NSSO quinquennial data (Chadha & Chadda, 2020b). In India, Poverty is estimated based on consumption levels. Data were collected by the National Sample Survey Office under the Ministry of Statistics and Programme Implementation (MOSPI) (Government of India, 1993). Data were collected on Uniform Resource Period (URP) till 1993–1994 and from 1999 to 2000 onwards, NSSO switched to mixed reference period (MRP). In 2012, the modified mixed reference period (MMRP) was followed (Government of India, 2013).

The head count ratio was used in this research. The percentage of the population who live in poverty is gauged by the head count ratio (Dev & Ravi, 2007). As seen below, it is defined as the proportion of the population whose income is below the poverty line:

$$\text{Head count ratio} = \frac{\text{No. of Poor People}}{\text{Total Population}}$$

Any decrease in this percentage would indicate more inclusivity as head count ratio is an indicator of abject poverty (Chadha & Chadda, 2020b).

Disparities in Income. Increasing participation of the unprivileged in the development process is another evidence of the decline in relative poverty. The difference between the areas under the Lorenz curve for a population in which everyone would receive the same income is known as Gini coefficient. The relative poverty of the society is shown by the Gini coefficient, a statistic that measures distributional inequality. According to Xiao et al. (2014), Gini coefficient is depicted by the regressive linear expression known as the Lorenz curve. This parameter oscillates from 0 to 1.

The Gini coefficient for India was calculated by the World Bank (Datt, 1999) and the United Nations Development Programme (UNDP; Radhakrishna & Panda, 2006). The present study makes use of the above-calculated indices of the Gini coefficient and it is in percentage form (per cent) (Dev & Ravi, 2007). *Greater inclusivity of growth would be indicated by any drop in the Gini coefficient over the time period* (Chadha & Chadda, 2020b).

Fair Opportunities for Employment Options. This is the second element of inclusive growth that has been selected. A growth process that creates jobs would encourage broad-based economic growth, which as a consequence, guarantees access to potable water, adequate sanitation, and the provision of healthcare and education. Additionally, it pertains to the development of marginalised groups including SCs, STs, and OBCs as well as some minorities who endure exclusion. Assuring the balanced growth of all social divisions, it also consistently closes the gender gap. Therefore, a growth plan that creates jobs will be inclusive and long-lasting provided it offers equal access to all social categories (Chadha & Chadda, 2020b; Government of India, 2013).

The variables of this aspect used to generate the equitable and inclusive index are described below from 1985 to 2016.

The Proportion of Men and Women Who Participate in the Labour Force.   An indicator of the workforce in an economy is the labour force participation rate (LFPR). According to various rounds of NSSO quinquennial statistics on the employment and unemployment situation in India, the Government of India (2015) and the World Bank Open Data (2016), the LFPR refers to the aggregate number of persons who are now employed or looking for work as a percentage of the overall populace. Farzana et al. (2012) studied that better labour market opportunities for females in the market empowered them and also associated with better educational outcomes for their children. The number of women in the labour force as a percentage of men in the labour force is the series used to indicate the female LFPR (Dogan & Akyuz, 2017). Therefore, for growth inclusivity, a larger female-to-male ratio in LFPR may reveal the rising percentage of women participating in labour (Chadha & Chadda, 2020b).

MGNREGA's Employment Creation Programme.   The generation of possibilities for employment at all levels of society and the strengthening of those at the bottom of the social ladder are two examples of inclusive growth. For instance, MGNREGA fosters inclusivity by guaranteeing employment and income for every rural household for a predetermined number of days each year. Sanyal (2014) and Pal et al. (2018) mentioned that MGNREGA provides employment to unskilled workers in rural areas and was very essential for economic development, by creating community/productive assets at the level of villages. The Government of India (2016a) provides data on the total number of person–days generated (Chadha & Chadda, 2020b).

The Percentage of the Workforce that Belongs to the SC and ST Classifications.   Increased work opportunities for the underprivileged and excluded groups would be the cornerstone of an inclusive growth plan for development. The advantages of prosperity should cascade down to society's impoverished and oppressed groups, particularly the SC and ST classes. The notion of equal access to work prospects was not supported by the Government of India over the previous three decades. Though it is said that during the last few decades, the percentage of SCs and STs in the government sector has increased, they have not actually been empowered (Thorat & Senapati, 2006). The proportion of SC and ST classes in total employment used in this study as a proxy for inclusive growth demonstrates social access and inclusion (Basole, 2018). The information was gathered from several series of the Handbook on Social Welfare Statistics and the NSSO quinquennial data on the employment and unemployment situation among social groups in India (Chadha & Chadda, 2020b).

Increasing Economic and Social Inclusion.   This is the third pillar of inclusive growth. In order to reduce the gap between the rich and the poor and to more fairly distribute the growth surplus, inclusive growth places a significant focus on involvement (OECD, 2012). The government offers financial support and micro-finance services for the financial inclusion of the economically deprived, including as SCs, STs, OBCs, and the disabled, through a number of programmes. For everyone to flourish socially and economically, there must be equal opportunity, liberty, and integrity. Due to the reservations for SCs, STs, and women, India's democratic system of government offers opportunities for all groups to be strengthened and included. The Panchayati Raj Institution (PRI), which oversees primary democracy, gives local citizens more relevance (Chadda, 2020b).

The indicators for this component used to build the inclusive growth index from 1985 to 2016 are as follows:

The Index of Gender Parity. When comparing the number of male and female students enrolled in primary, secondary, and higher education, the gender parity index (GPI) is calculated (Government of India, 2016b). Madgavkar et al. (2016) stated that gender inequality hampered economic development. According to the study, eliminating the gender gap in education levels will indeed encourage more women to enter the workforce and contribute to the family decision-making process also. Inclusive growth in India would be achieved by raising the GPI. In the several releases of Education Statistics at a Glance, the Ministry of Human Resource department publishes the data about GPI (ratio). GPI is calculated as shown below:

$$\text{Gender parity index} = \frac{\text{Gross enrolment ratio of girls}}{\text{Gross enrolment ratio of boys}}$$

The Gender Balance in Parliament. Only through taking steps and measures to uplift women might the goal of improving the socio-economic situations of women be achieved. Women cannot be empowered until they are given adequate representation in the political system. Women would make the democratic development of the economy and society more inclusive if they were given equal participation in the political system and allowed to have a prominent role in decision-making (Chaturvedi, 2016). According to UNDP's Human Development Reports (HDRs) and the Elections Commission of India's Electoral Statistics Pocketbook, the proportion of women holding parliamentary seats as a percentage of men (Rai, 2017) is calculated (Chadha & Chadda, 2020b).

The Overall Enrolment for the Reserved Group. Excluding marginalised groups from the redistribution or benefit-sharing process hinders their involvement in prosperity and reduces the inclusivity of development (Thorat, 2011). The primary task is to ensure that government policies reflect the wide vision of education for all. Providing appropriate solutions to a diverse range of learning requirements in formal and informal educational contexts is the focus of inclusive education. Education is the finest tool for promoting inclusion since it gives impoverished groups more power (Padhi, 2016). The data were obtained in the form of percentages from the Handbook on Social Welfare Statistics' various reports (Chadha & Chadda, 2020b; Dash & Bhatia, 2011).

Political Representation by Reserved Classes. The process of providing the populace with political resources and enabling them to actively take part in the forming and distribution of power for national progress is known as political empowerment. As the most effective means of halting their socio-economic, educational, or other backwardness, an equitable and inclusive policy will seek to strengthen the SC and ST sectors through their political mobilisation (Chaturvedi, 2016). For data analysis, the ratio of seats occupied by SCs and STs to those that were available was employed (Pande, 2003). The Electoral Statistics

Pocketbook, published by the Indian Election Commission, contains information about the political participation of SCs and STs (Chadha & Chadda, 2020b)

Independent Variables: Selecting Indicators of Social Sector Development

Social sector development is bifurcated into two services, viz. Social Services and Economic Services. Social services are classified into seven indicators and these are 'Education, Sports, Art and Culture'; 'Medical and Public Health'; 'Family Welfare'; 'Water Supply and Sanitation'; 'Housing and Urban Development'; 'Welfare of underprivileged Classes'; 'Labour and Employment' and 'Social Security and Welfare'. Economic Services are categorised into 'Rural Development' and 'Food Storage and Warehousing'.

Deb (2017) investigated the relationship between social and economic development. This study constructed a multi-dimensional social development index of 29 states and union territories of India. The six main dimensions to construct the index were selected namely demographic dimension, health dimension, education dimension, basic amenities, economic dimension, and social dimension. Furthermore, these dimensions are represented by a subset of indicators like total fertility rate, percentage of institutional deliveries, the prevalence of contraception, percentage of undernourished children, infant mortality rate, literacy rate, school attendance rate, pupil–teacher ratio, households which have access to safe drinking water, toilet facility, households that live in pucca house, families have electricity connection, head count rate, unemployment rate, monthly per capita expenditure, disparity ratio in literacy rates of underprivileged classes, educational and employment deprivation of underprivileged classes.

Indicators of social sector development: The explanatory variables of Models 1 and 2 are elaborated below.

Expenditure Incurred on Different Components of Social Sector Development. The expenditure incurred by the Government of India on different components of the social sector has been selected as an independent variable for Model 1. The expenditure share of each component was used out of the total expenditure incurred by the Government (Pattayat & Rani, 2017). Guhun (1995), Prabhu (1997), and Sen (1997) stated that the social welfare of the masses has been the objective of India's economic policy for strengthening the social sector. In order to boost the chances of equal economic involvement and so support inclusivity, social sector development placed a priority on providing additional means of subsistence, modern comforts, and services for decent living in both rural and urban areas. The relationship between social sector development and economic growth was studied by Pattayat and Rani (2017), Anand et al. (2014), Gupta (2014), Sharma (2014), and Kolawole (2016). An increase in spending on the social sector would make the growth inclusive.

Gross Enrolment Ratio. Education plays an essential role in the development of the economy. Better infrastructure and accessibility should be provided to improve the quality of schooling. The main emphasis of campaigns like Education for All and Millennium Development Goals (MDG) has been on increasing enrolments to have basic literacy, hence, universal school attainment can be attained (Hanushek, 2013). Education plays a significant contribution towards human development; an increased number of enrolments in the different levels of education has importantly resulted in the outcome of the reduction in poverty (Tilak, 2005). Growth will be more inclusive if the gross enrolment ratio of government schools rises and access to education increases.

Pupil Teacher Ratio. The quality of education will be improved by lowering drop-outs and improving the retention ratio, student–teacher ratio, and student–classroom ratio. Simply enrolling students in school is not enough. Along with gross enrolment ratio, the pupil teacher ratio is very important. Increased student scholarships, more programmes to provide interest subsidies on student loans for professional courses, more schools, universities, and colleges, special grants for the construction of women's hostels, and increased teacher numbers to ensure that everyone has access to education are several of the significant policy initiatives for education that have been implemented (Kumar, 2012). To bolster the growth, the pupil teacher ratio is important and this variable is used in ratio form (Dash & Bhatia, 2011).

Healthcare Infrastructure. Further with the inception of National Rural Health Mission (NRHM), India made tremendous progress towards delivering the rural poor with available and affordability healthcare facilities. The number of institutions providing medical education, the availability of beds, and the number of nurses and doctors in hospitals have also increased. By increasing the personnel in the public health sector and by improving health facilities, the main focus of the government was the removal of inequalities as it covered the inaccessible remote areas and poor-performing districts (Parshad et al., 2013). As per International Institute for Population Sciences (IIPS) and ICF (2017), it was found that 56 per cent of urban India and 49 per cent of rural India prefer private healthcare. No doubt, the percentage of households using the public sector for healthcare had increased over the last decade but this number was less as compared to private healthcare. Ghosh and Dinda (2017) examined different aspects of healthcare services facilities and health infrastructure available in India. The research employed percentage estimates for the beds provided for the 1,000 population, the proportion of physicians and nurses available, and the increase in health centres offered per 1,000 people. The results showed a strong association between health infrastructure and economic development in India. Increasing healthcare infrastructure and personnel would make the growth inclusive.

The Percentage of People Who Recovered from an Illness Under the Category of Epidemiology Out of the General Population. The performance of public health had been active in India as diseases like malaria, tuberculosis, leprosy, and high maternal and child mortality were grappled through a concerted action of the government. A lot has been achieved in this domain including the eradication of smallpox and polio eradication, a decrease in mortality rates, and awareness about the HIV pandemic (Lakshminarayanan, 2011). Several cases of diseases like malaria, tuberculosis, leprosy, chikungunya, dengue, kala-azar, and polio available per 1,000 population were compiled (Dua, 2005). Thus, by eradicating epidemiological diseases, growth will be more inclusive as it would increase the productive capacity of a person which further eliminates poverty.

The Proportion of Vaccinated Children in the Target Child Population. Immunisation is a cost effective and efficient intervention to overcome the problem of childhood mortality and morbidity worldwide. The public health infrastructure offered vaccination, medical treatment, and rehabilitation services. Several initiatives were taken to improve the quality of services and to reach more remote, destitute, and unreached areas (Ranjan, 2014). The number of cases covered for MCV1, IPV1, Hib3, HepB_BD, HepB3, BCG, DTP1, DTP3, PCV3, Pol3, RCV1, and RotaC has been showing the increasing trend. Data (percentage form) since 1980 was estimated by WHO UNICEF by taking the number of vaccinations received by children (as the numerator) and target population data (as the denominator) (Burton et al., 2009; WHO, 2018). Thus, this component will also bolster inclusive growth, if more children would be covered.

Percentage of the Population Who Have Access to Potable Water, Availability of Toilets, and Provision of Sewage Treatments. The Government of India had initiated several programmes related to the supply of improved water quality, however, the equal realisation of the right to water for everyone was not ensured. Assessing outcomes related to economic sustainability as well as equal access to the programme may result in improving the poor conditions of people (Samra et al., 2011). The data have been compiled from the various reports of the National Health Profile. The population who accessed potable water out of the total population was used in percentage form to do further analysis. The Government of India implemented the Total Sanitation Scheme (TSC) in 1999 and later it was renamed Nirmal Bharat Abhiyan to provide sewage treatment and construct toilets in each house after getting financial assistance from the government in rural areas. Eighty per cent of the beneficiaries had constructed bath-cum-toilet facilities. Various Annual Reports of the Ministry of Drinking Water & Sanitation provided data on the availability of toilets and sewages (percentage form). A widespread approach to economic development is to enhance access to potable water and basic sanitation to poor, which offers them a great deal of opportunity (WSP, 2011).

Percentage of the Population Receiving Benefits Under Housing Schemes. The Reserve Bank of India undertook several initiatives to promote affordable housing. Affordable housing for Economically Weaker Section (EWS) and Low Income Group (LIG) could boost economic growth (Palayi & Priyaranjan, 2018). The data were obtained from studies conducted by the Technical Group on Urban Housing Shortage as well as from the number of annual publications produced by the Ministry of Housing and Urban Poverty Alleviation. Out of the targeted population, the population who received the benefits has been used (percentage form). The Government of India aims for achieving inclusive growth by providing all basic needs to the needy.

Welfare of Underprivileged Classes. Zohir (2011) re-conceptualised the concept of inclusive growth and stressed the concept of complete inclusion. Balanced development will take place when all spheres of human society are included. Sections of society that are marginalised and underprivileged ought to have access to all government policies and programmes that promote education and health. Similarly, to this, despite the fact that women are well-equipped and competent to work full-time, as a consequence of institutional and societal impediments, they have actually been neglected in their full involvement in decision-making at the family and political levels. Shilpi Samriddhi Yojana, Ajivika Micro Credit Yojana, Term Loan Laghu Vyavsay Yojana, Mahila Samriddhi Yojana, Educational Loan Scheme, VETLS Scheme, and Micro Credit Finance, beneficiaries were added (absolute form) (Government of India, 2007). So, participation in this section is essential to have inclusive growth.

Construction Workers Employed.   Construction-related employment can provide additional opportunities in terms of short-term employment and improved infrastructure. There may be compounding implications on jobs and income across the economy as a result of the enhanced infrastructure that is developed, which may help to boost economic performance in other areas (International Labour Organisation, 2018). The Construction Workers' Federation of India provided data on the construction workers and the data were used in absolute numbers. These will be very helpful to boost inclusive growth.

Social Security and Welfare Schemes.   Good social protection policies have always been consistent with the growth process. Both the central and state governments had initiated many social security and welfare programmes like National Social Assistance Program, Employee State Insurance Programmes, and other social security schemes. These social security and pension schemes covered the significant support of the programmes to old-aged persons, widows, and employees. There had been a strong association between social security schemes and the protection of working conditions and rights at work for employees (Devadasan & Kalicharan, 2016). This component will help the poor section to have a better life and make growth inclusive. Reports on Social Security, Development Commissioner, Ministry of Micro, Small and Medium Enterprises and various annual reports of Ministry of Labour and Employment provide the data (absolute) for the same.

Benefits Provided to Rural Population.   The government had implemented various schemes for generating better productive employment opportunities, facilitating good social infrastructure, and providing basic amenities like potable water, free electricity, construction of roads, sanitation and sewerage facility, housing and housing facilities, food at discounted prices, and access to education for the poor masses of India (Mondal, 1993).

The data for the population's access to electricity in rural India were provided (percentage form) by World Bank Open Data Series. Various Reports of Basic Road Statistics in India and the Ministry of Rural Development provide data on the length of road works completed and the length of total road works to be completed. The data are used in ratio form (rural roads completed as a percentage of total road length). Various series of NSSO reports on Consumption Expenditure provide data on rural food consumption (absolute number). The data were compiled from various reports of Education Statistics at a Glance and Selected Socio-Economic Indicators, 2011, on literacy rates (percentage form).

Rural Poverty Rate. Eradicating poverty in rural areas would result in more inclusive growth in India. Thomas and Chittedi (2015) stated that the government framed numerous policies for reducing poverty. These growth-oriented policies will ensure broad-based per capita income growth and then the benefits of the growth would percolate to the downtrodden members of society. For rural poverty, the head count ratio has been used and taken from Planning Commission Data and World Bank Open Data.

Food Grains Procured by FCI (Lakhs Tons). To ensure food security, FCI procures food grains for effective market intervention. Manap and Ismail (2019) stated that better food security has a positive association with growth and that lead to poverty elimination, more employment, and better life expectancy. Various Reports of the Handbook of Statistics on the Indian Economy (2002–2003), Ministry of Consumer Affairs, Reserve Bank of India, and Food and Public Distribution Department of Food and Public Distribution provide the data for the same (absolute numbers).

In order to achieve the goals of redistribution of wealth and social fairness, India used a trickle-down method of growth, but towards the completion of the Fourth Five Year Plan, it failed. Human development and welfare initiatives have since come into prominence. As the primary objective and cornerstone of their growth strategy, Indian planners aimed to eliminate both poverty and inequality. The policymakers pondered about strengthening social sector development and employing a people-centred strategy to boost people's capability and capacity, reflecting Sen's philosophy. Indian economic strategy aims to increase social welfare and public participation in the development of an economy. As a result, measures based on equity, increasing employment, and eliminating poverty and so promoting inclusive growth continued to be the primary concern (Anand et al., 2014; Kakwani & Pernia, 2000; Klasen, 2010; Kundu & Varghese, 2010). *Table 2 displays the set of data and relevant data sources that were used in the research.*

Limitations of the Study and Suggestions for Future Research

The present research endeavour is based on secondary data. There have been certain limitations of the study that need to be discussed:

- The chosen canvas of the study is too large, so some finer details might have been overlooked.
- Inclusive growth is a vast concept. But in the present study, a restrictive approach, though quite representative connotations of inclusive growth were included (as emanating from our vast study of the relevant literature on the subject).
- Interstate and interdistricts comparisons could have been performed to get a better picture which may constitute a part of the future research on the subject.

Chapter 4

Social Sector Development: Programmes and Policies in India

Indian economy, at the time of independence, was characterised as rural and agricultural wherein the majority of people earned their livelihood from agriculture and related pursuits, based on customary and low-productive techniques. The state failed to be self-sufficient in food and raw materials despite the massive population engaged in agriculture. Thus, independent India inherited a stagnant economy, plagued with problems of deprived and decadent industrialisation, low agricultural output, low national income per capita, considerable unemployment and underemployment, and rampant poverty and deprivation. Later, post-independence, the Indian economy passed through another major crisis along with its inheritance of the said fragile economic state and was caught up in a vicious circle of poverty. India was, thus, in dire need of rapid growth and social justice for the poor masses (Kapila, 2010).

India's main objective is to build an affluent pattern of society where every person has equal rights and access to basic needs. Economic growth would be balanced if the economy has self-sufficiency and equal opportunity, and is also free from rampant poverty and unemployment. The Planning Commission was established in March 1950 to initiate national economic development through the Five Years Planning process (Parikh, 2002). The sustainable strategy of poverty alleviation is aimed at channelising productive employment opportunities to downtrodden masses of society for both the economic betterment of the people and social transformation (Roy, 2014).

Social Sector Development Programmes Since 1950

The underutilisation of potential resources as well as the underestimation of the potentialities of these resources is often viewed as the root cause of all other associated problems of an underdeveloped economy. An economic and social change strategy has to be adopted simultaneously for promoting the development of such an economy, concomitance with two wider objectives of generating full employment, and the removal of economic inequalities by providing social security benefits. Hence, the main concern is to improve the welfare of the deprived

Social Sector Development and Inclusive Growth in India, 67–97
Copyright © 2023 by Ishu Chadda
Published under exclusive license by Emerald Publishing Limited
doi:10.1108/978-1-83753-186-820231005

population by employing multiple pathways like more productivity and income, improving education and health, and providing better accessibility of the other basic amenities of the people by creating a balance between the social and economic development (Chadha & Chadda, 2018).

Numerous social sector development programmes have been launched to achieve the foremost objective of poverty eradication and social justice since 1950. These programmes are categorised as follows:

(1) Human development programmes.
(2) Education, health, and family welfare schemes.
(3) Water supply and sanitation schemes.
(4) Housing and urban development.
(5) Labour and employment and social services benefits.
(6) Rural development programmes.
(7) Schemes related to public distribution system (PDS).

Programmes Related to Human Development

Community Development Programme (CDP) (1952–1968)

The First Five Year Plan emphasised raising the standard of living of the people. After independence, the CDP was instigated in October 1952. CDP was a process in which the efforts of the people were united with government authorities to improve the economic, social, and cultural conditions. The main focus was to induce people's participation in rural development and maximise the utilisation of local resources by available resources (Lawania, 1992).

The fundamental objective of community development in India was the upliftment of the masses through comprehensive economic development, social justice, and democratic growth. Thus, the programme was multi-dimensional and formulated to provide an administrative framework through the district, tehsil, and village levels. The main objectives of this programme were focussed on escalating agricultural production, ameliorating the extant village crafts and industries and establishing new ones, bestowing the basic necessary health services and upgrading the health practices, indulging the needy person to have basic educational facilities for their children along with the additional adult education programme. It aimed to promote recreational facilities and programmes and also wanted to work on improving housing and living conditions (Government of India, 1952).

The CDP in India contributed to the creation of basic socio-economic infrastructure in rural areas and improved the production base of the rural economy. CDP in India was considered a task-oriented programme rather than a process-oriented programme (Government of India, 1963).

Table 3 depicts the blocks covered during CDP and the expenditure incurred by blocks for the development. On the completion of the First Five Year Plan, 248 blocks covered approximately 1.23 lakh villages, that is, fifth of the total population. By the end of the Second Five Year Plan, approximately 2.47 lakh villages of 3,000 blocks had been included in 70 per cent of all rural areas, and by 1964, it covered the entire population of the country covering 5,256 blocks.

Table 3.   Villages and Development Blocks Covered Under CDP.

Five Year Plan	Villages	Blocks	Expenditure (Rs. Crores)
1st	122,957	248	79.03
2nd	247,043	3,000	222.11
3rd + plan holiday	268,588	2,008	361.85
Total	638,588	5,256	662.99

Source: Government of India (various issued-d), *Five Year Plan Documents*. New Delhi: Planning Commission.

Table 4 describes the year-wise actual expenditure incurred on the CDP during the years from 1952–1953 to 1967–1968. The period registered frequent fluctuations in both, the actual amount spent as well as the percentage share. The investment made during the First Five Year Plan hovered between a high of 6.31 per cent and a low of 0.78 per cent, whereas in the Second and Third Five Year Plans, a downward trend has been initiated.

Table 4.   Actual Expenditure Incurred on CDP and its Percentage on the Total Expenditure.

Years	Actual Expenditure (Rs. Crores)	Percentage on Total Expenditure
1952–1953	4.13	0.78
1953–1954	10.66	3.10
1954–1955	25.48	5.35
1955–1956	38.76	6.31
1956–1957	31.86	5.03
1957–1958	37.08	4.91
1958–1959	46.81	4.67
1959–1960	47.31	4.68
1960–1961	59.05	5.28
1961–1962	55.00	4.88
1962–1963	58.85	4.24
1963–1964	55.84	3.27
1964–1965	59.00	2.97
1965–1966	59.77	2.61
1966–1967	40.00	1.87
1967–1968	33.69	1.50

Source: Government of India. (various issues-d). *Five year plan documents*. Planning Commission.

Nayar (1960) studied that CDP was very efficient and comprehensive and reached out to a large number of people. During the First Five Year Plan, 77.5 million people were covered with an expenditure of Rs. 460.2 million. But CDP failed to achieve the goals due to a lack of people's participation, uneven distributions, and non-achievement in agricultural production as per expectations. It instead resulted in gnawing poverty, malnutrition, illiteracy, poor health conditions, and exacerbation of the food crisis in India (Karunaratne, 1976).

Minimum Needs Programme (MNP; 1974–1985)

The Government of India (1974) conceptualised the MNP as an investment in human welfare during the Fifth Five Year Plan. Experiences from the previous plans made it obvious that neither growth nor social consumption could be sustained unless these are mutually supportive. The provision of free services earmarked through public agencies was expected to improve the consumption levels of those living below the poverty line (BPL) and which further resulted in the enhanced productive efficiency of both the rural and urban workers. This integration of social consumption programmes with economic development programmes was expedient to accelerate growth and social justice. The programme was designed to raise the living standards and in removing the regional inequalities in development. In the previous programmes, the primary focus was on the development of infrastructure and production, while the social sector was not given due importance.

Table 5 explains the expenditure incurred on the MNP from the years 1974–1975 to 1984–1985. From 1974 to 1985, the investment made in upgrading the infrastructure related to education showed an increasing trend of approximately Rs. 200 crores and Rs. 21 crores, respectively, both in elementary education and adult education. The actual outlays incurred on rural health, rural water supply, rural electrification and rural housing also escalated during the same period by approximately Rs. 35 crores, Rs. 100 crores, Rs. 107 crores, and Rs. 60 crores, respectively. While the expenditure incurred on rural roads declined in this period. Also, environmental improvements in urban slums and nutrition indicated a rising trend with Rs. 4 crores and Rs. 90 crores, respectively, during this programme.

Table 6 highlights the educational infrastructure achievements and health expansion in India from 1970 to 1990. The number of schools, colleges, and universities also increased from the year 1970 to the year 1990 in India. A rising trend for health centres in rural areas is evident from the table. There were openings of many sub health centres (SHC), primary health centres (PHCs), and community health centres (CHCs) in rural areas. The number of institutions that provide medical education, the availability of beds, number of nurses and doctors in hospitals has also shown a rising trend. The number of dispensaries, hospitals, and beds rose from 16 thousand to 3.5 lakhs approximately in the year 1970 to 39 thousand and 81 lakhs approximately in the year 1990, respectively. The number of nurses and doctors also climbed up from 80 thousand to 3.5 lakhs and from 1.5 lakhs to 3.9 lakhs approximately from 1970 to 1990.

Table 5.   Expenditure Incurred on MNP (Rs. Crores).

S. No.	Services	1974–1978	1978–1979	1979–1980	1980–1981	1981–1982	1982–1983	1983–1984	1984–1985
1	Elementary education	230	32	61	97.94	108.18	143.43	196.54	256.01
2	Adult education	1	4	7	9.38	9.89	11.28	17.38	21.40
3	Rural health	74	33	33	48.05	62.84	67.53	91.68	109.76
4	Rural water supply	262	133	188	211.91	259.54	307.79	360.51	366.08
5	Rural roads	231	152	182	43.41	51.04	52.94	54.63	46.20
6	Rural electrification	103	34	45	203.25	232.18	204.15	308.79	211.78
7	Rural housing	50	22	53	54.54	76.54	92.31	110.51	119.71
8	Environmental improvements of urban slums	38	10	16	21.69	26.52	27.15	35.23	42.33
9	Nutrition	49	20	22	28.58	35.37	68.41	117.79	139.72
10	Total	1,038	440	607	718.75	861.10	974.99	1,293.06	1,312.99

Source: Government of India. (various issues-d). *Five year plan documents*. Planning Commission.

Table 6.   Educational Infrastructural Development and Expansion of Health Services in India.

Indicators	1970	1980	1990
Infrastructure development			
No. of primary schools	408,378	494,503	560,935
No. of upper primary schools	90,621	118,555	151,456
No. of senior secondary schools	37,051	51,573	79,796
No. of colleges for general education	2,285	3,421	4,862
Colleges for professional education	992	3,542	886
No. of universities	82	110	184
Health centres			
SHC/PHC/CHC*	33,601	57,363	153,505
Dispensaries and hospitals (all)**	16,042	23,555	38,605
Beds (private and public)**	346,855	569,495	810,548
Nursing personnel	80,620	143,887	340,208
Doctors	151,129	267,810	394,068

Sources: Government of India. (2014). *Educational statistics at a glance*. Ministry of Human Resource Development. Government of India. (2013). *Human resources in health sector, Central Bureau of Health Intelligence*. Ministry of Health and Family Welfare.

Notes: 1. Professional education includes engineering, technology, architecture, and medical (ayurveda, homeopathy, unani, allopathy, nursing, and pharmacy) and teaching training colleges.

2. SHC/PHC/CHC: sub-centre/primary health centre/community health centre.

3.*Rural Health Statistics as on 31 March of every year, Central Bureau of Health Intelligence; ** as on 31 January of every year.

The important policy initiatives taken for higher education include the increasing number of universities and colleges, special grants for the construction of hostels for women, scholarships to students, schemes to provide interest subsidies on educational loans for and professional courses to make sure that everybody should be educated (Kumar, 2012). Although various efforts had been initiated by the government, one-third of the population was still found to be illiterate. The problems lie in the implementation of schemes for all levels of education in India which include inadequate quantitative expansion, poor quality of education, and a high degree of inequalities (Mercy, 2007).

Kumar and Kumar (2008) studied that the amount of spending made by the private health sector was much more than the public health sector. Governmental efforts to provide health facilities to the people had been quite disappointing because the number of public hospitals and beds in public hospitals increased from 2,832 to 4,084 and from 2.11 lakh to 4.2 lakh, respectively, from 1974 to 2002 while in private sector hospitals and beds went up to 644 to 11.35 thousand and 5.75 thousand and 2.6 lakh, respectively, in the same period.

Twenty Point Economic Programme (TPP; 1975–Ongoing)

The TPP was initiated in 1975 and updated in 1982, 1986, and 2006. It is very important to achieve the objectives of development, that is, eradication of poverty and improving the quality of life of the masses. TPP 1982 and TPP 1986 had been revised in agreement with the priorities of the government as contained in the National Common Minimum Programme (NCMP), the Millennium Development Goals (MDGs) of the United Nations, and South Asian Association for Regional Cooperation (SAARC). The Programme was again updated in 2006 and was called TPP 2006. It focussed on eliminating poverty, increasing efficiency and productivity, removing inequalities, and eliminating social and economic differences (Government of India, 2006).

TPP 2006 encompassed the benefits for both rural and urban population to improve their quality of life-based on 20 points and 66 monitorable items. This programme included socio-economic aspects like poverty, employment, education, housing, health, agriculture, land reforms, irrigation, drinking water, and the environment.

TPP aimed at the socio-economic development of the country which covered schemes like poverty eradication, good education and health, food security, housing for all, women and child welfare, and social security. States like Himachal Pradesh, Rajasthan, Uttarakhand, Tamil Nadu, and Gujarat had achieved the targets while states like Assam, Mizoram, Bihar, West Bengal, Sikkim, and Chhattisgarh required more improvement to achieve the targets stated in TPP 2006. TPP improved the living standard of the poor and downtrodden sections of society. The efforts had also been put into streamlining production, procurement, and distribution of essential commodities, implementation of agricultural land ceiling and distribution of surplus land, development of handloom sector, workers association in the industry, apprentice scheme to enlarge employment and training, etc. (Government of India, 2010).

Bharat Nirman Programme (BNP; 2005–Ongoing)

BNP, a flagship programme, was inaugurated by the Government of India during 2005–2006. It was a time-bound business plan for four years which was further extended in the Twelfth Five Year Programme. The BNP and other flagship programmes focussed on improving the living conditions of poor people by providing them with upgraded infrastructure indicators like electricity, irrigation, banking, communication, health, and transport (Government of India, 2013).

The main focus of the BNP was to create a rural infrastructure covering irrigation facilities, rural roads, electrification, housing development, potable water and sanitation, and telecommunication connectivity with the intention of more growth potential for rural India.

Das (2013) aptly stated that BNP was implemented in two phases. The investments made in Phases I and II improved the rural economy and reduced the gap between rural and urban areas of India. The main motive of BNP is the percolation of growth benefits uniformly, reduction of poverty, generation of productive employment opportunities, assurance of social security benefits, expanding access to education, improving the standard of health, and better hygiene and sanitation. The outcomes stated that 60 per cent of households were constructed for rural households under Indira Awaas Yojana (IAY) during 2005–2010. The work done was 62.17 per cent for the construction of road connectivity with the rural areas under Pradhan Mantri Gram Rozgar Yojana for the same duration. For telecommunication, 92.5 per cent of villages were covered and under Accelerated Irrigation Benefits Programme (AIBP), 73 per cent of villagers benefited. Under the Accelerated Rural Water Supply Programme (ARWSP) rural households covered were 89 per cent. Rajiv Gandhi Vidyutikaran Yojana, BPL rural households, rural households, intensive electrification, and electrification of villages covered were 38.4 per cent, 25.7 per cent, 29.7 per cent, and 61.9 per cent, respectively.

Lalvani (2010) viewed that BNP achieved the desired results but many general and specific problems were witnessed. The government focussed on more coverage of the rural areas rather than the good quality of the services. People were not aware of the possible benefits of this programme. To improve the performance of BNP, the government must adopt measures to remove the problems of underutilisation of funds, improve the quality of roads constructed, and declare more incentives to attract private participation. Efforts should be made to educate the masses, so people could be more responsive towards the benefits and aware of their rights too.

Education, Health, and Family Welfare Schemes

Integrated Child Development Services (ICDS; 1975–Ongoing)

The Government of India commenced the ICDS in 1975 in 33 blocks with 4,891 Anganwadi Centres (AWCs) which further extended to the entire country in the year 2005. It was introduced for improving the health and well-being of mothers and children by providing health and nutrition education, health services, supplementary food, and preschool education. ICDS is the largest outreach programme operated through AWCs. AWCs are managed by anganwadi workers (AWWs) and anganwadi helpers (AWHs) (Government of India, 2009).

The Government of India (2014) observed that ICDS aimed at reducing morbidity, mortality, and malnutrition. The beneficiaries of the scheme are the children of the age group of 0–6 years, pregnant women, and lactating mothers. The objectives of ICDS are to improve the nutritional and health status of children in the age group 0–6 years; to lay the foundation for proper psychological, physical, and social development of the child; to reduce the incidence of mortality, morbidity, malnutrition, and school dropout; to achieve effective coordination of policy and implementation among the various departments to promote child development; and to enhance the capability of the mother to look after the normal health and nutritional needs of the child through proper nutrition and health education (Government of India, 2009).

Table 7 explains the achievement of ICDS from the year 1975 to the year 2015. In the year 1975, 33 blocks were operated which had increased to 7,729 in the year 2015. In the year 1975, 4,891 AWCs had been sanctioned which increased to

Table 7. Physical Performance of ICDS.

Year	No. of Operational Projects	No. of Operation AWCs	No. of Supplementary Nutrition Benefits (in Lakh)	No. of Preschool Education Beneficiaries (in Lakh)
1975	33	48,91	NA	NA
1985	1,130	162,061	NA	NA
1995	3,397	375,801	NA	NA
2005	5,237	754,148	685.23	279.81
2010	6,509	1,142,029	884.34	354.93
2015	7,729	1,761,857	1,229.41	415.31

Source: Government of India. (various issued-a). *Annual reports*. Ministry of Women and Child Development.

NA, not available.

1,761,857 AWCs in 2015. Supplementary nutrition benefits and preschool education beneficiaries had also shown rising trends from 1975 to 2015.

Ranjan (2014) indicated that several initiatives were taken to improve the quality of services as the increased budgetary allocations for ICDS indicated that the projects could be reached in more remote, destitute, and unreached areas. India ranked 46 among 193 countries with the highest under-five child mortality rate.

Despite such results, ICDS lagged. States with the highest incidence of child undernutrition and malnutrition received the least coverage and funds also. The AWCs had insufficient infrastructure as well as storage space. More than 60 per cent had no toilet facilities and approximately 49 per cent of the AWCs had not had enough space for outdoor and indoor activities. In addition to this, 50 per cent AWCs had no separate space for the storage of materials. Similarly, the number of cooking and service utensils was considered insufficient in 42 per cent and 37 per cent of AWCs, respectively (Government of India, 2011c). Approximately 44 per cent of the AWCs did not have preschool education kits and about 37 per cent reported the non-availability of materials/aids for nutrition and health education. Between 1999 and 2005, only Rs. 1.79 crores had been used on procuring medicines for the treatment of diarrhoea, respiratory tract diseases, and skin and eye infections as compared to Rs. 10.4 crores that were allocated for these purposes (Awofeso & Rammohan, 2011).

Mid-Day Meal (MDM) Scheme (1995–Ongoing)

A programme launched by Madras Municipal Corporation for the deprived and destitute children in 1925 called MDM Programme. Later on, Gujarat, Kerala, Tamil Nadu, and Pondicherry also initiated the same programme by using their resources for primary-level class children in the mid-1980. From 1990 to 1991, 12 more states also started this scheme by deploying their funds and resources.

The National Programme of Nutritional Support to Primary Education (NP-NSPE) launched MDM as a Centrally Sponsored Scheme on 15 August 1995. MDMs aimed to encourage enrolment, retention, and attendance and simultaneously improve the nutritional levels among children. It initially started in 2,408 blocks in the country, and by the year 1997–1998, it was introduced in all blocks of the country (Government of India, 1995),

Kainth (2013) stated that the MDM Programme was to encourage poor children to attend school regularly and also help them to concentrate on classroom activities. It aimed for improving the nutritional status of children of I–VIII grades in government, local bodies and government aided schools, Educational Guarantee Scheme (EGS), and Alternative and Innovative Education (AIE) centres especially covering the drought-affected areas.

Uma (2013) highlighted that the enrolment statistics improved and the number of dropouts diminished but the quality of education decreased. The study explained that the quality of education decreased because the teachers were involved in various other duties like storing meals and supply of meals. The cooked MDM Scheme had only contributed to the retention of children in schools across the country but it was not able to attract fresh enrolments in school. The attention towards teaching and learning activities had reduced which resulted in the loss of studies. There was a lack of basic infrastructural facilities and manpower in the schools (Government of India, 2010).

Sarva Shiksha Abhiyan (SSA; 2000–2001–Ongoing)

SSA is a widespread and coordinated programme, commenced with the motive of achieving Universal Elementary Education (UEE) throughout the country. SSA was proposed for the children of 6–14 age groups, to provide them access to formal education by the year 2010, implemented in partnership with the state governments and local self-governments. It was an initiative to universalise and improve the quality of education through decentralised and context-specific planning to achieve the objectives (Government of India, 2004).

The goals of the SSA mission were the enrolment of children in school, the opening of education guarantee centres and alternate schools, a back-to-school camp by 2005; retention of all children by 2010. It also focussed on reducing the gender and social category gaps in enrolment, retention, and learning achievement levels of children at the primary and upper primary stages (Government of India, 2010).

Table 8 shows that the gross enrolment ratio increased from 78.6 per cent to 114 per cent from the period 1970 to 1990 at the primary level. At the upper primary level, it was raised to 62.1 per cent from 33.4 per cent, and the dropout rate reduced to 42.6 per cent in 1990 from 67.0 per cent in the year 1970 by 25 per cent at the primary level of schooling. At the elementary and secondary levels, the dropout rate had shown a declining trend of 17.5 per cent and 11.2 per cent, respectively during the period from 1970 to 1990. Numerous schemes were launched by the Government of India to promote social equality. The main emphasis was on the UEE, which consisted of various schemes like SSA, District Primary

Table 8. Educational Achievements Since 1970.

Indicators	1970	1980	1990	2000	2010	2011	2013
Gross enrolment ratio							
Primary (I–V) 6–10 years	78.6	80.5	114	85.9	115.5	120.3	99.3
Boys	95.5	95.8	85.5	95.7	114.9	120.82	98.1
Girls	60.5	64.1	100.1	104.9	116.3	119.78	100.6
Upper Primary (VI–VIII) 11–13 years	33.4	41.9	62.1	49.9	85.2	104.12	87.4
Boys	46.5	54.3	76.6	58.6	87.5	104.21	84.9
Girls	20.8	28.6	47	66.7	82.9	104.03	90.3
Dropout rate							
Primary	67.0	58.7	42.6	40.7	34.8	22.3	19.8
Elementary	77.9	72.7	60.9	53.7	40.8	30.3	36.3
Secondary	82.5	82.5	71.3	68.6	50.3	39.3	47.4

Source: Government of India. (2014). *Educational statistics at a glance*. Ministry of Human Resource Development.

Education Programme (DPEP), MDM Scheme, Teacher Education Scheme, and Kasturba Gandhi Balika Vidyalaya Scheme for promoting inclusive education across all level of education (Kumar, 2012).

The infrastructure of schools regarding the facility of drinking clean water, toilet facilities, provision of electricity, computer know-how, classroom infrastructure, and additions in personnel were also improved. Despite the SSA norms, the quality of education varied across the states of India. This programme required more community participation and parental involvement with effective and better linkages with support centres to have desired results. It also required effective community-based monitoring activities along with the district-level monitoring teams. There needed to be coordinated efforts to strengthen the programme to accomplish the desired outcome (Government of India, 2010).

National Rural Health Mission (NRHM; 2005–2012)

NRHM commenced on 12 April 2005 throughout the country. The special focus of NRHM was on 18 states including eight Empowered Action Group (EAG) states: the North Eastern States, Jammu and Kashmir, and Himachal Pradesh to impart approachable, reasonable, and reliable quality health services even to the poorest households in the remotest rural regions. The thrust of this programme was thus on establishing a fully functional, community owned and decentralised health delivery system to ensure simultaneous execution of determinants of health like water, sanitation, education, nutrition, and social and gender equality to make India disease-free (Government of India, 2010).

The NRHM (2005) effectively contributed by expanding the health facilities and also made people aware of the benefits distributed to them. The main focus of NRHM was to remove the inequalities by increasing the personnel in the public health sector and by improving health facilities, by covering inaccessible remote areas and poor-performing districts (Government of India, 2011c).

Table 9 emphasises the progressive expansion of health services reflected in the demographic, epidemiological, and infrastructural indicators from 1991 to 2013. The life expectancy which was 59.4 per cent in the year 1991 had augmented to 68.3 per cent in the year 2013. The crude birth rate had declined from 25.9 per cent in 1991 to 21.6 per cent in 2013. The crude death rate was 9.8 per cent in 1991 and declined to 7.0 in 2013. The infant mortality rate had come down from 80 per cent to 42 per cent in 1991 and 2013, respectively. The mother mortality ratio dropped from 398 in 1991 to 212 in the year 2011. Malaria had reduced to 1.31 million cases in the year 2011 which used to cause 2.12 million cases in 1991. Leprosy has been eliminated as a public health problem in 32 states and 83 per cent of districts. Smallpox and guinea have been eradicated, and the last cases occurred in the country in May 1975 and July 1996, respectively. Polio eradication is very bright soon.

The above table shows an upward trend from 725 to 1.7 lakh approximately health centres in rural areas. There are openings of many SHCs, PHCs, and CHCs in rural areas. The number of institutions providing medical education, the availability of beds, and the number of nurses and doctors in hospitals have also increased. The number of dispensaries and hospitals and beds has risen from 38 thousand and 8.1 lakh approximately in the year 1991 to 63 thousand and 21 lakhs approximately in the year 2013, respectively. The number of nurses and doctors has also climbed up from 3.4 lakh to 5.5 lakh and 3.9 lakh to 9.2 lakh approximately during the period 1991–2013.

There is a lower contribution on the part of the public sector as compared to the private sector in health care. Mukhopadhayay (2008) stated that the public normally preferred the private healthcare sector as compared to the public health sector. Private healthcare institutions were more attentive to the needs of patients, offered better services, had negligible waiting time, and the manners and skills of doctors and other personnel were better.

With the advent of NRHM, India made remarkable achievements in providing affordable healthcare facilities to the rural poor. A significant number of CHCs, PHCs, and SHCs had been opened to rural health services in India. However, the functioning of CHCs, PHCs, and SHCs on a 24×7 basis was still below the required level. There was a shortage of human resources in public health institutions with shortfalls of even specialists/post-graduate doctors, gynaecologists, staff nurses, and anaesthetists in almost all the states. States like Madhya Pradesh, Jharkhand, Assam, and Tamil Nadu worked quite efficiently. However, in most of the districts in Uttar Pradesh, Orissa, and Jammu and Kashmir, the mobile medical units had failed to achieve the desired results (Parshad et al., 2013).

Table 9. Expansion of Health Services.

Indicators	1991	2001	2011	2013
Demographic change				
Life expectancy rate	59.4	64.6	65.9	68.3
Crude birth rate	29.50	26.1	21.8	21.6
Crude death rate	9.80	8.4	7.1	7.0
Infant mortality rate	80	66	44	42
Mother mortality ratio	398	301	212	NA
Epidemiological shifts				
Malaria (cases in millions)	2.12	2.02	1.31	NA
Smallpox (no. of cases)	–	–	–	–
Guinea worm disease (no. of cases)		Eradicated	–	–
Polio (cases in millions)		265	NA	NA
Infrastructure development				
SHC/PHC/CHC*	153,505	163,181	176,820	177,248
Dispensaries and hospitals (all)**	38,605	38,832	43,328	63,302
Beds (private and public)**	810,548	1,068,214	1,894,968	2,124,646
Nursing personnel	340,208	382,901	488,538	558,956
Doctors	394,068	622,105	883,812	922,177

Sources: 1. Government of India. (2013). *Human resources in health sector, Central Bureau of Health Intelligence*. Ministry of Health and Family Welfare.

2. Government of India. (2013). *Health finance indicators, Central Bureau of Health Intelligence*. Ministry of Health and Family Welfare.

Notes: 1.SHC/PHC/CHC: sub-centre/primary health centre/community health centre.

2. *Rural health statistics as on 31 March of every year, Central Bureau of Health Intelligence, ** as on 31 January of every year.

3. NA, not available.

Water Supply and Sanitation

ARWSP (1972–2008)

During the mid-sixties, the water supply schemes were executed in the reachable villages and ignored the remote rural areas. The government of India introduced ARWSP to provide safe and potable drinking water to the rural population, covering more remote and destitute villages (Government of India, 1975). With the commencement of the MNP in 1974–1975, ARSWP was discontinued. However, the government resumed ARSWP in the year 1977 because some remote villages did not have access to safe drinking water. Later on, in the year 2009, ARSWP was reintroduced with the new name called National Rural Drinking Water Programme (NRDWP).

The main goals of the programme were to ensure coverage of all rural habitations in the remote and hard-core rural areas of India, to provide access to a minimum of 40 litres per capita per day (LPCD) of safe drinking water, to ensure the sustainability of systems and sources, to institutionalise water quality monitoring and surveillance, and to tackle the problem of water quality in affected habitats. The main objective of this programme was to ensure full coverage of all habitations of the state by selecting suitable sources and schemes scientifically and cost-effectively to ensure the supply of the required quality and quantity of water besides ensuring the sustainability of sources and schemes (Government of India, 2007).

Table 10 explains the access to potable water supply and sanitation facilities in rural and urban areas of India. In rural and urban areas, access to potable water supply had increased from 1.9 per cent to 91 per cent and 41.9 per cent to 97 per cent, respectively, from 1961 to 2015. Sanitation facilities had also gone up from 0.7 per cent to 30 per cent and 14 per cent to 70 per cent in rural and urban areas, respectively, over the same period.

Kumar and Das (2014) studied that despite many efforts, India still lagged in providing sanitation facilities. Due to a lack of basic sanitation facilities, polluted water, and unhealthy conditions, about 70 per cent of India's rural and slum population still faced waterborne and vector-borne diseases. The benefits of this scheme had not been equally distributed because the benefits were enjoyed by the economically better-off sections of the community. The poor, vulnerable, and destitute people had been underprivileged of their due and opposite share. The main constraint seemed to be the inconvenient locations of the government for public supply junctions as people belonging to tribal and desert areas were not able to use such sources. This is because of a lack of community support,

Table 10. Physical Achievements Under Water Supply and Sanitation Component.

Indicators	1951	1961	1971	1981	1991	2001	2011	2015
Access to potable water supply								
Rural	NA	1.9	3	31	56.3	73.9	76	91
Urban	NA	41.9	62	72.9	77.8	83.8	92	97
Sanitation facilities								
Rural	NA	0.7	1	2.4	9.5	17.4	25.2	30
Urban	NA	14	20	28.4	45.9	60.1	63.9	70

Source: Government of India. (various issues-a). *Annual reports*. Planning Commission.
Note: NA, not available and P, projected.

participation, and contribution to the implementation and operation as well as maintenance of the programme concerned (Government of India, 1980).

NRDWP (2009–Ongoing)

The ARWSP was reintroduced with the new name called NRDWP in 2009. NRDWP was initiated with the target of covering the whole of rural India. It is intended to ensure ample potable water for drinking, cooking, and other fundamental needs of rural households. This basic requirement was assuring the minimum water quality standards reachable to the remotest rural areas. It was observed that the requirement of 40 LPCD under ARSWP was insufficient for providing enough water to tail-end villages. So, LPCD approach adopted the cloak of the water security approach, and 24×7 hours supply was ensured to households to fulfil the basic minimum requirement, that is, domestic and cattle (Mankad, 2013).

The Government of India (2009) restructured ARWSP by considering the following objectives and renamed it NRDWP 2009. The objectives were to ensure the provision of safe and adequate drinking water supply to all uncovered, partially covered, and quality-affected habitations in the rural areas of the country; to ensure that all schools and anganwadis have access to safe drinking water; to enable Gram Panchayat (GPs) and Village Water and Sanitation Committee (VWSCs) to plan, manage, operate, and maintain local water sources and water supply; to provide enabling support and environment for Panchayati Raj Institutions (PRIs) and local communities for this purpose; to enable rural communities to monitor and keep surveillance on their drinking water sources, water supply, and initiate corrective action to have contaminants free water; and provide access to information through online reporting system with information in the public domain to bring in transparency and informed decision making.

The Government of India (2013) stated that several states fell behind in the implementation of the programme. Beneficiaries faced deficiencies like delay in procurement processes, delay in preparatory activities, even longer time taken for completion of legal formalities, and subsequently late release of funds, etc. It had been observed that Gram Panchayats and communities were not involved in the planning, implementation, monitoring, and Operations and Maintenance (O&M) of their rural water supply systems. Poor implementation of schemes leads to non-functionality or low yield of many schemes especially piped water supply schemes. Depletion of the groundwater-based drinking water sources due to over-extraction by irrigation/industry, contamination of drinking water sources due to untreated sewage, open defecation, untreated industrial effluents, and leaching of fertilisers and pesticides were some of the problems faced by the people (Mojumdar, 2013).

Total Sanitation Campaign (TSC; 1999–2012)

TSC was launched in 1999. It emphasised more human development and capacity development activities for increasing awareness among the rural people to generate the demand for sanitary facilities. This programme was being introduced to the masses to convince them of good sanitation practices within their households and conjointly in the school. TSC provided separate toilets for boys and girls in all the schools/anganwadis in rural areas within the country. The programme was revised in 2012 and was renamed Nirmal Bharat Abhiyan (NBA) which was further restructured in 2015 as Swachh Bharat Abhiyan (SBA) (Government of India, 2011c).

TSC aimed at targeting the people for having sanitation practices in the living and more associated areas to have a hygienic environment. The objectives of the programme were to bring an improvement in the general quality of life in the rural areas; accelerate sanitation coverage in rural areas by providing toilet facilities to all masses by 2007; motivate communities and PRIs to promote sanitation facilities through awareness; include the schools/anganwadis in rural areas with sanitation facilities and promote hygiene education and sanitary habits among students; encourage cost-effective and appropriate technologies for ecologically safe and sustainable in sanitation; and develop community managed environmental sanitation systems that specialised solid and liquid waste management (SLWM).

Apart from such efforts, TSC had led to poor sanitation which further led to a higher incidence of disease. Many incentives including cash were given to BPL households to construct toilets in their own houses and promote the usage of individual household latrines (IHHL) in the community. Grants-in-aid were also provided for the construction of school toilet units, anganwadi toilets, and community sanitary complexes (CSC) with SLWM. The Government of India also launched the Nirmal Gram Puraskar (NGP) to improve TSC. NGP brought the movement in the community for attaining the Nirmal Status by effectively increasing the sanitation coverage in rural areas across the country. The TSC is being renamed NBA as it gained importance in NGP (Government of India, 2013).

(a) *NBA:* The Government of India (2011c) mentioned that for implementing TSC, a strategy was selected to make this programme community-led and people-centred. A demand-driven approach was adopted which emphasised awareness creation and demand generation for sanitary facilities in houses and schools. The NBA was implemented in two phases. The first phase was to conduct a preliminary survey and prepare the project implementation plan (PIP) at the district level to identify SLWM modes. The second phase was to implement the plan, that is, construction of IHHL, CSC, bathing cubicles, washbasins, and institutional toilets in schools and anganwadis. According to the Census (2011), only 5.48 crore households (32.7 per cent) had access to toilets which means that 67.3 per cent of the rural households in the country still did not have access to sanitation facilities. Later as per the Baseline Survey, 2012– 2013, carried out by the Ministry through the states, only 40.35 per cent of rural households had been found to have access to toilets (Government of India, 2014).

(b) *SBA:* Under the new programme, NBA was restructured in the year 2015 with the new name Swachh Bharat Mission for accomplishing two sub-missions – Swachh Bharat Mission (Gramin) and Swachh Bharat Mission (Urban). Under the NBA, the major constraint is the lack of funds for increasing the coverage of toilets at an adequate pace. The proposed investment was Rs. 1.34 lakh crores and Rs. 62,000 crores for rural and urban areas, respectively, over the next five years. This overall investment was made by the government in collaboration with private-sector players. The highest degree of policy priority accorded to sanitation with the introduction of SBA could go a long way towards achieving an open defecation-free India in the coming years (Kaul, 2015).

Housing and Urban Development

Indira Awas Yojana (IAY) (1985–Ongoing)

Government also initiated programmes related to housing development. IAY, a rural housing programme across the country is the largest and most inclusive rural housing programme. The genesis of this programme was the wage employment programmes, which commenced National Rural Employment Programme (NREP, 1980), and the Rural Landless Employment Guarantee Programme (RLEGP, 1983). The houses were constructed for the labourers under these programmes. Later on, in the year 1985, RLEGP commenced a programme called IAY for the construction of houses for Scheduled Castes/Scheduled Tribes (SCs/STs) and freed bonded labourers. Then this programme shifted as a sub-programme under a scheme named Jawahar Rozgar Yojana (JRY) in 1989. In the years 1993–1994, IAY broadened its scope and started to cover BPL non-SCs/STs (Government of India, 2010).

The main focus of IAY was to help rural BPL SC/ST families, freed bonded labourers, and non-SCs/STs by providing them financial assistance for the construction or renovation of houses (Government of India, 2012b). But the IAY scheme was not implemented as per the implementation guidelines of the programme. The selection procedure of eligible beneficiaries was not done according to the prescribed norms as many illegitimate beneficiaries were selected under this scheme. The shortage of houses was also determined. The authorities failed to exercise due diligence in the construction activity and houses costing Rs. 7.88 crores were constructed in 12 blocks of 8 selected districts of 5 states. In 48 selected districts of 9 states, 61,293 houses remained incomplete even after the lapse of two years. In the majority of the states, the IAY beneficiaries were deprived of safe drinking water, free electricity connection, and sanitary toilets due to non-convergence with other schemes as earlier envisaged. There were deficiencies in the system of approval and release of funds by the Ministry. The short and delayed release of the state share, misappropriation, and diversion of funds were also observed (Government of India, 2014).

Rajeev Awas Yojana (RAY; 2009–Ongoing)

The Government of India aims for a slum-free nation with the target of achieving inclusive growth by providing all basic needs. An integrated approach collaborated under RAY which aimed to bring a formal system for those who lived in extra formal spaces and were in denial of basic amenities by providing them a decent shelter. RAY provided support to states/union territories to redevelop all existing slums in a comprehensive way to develop urban slums and create new affordable housing stock (Government of India, 2011a).

The Government of India (2009) approved RAY for the development of slum areas that further cause the growth of the urban poor also. RAY encouraged dealing with urban slums by fixing all notified as well as non-notified slums under the formal system so that urban slum families could have the basic essential facilities. If somehow, the formal system was unable to fulfil the requirements of the people living in slum areas, then corrective steps could be followed immediately. RAY had the objectives of improving and provisioning housing, basic civic infrastructure, and social amenities in intervened slums; enabling reforms to address some of the causes leading to the creation of slums; facilitating a supportive environment for expanding institutional credit linkages for the urban poor; institutionalising mechanisms for prevention of slums including the creation of affordable housing stock; strengthening institutional and human resource capacities at the municipal, city, and state levels through comprehensive capacity building and strengthening of resource networks; and empowering community by ensuring their participation at every stage of decision making through strengthening and nurturing Slum Dwellers' Association/Federations.

Das Simpreet and Bhise (2014) viewed that under the pilot phase of RAY, the government approved 55 projects in 48 cities across 16 states. Later on, 42,488 dwelling units (DUs) were approved under RAY across 55 cities. Jaipur, Bhubaneswar, Sirsa, Vijayawada, Alwar, Kota, Chennai, Indore, Ajmer, and Rai Bareli got 19,564 DUs passed under the total RAY projects. Out of 16 states, only 8 states had acquired more than 75 per cent of the projects. Rajasthan, Madhya Pradesh, Haryana, Karnataka, Andhra Pradesh, Chhattisgarh, Uttar Pradesh, and Tamil Nadu managed to get the pilot projects. In addition to it, many rental slum dwellers were also included in the list. While conducting pre-survey, survey, and post-survey, it had been observed that participation and contribution of the community were not shown. So, measures must be taken to ensure the proper implementation of RAY.

Labour and Employment and Social Services Benefits

Integrated Rural Development Programme (IRDP; 1978–1999)

IRDP and allied programmes were launched in 1978 and this scheme was replaced by Swarnajayanti Gram Swarozgar Yojana (SGSY) in 1999. This programme focussed on income-generating assets and employment opportunities for the rural poor to improve their standard of living (Mukhopadhyay & Saha, 2005). For the proper implementation of IRDP in rural areas, an autonomous agency called the District Rural Development Agency (DRDA) was appointed. It was responsible for implementing, coordinating, supervising, and monitoring the IRDP at the district level. Selection of IRDP beneficiaries was made by village level workers (VLW) by following the Antyodaya, that is, selecting the poorest from the poor first (Roy, 2014). The small farmers and landless labourers were given subsidised credit, training, and infrastructure to increase their source of income. In this scheme, agricultural labourers and small farmers were encouraged to adopt new skills to involve in vocations other than cultivating the land. It included fishery, animal husbandry, and forestry (Yesudian, 2007).

There has been a shift in achieving desired results by selecting the needy beneficiaries like educated unemployed rural youth BPL so that extraordinary results could be achieved via investing in infrastructure. The beneficiaries were eligible for subsidies of up to 50 per cent of project costs, subject to a ceiling of Rs 7,500 (Government of India, 2000).

The survey conducted by National Bank for Agriculture and Rural Development (NABARD) showed the leakage in the implementation of the programme. It was found that only 22 per cent of the eligible beneficiaries or 18.7 per cent of all beneficiaries had been able to cross the poverty line. However, a person whose income was more than Rs. 3,500, lives above the poverty line. About 47 per cent of eligible beneficiaries were non-eligible beneficiaries under this scheme. The selected districts in states like Punjab, Haryana, Uttar Pradesh, and Maharashtra showed a better performance with more than 40 per cent rising above the poverty line, while Rajasthan, Tamil Nadu, and Andhra Pradesh showed 10 per cent or less performance (Rath, 1985). The IRDP suffered from several defects which include sub-critical investment, unviable projects, illiterate, and unskilled beneficiaries with no experience in managing an enterprise, indifferent delivery of credit by banks, overcrowding of lending in certain projects such as dairy, less emphasis on activities like trading, service, and even simple processing, poor targeting, and selection of non-poor (Government of India, 2014).

SGSY (1999–2013)

SGSY was executed in the year 1999 with the help of state governments, PRIs, banks, DRDA, and non-governmental organisations to safeguard the interest of vulnerable and weaker sections. This programme aimed at micro-enterprise development in rural areas with an emphasis on organising the rural poor into self-help groups, capacity-building, women and children development, planning of activity clusters, infrastructure support, technology, credit, and marketing linkages (Roy, 2014).

Before 1999, many self-employment generation programmes were implemented but did not give the desired results. So, many programmes collaborated to form SGSY in 1999. The main objective was to rectify the situation of lack of proper social intermediation, and the absence of desired linkages which were targeted earlier, on self-employment programmes. This programme focussed on organising the poor into self-help groups via the process of mobilisation, training, and capacity building (Dev & Rao, 2002). Sunkari (2014) highlighted that through SGSY many women were empowered and earned on their own. The formation of SHGs had helped poor women to develop both economic and social strength. It was also demonstrated that the SHGs have enhanced the status of women as participants, decision-makers, and beneficiaries in the democratic, economic, and social spheres of life. Despite such results, there had been problems like the marketing of products and non-transparency of funding patterns. Roy (2014) stated that SGSY had not achieved success due to a lack of capacity building of the beneficiaries, a smaller number of community institutions, and weak linkages with banks. It was also found that several states had not been able to fully utilise the funds provided by the SGSY scheme. However, despite these drawbacks, this programme was successful in eradicating rampant poverty in rural areas.

Prime Minister Rozgar Yojana (PMRY; 1993–2007)

PMRY was a credit-linked subsidy scheme, initiated in 1993 to fulfil the needs of less educated and unemployed youth living under BPL. This scheme helped poor people to establish micro-level self-employment ventures in industry and service sectors by bestowing them with some financial grants (Government of India, 1993). The objective of the scheme was to provide productive employment opportunities to have hurdle-free life. The micro-enterprises covered manufacturing, service, and business ventures. The PMRY targeted the setting up of seven lakhs micro-enterprises to generate employment for 1.4 million persons by the end of the Eighth Five Year Plan (Government of India, 1993).

The evaluation of this scheme was done in three phases: firstly in 1996–1997 followed by 2000–2001, and 2005–2006. The proportion of SCs/STs increased from about 12 per cent in the first round to 13 per cent in the second and further increased to 21 per cent in the third round. No such improvement had been observed in the share of women beneficiaries under this scheme. The average amount of loan disbursed had been increased to Rs. 64,000 in the third round from Rs. 57,000 in the second round. The employment generation was higher in the first round at 2.5 per unit which decreased to 1.95 per unit in the third unit. The share of rural beneficiaries had plummeted from 49.9 per cent to 39.1 per cent. The average rate of recovery of loans was 29 per cent and 38 per cent in the second and third rounds, respectively. Lack of awareness along with the selection of non-eligible beneficiaries was one of the main reasons for the failure. Non-eligibility led to more non-performing assets. So, it required more awareness among people to increase the participation of women and the needy beneficiaries of underprivileged classes (Government of India, 2010).

(a) *Prime Minister Employment Generation Programme (PMEGP; 2008):*
A new centrally sponsored scheme was launched in 2008 called PMEGP. This scheme was a collaboration of merging PMRY and the Rural Employment Generation Programme (REGP) for the generation of employment opportunities through the establishment of micro-enterprises in rural as well as urban areas. Khadi and Village Industries Commission (KVIC) implemented PMEGP at the national level and state KVI boards and District Industries Centres (DICs) worked at the field level (Government of India, 2008).

This programme was mainly for micro-level entrepreneurs. It focussed on empowering entrepreneurs through skill development and entrepreneurial development programmes. Micro-enterprises were set up to create more employment for unemployed youth belonging to both rural and urban areas. The main objectives of PMGSY were to generate employment opportunities in rural and urban areas of the country through self-employment ventures/ projects/micro enterprises. It would bring the traditional and prospective artisans, rural and urban unemployed youth altogether and give them self-employment opportunities; continuous and sustainable employment for their better livelihood. It would increase the wage-earning capacity of artisans and also contribute to the growth of rural and urban employment. It also facilitates the participation of financial institutions for higher credit flow to micro-enterprises.

This scheme was enacted as very beneficial for the unemployed youth of the country covering 16 lakhs unemployed persons. The government provided a margin money subsidy between 25 and 35 per cent of the project cost, depending upon the category of the entrepreneur and the balance amount being covered by the banks. An outlay of Rs 8,060 crores (Rs 7,800 crores margin money subsidy plus Rs 260 crores under backward and forward linkages) had been approved by the Planning Commission for PMEGP in the Twelfth Five Year Plan to set up about Rs 3.39 lakh projects and create 27.12 lakhs employment. About 91.7 per cent of the units financed were working till 2013–2014 and the average income of the beneficiaries increased by 61 per cent. PMEGP also undertook activities like organising entrepreneurship development and other training programmes, awareness camps, workshops, e-tracking, web management, publicity, and physical verification of units. The PMEGP scheme indicated success in generating employment opportunities in rural and urban areas of the country (Government of India, 2014).

Mahatma Gandhi National Rural Employment Guarantee Act (MGNREGA; 2005–Ongoing)

The Maharashtra Government introduced the EGS in 1970 which was later on launched as a nationwide Food for Work Programme in 1977 to generate employment and utilise the surplus food grains for rural as well as urban development. In 1980, the Food for Work Programme was renamed as NREP. Later on, NREP and RLEGP were merged in 1989 into JRY. Jawahar Gram Samridhi Yojana (JGSY) collaborated with Employment Assurance Scheme (EAS) in 1996 and the JRY was revised in April 1999 and renamed Sampoorna Grameen Rozgar Yojana (2001). National Food for Work Programme and Sampoorna Grameen Rozgar Yojana (SGRY) was amalgamated with MGNREGA in 2005. The main objective of MGNREGA was to provide guaranteed employment by ensuring at least 100 days of guaranteed wage employment in a financial year. It is helpful to enhance the livelihood security of every rural household if the volunteer adult member of the household is prepared to do unskilled manual work (Government of India, 2005).

To follow the approach of inclusive growth, MGNREGA enrooted as a very effective programme. It covered social protection, livelihood security, and democratic empowerment. It was a demand-driven programme where the provision of work was triggered by the demand for work by wage seekers. It provided a legal guarantee of wage employment. The objectives of MGNREGA included providing social protection for the most vulnerable people living in rural India; ensuring livelihood security for the poor through the creation of durable assets, improved water security, soil conservation, and higher land productivity; strengthening drought-proofing and flood management in rural India; aiding in the empowerment of the marginalised communities, especially women, SC, STs through the processes of rights-based legislation; strengthening decentralised, participatory planning through the convergence of various anti-poverty and livelihoods initiatives; and deepening democracy at the grass root levels by strengthening the PRIs, effecting greater transparency and accountability in governance (Government of India, 2012a).

Table 11 shows the achievements of MGNREGA. The share of SCs had increased initially from 25 per cent in 2006–2007 to 31 per cent in 2010–2011 but later on, it had shown a declining trend and in the year 2014–2015, the SCs share became 23 per cent. The participation of STs had fallen from the initial years from 36 per cent to 17 per cent in the same period. Women participation augmented throughout the decade from 40 per cent to 55 per cent ensuring equitable access to work, decent working conditions, equal payments of wages, and decision-making power (Government of India, 2016a).

Total expenditure incurred on MGNREGA showed an increasing trend from 2006 to 2016 from Rs. 8,824 crores to Rs. 36,032 crores. Expenditure incurred on wages also indicated the rising trend. Works taken up during the programme and the work completed both increased, thus targets were not achieved as per decided. The social inclusion of vulnerable classes was one of the main objectives of MGNREGA. Through the MGNREGA, multiple impacts had been seen such as the creation of durable assets, improvement in the bargaining power of agricultural labourers, generation of employment, financial inclusion, the institutionalisation of transparency and accountability measures in governance, and strengthening PRIs. Most importantly, the MGNREGA had become a platform across the country for mobilising informal labour and powering them to claim their basic rights as workers (Sanyal, 2014).

Instead of such achievements, MGNREGA participation declined over recent years. Employees appointed under the popular job scheme of the MGNREGA system stated that they were often not paid in full or compelled to pay bribes to get tasks, and were not learning any new abilities that could enhance their long-term leads and break the pattern of hardship. There was a lack of grievance redressal mechanism, 15 days time frame to provide jobs after demand via application was not met, and in some states job cards were not made. And the method of measurement of work was as such that it resulted in corruption and fewer wages for real and legitimate workers. There were also widespread instances of fake job cards (dead job cards). Moreover, the type of work done under MGNREGA was not done correctly. This appeared to be a huge loss of public money (Sushmita, 2015).

Table 11.   Achievements of MGNREGA.

Year	Social Inclusion (In Crores)			Total Person days	Employment Days Per Household (In Days)	Expenditure Incurred (In Crores)		Works (In Lakhs)	
	SCs	STs	Women			Expenditure on Wages	Total Expenditure	Works Completed	Works Taken Up[a]
2006–2007	23 (25)	33 (36)	36 (40)	90.5	43	5,842 (66)	8,824	3.9 (46.4)	8.4
2007–2008	39.4 (27)	42 (29)	61 (43)	143.6	42	10,739 (68)	15,857	8.2 (46)	17.9
2008–2009	63.4 (29)	55 (25)	103.6 (48)	216.3	48	18,200 (67)	27,250	12.1 (43.8)	27.8
2009–2010	86.5 (30)	58.7 (21)	136.4 (48)	283.6	54	25,579 (67)	37,905	22.6 (48.9)	46.2
2010–2011	78.8 (31)	53.6 (21)	122.7 (48)	257.2	47	25,686 (65)	39,377	25.9 (50.8)	51.0
2011–2012	46.2 (22)	41.5 (19)	101.1 (48)	218.8	42	24,660 (66)	37,303	14.3 (19.6)	73.6
2012–2013	53.0 (23)	41.5 (18)	117.6(51)	230.5	45	27,154 (70)	38,770	27.6 (34.1)	80.8
2013–2014	48.9 (22)	37.5 (17)	116.9(53)	220.4	45	26,535 (68)	38,602	25.5 (24.4)	104.6
2014–2015	38.2 (23)	28.3 (17)	91.5 (55)	166.3	44	24203 (67)	36,032	24.1 (25.6)	94.1

Source: Government of India. (2016). *Mahatma Gandhi National Rural Employment Guarantee Act 2005 – The Journey of a decade*. Ministry of Rural Department.

Note: ( ) denotes percentage.

[a]Total works have taken up=Spill over works + New works.

Rural Development

Intensive Agricultural Development Programme (IADP; 1960–1963)

For rural development, it was decided that to encourage the development of agriculture and allied activities focus must be shifted to it. An Agricultural Administrative Committee called Nalagarh Committee was established in 1958 and it was reported that agriculture had not been developed to the extent which was required. Initially, there was confusion and disagreement about the roles and responsibilities of the units of the programme implementation. The committee concluded that a streamlined agricultural administration was an urgent necessity and that the food situation of the country could be substantially eased if positive steps were taken to accomplish this goal. It was emphasised that special focus should be particularly on scientific and progressive agriculture in an intensive way and therefore, the IADP had been launched in 1960–1961 (Chandra, 2008).

This programme highlighted the adoption of known improvements in technology. The major emphasis was laid down on the organisation and operation in selected districts that further provided educational, technical, and service assistance to farmers in getting and utilising the new inputs in yield-increasing combinations (Malone & Johnson, 1971).

Evenson and Mohan (1974) observed that the IADP approach was a bit different from the earlier CDP approach. This programme was very effective due to its foremost focus on the rapid increase in agricultural production with technocratic methods and to provide an experimental programme developing new ideas.

Table 12 shows that the yields per acre of crops in the first group of selected districts were higher in 1961–1962 as compared to those in 1960–1961. Out of 23 cases, 19 cases had shown an improvement in the yield per acre. While in 1961–1962, it has been observed that the yield per acre declined in both IADP districts as well as in control blocks. The change in yields of both IADP and Controlled blocks in the period of 1960–1961 to 1962–1963 revealed that yield per acre increased substantially in IADP districts in 1961–1962 as compared to 1960–1961 because of favourable weather and in 1962–1963, yields per acre had been declined as the weather was reported as unfavourable in many yields (Rao, 1964).

Table 13 describes the average yields per acre of the second group of selected districts under IADP for two years, that is, 1961–1962 and 1962–1963. No significant results were shown in IADP districts and controlled areas. The basic policies of the government regarding credit, marketing, prices, industries, imports, investment, and land were not favourable for the efficient implementation of the programme (Government of India, 1969).

Table 12.   Yields in IADP and Control Blocks of First Group of Selected Districts (Quintals Per Hectare).

S. No.	Districts	States	Crop	Yield (IADP Districts)				Yield (Control Blocks)			
				1960–1961	1961–1962	1962–1963	Average	1960–1961	1961–1962	1962–1963	Average
1	Pali	Rajasthan	Maize	9.9	9.7	9.1	9.6	NA	7.9	10.5	9.2
			Bajra	1.7	3.2	2.5	2.5	NA	2.7	2.5	2.6
			Jowar	1.2	2.8	1.3	1.8	NA	2.8	1.3	2.1
			Wheat	9.5	10.4	9.4	9.8	NA	12.4	12.8	12.6
			Barley	10.3	11.8	10.8	11.0	NA	14.9	11.2	13.1
2	Thanjavur	Madras	Rice – first crop	15.2	17.0	15.4	15.8	NA	17.3	17.7	17.5
			Rice – second crop	14.4	17.0	17.7	16.4	NA	16.1	15.6	15.9
3	West-Godavari	Andhra	Rice – first crop	14.6	16.9	13.8	15.1	NA	17.9	14.5	16.2
			Rice – second Crop	10.9	15.2	18.2	14.8	NA	13.6	15.9	14.8
4	Shahabad	Bihar	Rice	10.8	12.9	11.8	11.8	NA	NA	NA	NA
			Wheat	8.0	6.8	7.0	7.27	NA	NA	NA	NA
			Gram	5.6	5.3	5.4	5.43	NA	NA	NA	NA
5	Raipur	Madhya Pradesh	Rice	–	9.8	7.9	8.85	NA	9.4	7.2	8.3
6	Aligarh	Uttar Pradesh	Bajra	2.7	5.2	7.9	5.27	NA	5.5	9.9	7.7
			Maize	2.4	5.0	13.4	6.93	NA	4.6	15.8	10.2
			Wheat	11.5	12.0	11.9	11.8	NA	15.0	13.5	14.3
			Barley	9.1	11.3	11.3	10.6	NA	15.8	12.3	14.1
			Gram	9.4	7.8	9.5	8.9	NA	12.4	8.6	10.5
			Pea	11.4	10.5	9.6	10.5	NA	15.4	14.7	15.1
7	Ludhiana	Punjab	Maize	–	20.1	11.4	15.8	NA	20.9	12.7	16.8
			Cotton	–	3.0	1.6	2.3	NA	3.0	1.4	2.2
			Wheat	15.6	17.6	17.5	16.9	15.9	17.6	15.4	16.3
			Grams	9.4	10.5	10.5	10.1	9.5	11.2	9.6	10.1

Source: Government of India (1969).

Note: NA, not available.

Table 13.   Average Yields in IADP and Control Blocks of the Second Group of Selected Districts of Two Years (Quintals Per Hectare).

S. No.	Districts	States	Crop	Yield (IADP Districts)	Yield (Control Blocks)
				Average	Average
8	Alleppey	Kerala	Rice	14.1	16.3
9	Palghat		Rice	16.8	15.5
10	Mandya	Karnataka	Rice	22.5	27.4
			Ragi	7.8	7.8
11	Surat	Gujarat	Rice	12.9	NA
			Jowar	8.7	8.5
12	Sambalpur	Odisha	Rice	9.6	8.7
13	Burdwan	West Bengal	Rice	18.2	15.7
14	Bhandara	Maharashtra	Rice	9.9	9.5
			Wheat	3.8	4.9
			Jowar	2.5	4.2
15	Cachar	Assam	Rice	12.9	NA

Source: Government of India (1969).

Note: NA, not available.

Intensive Agricultural Area Programme (IAAP; 1964–1967)

The government decided to extend the IADP under the name of the IAAP because of undesirable results. IAAP was adopted to accomplish the task of putting about 20–25 per cent of the cultivated area of the country under an intensive agricultural programme. This programme stressed the intensive development of improving crops like wheat, paddy, millets, pulses, and cotton for the high agricultural production in 114 selected districts. The selection of IAAP districts is more or less the same as the IADP district's selection criteria (Krishna & Swaminathan, 1971).

Table 14 explained that IAAP had 1,084 blocks in the year 1964–1965 and the number of blocks also increased to 1,410 in the year 1966–1967.

Table 14.   Number of Blocks Selected Under IAAP.

S. No.	Year	No. of Districts	No. of Blocks
1	1964–1965	114	1,084
2	1965–1966	114	1,285
3	1966–1967	114	1,410

Source: Government of India. (1961). *Third five year plan document*. Planning Commission.

Under this scheme, all the essential elements for increasing agricultural production such as the supply of fertilisers, pesticides, improved seeds and implements, and supply of adequate credit were provided to all farmers. While both the IADP and IAAP were concerned with the promotion of intensive agriculture, they operated within the importations set by existing crop varieties which had a relatively low response to fertilisers (Government of India, 1961).

High Yielding Varieties Programme (HYVP; 1966–1979)

The focus was shifted to increasing the productivity of crops and earnings, so, the HYVP was introduced in 1966. India faced the problem of an acute shortage of food grains in 1965–1966 and 1966–1967. The HYVP was a comprehensive package consisting of agricultural research, irrigation, supply of inputs (seeds, fertilisers, and credit), intensified agricultural extensive services, training, and supervision. This programme included five separate programmes designed for each crop, that is, paddy, wheat, maize, jowar, and bajra (Government of India, 1971).

HYVP is also known for the Green Revolution. The vagaries of monsoon rains, fluctuating production, and increasing demand for food grains by a rapidly rising population lead to chronic food deficiency. To attain self-sufficiency in food, HYVP came into action with objectives like using high-yielding varieties of seeds, increasing the use of fertilisers, and increasing irrigation (Government of India, 1971).

Table 15 explains the area and production of paddy, wheat, maize, jowar, and bajra from 1966 to 1979. Paddy, wheat, and maize show an increasing trend area-wise and production-wise during the implementation of HYVP. The area of paddy increased in the year 1979 to 39.42 million hectares from 35.25 million hectares in the year 1966 with production from 30.44 million tons to 49.33 million tons in the same period. The area and production of wheat also showed a growing trend during this period from 12.57 million hectares to 22.17 million hectares and 10.4 million tons to 31.83 million tons, respectively. Maize also indicated a rising trend area-wise and production-wise from 5.07 million hectares to 5.84 million hectares and 4.89 million tons to 6.39 million tons, respectively. While jowar and bajra showed a decreasing trend during the HYVP.

The area of jowar declined to 16.67 million hectares in the year 1979 from 18.05 million hectares while the production had increased from 9.22 million tons in the year 1966 to 11.65 million tons in the year 1979. Bajra also decreased from 12.24 million hectares and 4.47 million tons, respectively, to 10.58 million hectares and 3.95 million tons during the same period. This era brought effective change and this implementation of technological change in agriculture focussed on the use of pesticides, irrigation, machinery, improved implementations, and soil conservation. The successful adoption of these components of the new strategy increased agricultural production. The introduction of these components depends upon various factors like irrigation, size of the farm, capital, institutional credit, and extension services (Sadhu & Mahajan, 1985).

Sarma (1981) analysed the effects of HYVP in three phases. In the first phase, 1966–1971, HYVP proved an instant success and the area expanded rapidly with

Table 15.   Crop Production During HYVP (Area – Million Hectares, Production – Million Tons).

Year	Paddy		Wheat		Maize		Jowar		Bajra		Total	
	Area	Prod	Area	Prod	Area	Prod	Area	Prod	Area	Prod	Area	Prod
1966	35.25	30.44	12.84	11.39	5.07	4.89	18.05	9.22	12.24	4.47	115.30	74.23
1967	36.44	37.61	14.99	16.54	5.58	6.27	18.42	10.05	12.81	5.19	121.42	95.05
1968	36.97	39.76	15.96	18.65	5.72	5.70	18.73	9.80	12.05	3.80	120.43	94.01
1969	37.68	40.43	16.63	20.09	5.86	5.67	18.61	9.72	12.49	5.33	123.57	99.50
1970	37.59	42.22	18.24	23.83	5.85	7.49	17.37	8.11	12.91	8.03	124.32	108.42
1971	37.76	43.07	19.14	26.41	5.67	5.10	16.78	7.72	11.77	5.32	122.62	105.17
1972	36.69	39.24	19.46	24.74	5.84	6.39	15.51	6.97	11.82	3.93	119.28	97.03
1973	38.29	44.05	18.58	21.78	6.02	5.80	16.72	9.10	13.93	5.52	126.54	104.67
1974	37.89	39.58	18.01	24.10	5.86	5.56	16.19	10.41	11.29	3.27	121.08	99.83
1975	39.48	48.74	20.45	28.84	6.03	7.26	16.09	9.50	11.57	5.74	128.18	121.03
1976	38.51	41.92	20.92	29.01	6.00	6.36	15.77	10.52	10.75	5.85	124.36	111.17
1977	40.28	52.67	21.46	31.75	5.68	5.97	16.32	12.06	11.10	4.73	127.52	126.41
1978	40.48	53.77	22.64	35.51	5.76	6.20	16.15	11.44	11.39	4.57	129.01	131.90
1979	39.42	42.33	22.17	31.83	5.72	5.60	16.67	11.65	10.58	3.95	125.21	109.70

Source: Government of India. (2014). *Agricultural statistics at a glance*. Ministry of Agriculture.

an increase in fertiliser used under this program. In 1970–1971, two-thirds of irrigated area and 35 per cent of the total area planted with wheat was sown. While only 38 per cent of the irrigated area and 15 per cent of the total area planted with rice were sown. In the second phase, 1971–1975, fertiliser was used, irrigated areas, and food grain production stagnated, though irrigation picked up in the last year of the period. In the last phase, that is, 1975–79, irrigation, consumption of fertiliser, and the area also increased. The expansion of other crops was even more limited due mainly to the suitability of availability of HYVs to only limited areas. The application of fertilisers was inadequate and unbalanced. This was due to inadequate availability of credit, ignorance of gains, insufficient irrigation facilities, shortage of fertilisers in 1972–1973, and the hike in their prices in 1974 (Government of India, 1976).

This programme did not indicate an increase in the production of crops. Only wheat and rice production contributed to the growth in production and productivity of the country. The main reason for the rapid adoption of new varieties of wheat was the expected higher net income. It resulted in the procurements of large surpluses which enabled India to reduce wheat imports and attain self-sufficiency (Government of India, 1976). India still required about 10 years for achieving self-sufficiency in food grains. There is an urgent need for modernising marketing techniques (Krishna & Swaminathan, 1971).

Food Storage and Warehousing

Antyodaya Anna Yojana (AAY; 2000–Ongoing)

AAY was initiated in 2000 to ensure food security across the country. Therefore, this scheme was to create a hunger-free India and improve the PDS to serve the poorest of the poor in rural and urban areas. It had been seen that 5 per cent of the population was unable to get two square meals a day on a sustained basis throughout the year because they could not purchase the food grains at BPL rates as their purchasing power was so low (Government of India, 2000).

Khera (2011) mentioned that there were several defects in Targeted Public Distribution System (TPDS). With coverage of around 40 crores BPL families, TPDS suffered from the structural shortcomings and disturbances like growing instances of the consumers receiving inferior quality food grains in ration shops; deceitful dealers replace good supplies received from the Food Corporation of India (FCI) with inferior stock and sell FCI stock in the black market; illicit fair price shop owners have been caught in creating the large number of bogus cards to sell food grains in the open market; many Fair Price Shop (FPS) dealers resort to malpractice, illegal diversions of commodities, hoarding, and black marketing due to the minimal salary received by them; numerous malpractices made safe and nutritious food inaccessible and unaffordable to many poor thus resulting in their food insecurity; identification of the households to be denoted status and distribution to granted PDS services has been highly irregular and diverse in various states and regional allocation and coverage of FPS are unsatisfactory and the core objective of price stabilisation of essential commodities has not met.

The government introduced Aadhar Unique Identification Authority of India (UIDAI) cards to solve the problem of identification and distribution of PDS services along with direct cash transfers. Nation Food Security Act (NFSA) was passed to provide food and nutritional security in the human life cycle approach, by ensuring access to an adequate quantity of quality food at affordable prices for people to live a life with dignity and for matters connected therewith and incidental thereto. The Food Bill provides free nutritious meals to children and pregnant and lactating women. The attention was more on nutrient-rich foods including pulses that would be provided to the poor. The bill included subsidised rates for pulses for the poor. Currently, the food grains in the PDS shops come from a centralised warehouse which is often located far away. The bill insisted on decentralised storage of food grains like a warehouse in each cluster of the village, block, or district (Government of India, 2013).

India followed a trickle-down approach to embark on the path of development and then an inclusive growth strategy. No doubt, the government is spending huge sums of money to remove poverty in the nation; still, about 20 per cent of the country's population is poor. The social welfare of the masses has become both a tool and objective of Indian economic policy. Social sector expenditure eradicates poverty in the nation significantly but the reduction in poverty does not indicate a reduction in hunger, malnutrition, and deprivation. Poverty alleviation programmes could lead to an increase in incomes which could have additional spin-offs in the form of higher nutrition, better health, and productivity (Chadha & Chadda, 2018).

Among the physical performance of the social sector in India, some important findings are as follows:

- *Education*: Gross enrolment rate increased from 42.6 per cent to 99.2 per cent from 1951 to 2016 at the primary level. At the upper primary level, it had increased to 92.8 per cent from 12.7 per cent over seven decades. Dropout rate reduced to 19.8 per cent in 2015 from 64.9 per cent in the year 1961 at the primary level of schooling. At elementary and secondary levels, the dropout rate had shown a declining trend of 42 per cent and 35.1 per cent, respectively 1961–2015.

- *Health infrastructure*: Health centres in rural areas have shown an increasing trend from 725 to 1.9 lakhs during 1951–2015. The number of dispensaries and hospitals and beds had risen from 9 thousand and 1.1 lakhs, respectively, to 63 thousand and 21 lakhs during 1951–2015. The number of nurses and doctors also climbed up from 18 thousand to 5.5 lakhs and 61 thousand to 9.2 lakhs during 1951–2015.

- *Epidemic control*: Malaria has been reduced to 1.31 million cases in the year 2011 which used to cause 75 million in the 1950s. Leprosy has been eliminated as a public health problem in 32 states and 83 per cent of districts. Smallpox and guinea had been eradicated.

- *Housing development*: It was targeted to achieve the construction of three lakhs dwelling houses but 83,967 houses were constructed in urban India at the end of 2014–2015. There is still a shortage of 14.8 million houses in 2015 in rural areas.

- *Drinking water and sanitation*: 70 per cent of India's rural and slum populations are exposed to water- and vector-borne diseases due to a lack of basic sanitation facilities, unsafe water, and unhygienic conditions.

The vision of inclusiveness must go beyond the traditional objective of poverty alleviation to encompass equality of opportunity, as well as economic and social mobility for all sections of society, with affirmative action for SCs, STs, OBCs, minorities, and women. Inclusive development includes social inclusion along with financial inclusion and its major dimensions like poverty alleviation and employment generation.

Chapter 5

Growth and Development of the Social Sector in India

Free India inherited a dilapidated and shattered economy with rampant poverty and retrogressive socio-economic antecedent of a monolithic population. Not only the income needed to be pushed up, but it needed to be fairly distributed. The socio-economic traits of the population needed to be braced up to make growth inclusive. The social sector is based on a welfare motive that has an imperative role to support the economy and society so that it leads to the reduction of regional disparities and poverty alleviation through employment generation. Earlier, human development incorporated health and education as the major components, but recently, with an ever-rising concern of the government and policymakers, the development of infrastructure and other components of the social sector are also considered extremely important ingredients for economic development (Nayak & Mishra, 2014).

To remove poverty and for equal distribution of income among the masses, the government must invest in social sector development to make growth inclusive. The expenditure incurred on social sector development will create more opportunities for employment which further leads to more income for deprived classes. Human development is a much wider notion than human capital. Social Sector development provides the rationale for the growth strategy as it develops human resources by empowering them through better access to education and health, potable water and sanitation practices, housing and urban development, and the welfare of marginalised classes (Jain & Runa, 2014).

Sen-Bhagwati Debate

The trickle-down approach based on the Nehruvian/Mahalanobis model was advocated by Jagdish Bhagwati. After independence, India, till the Fourth Five Year Plan, experimented with this approach and failed. Sen and Dreze continued to profess the human development approach to economic development by reinforcing the social sector development, which India started emphasising since the Fifth Five Year Plan. Even otherwise, since independence, due to gnawing poverty and deprivation of the masses, social sector development had been given prime importance, to promote democratic inclusive growth.

Social Sector Development and Inclusive Growth in India, 99–124
Copyright © 2023 by Ishu Chadda
Published under exclusive license by Emerald Publishing Limited
doi:10.1108/978-1-83753-186-820231006

Bhagwati and Panagariya pointed out the two stages of reforms, that is, Track I and Track II reforms, which are necessary for long-term economic development. It was mentioned in their book, *Why Growth Matters: How Economic Growth in India Reduced Poverty and Lessons for other Developing Countries* (Bhagwati & Panagariya, 2013). Track I reforms aimed at facilitating the growth of gross domestic product (GDP) and reducing the poverty through this economic growth and Track II reforms focussed on providing better healthcare facilities, improving access to education, and guaranteeing productive employment in rural and destitute areas. The growth would be possible only if government revenue was increased by economic growth and could be trickled down to grass root level because of democracy.

Drèze and Sen (2013) in their book, *An Uncertain Glory: India and Its Contradictions* stated that the sequencing of Track I and Track II reforms mentioned by Bhagwati and Panagariya had been repugnant to economic development. According to them, a far better pattern of economic development is one which focussed on Track II reforms which emanated Track I reform eventually as improvements in education and health lead to more human productivity, and human development and ultimately increase the GDP. In India, a large section of the population faced the pitiable state of health, education, and other social indicators that were left behind in the model of development (Dasgupta, 2013).

Amartya Sen, in his views on social spending, mentioned that economic growth must be an adjunct to social improvement and the government must incur expenditure on education, healthcare, welfare of marginalised classes, and food subsidy programmes. While Bhagwati, in his views on the free market corner, disagreed with Sen and stated that India should concentrate exclusively on economic growth because of market deregulation which will consequently direct for improving the living standard of the poorest (Acharya, 2013). Sen believed that India ought to devote more attention to upgrading the social infrastructure which raises the efficiency and productivity of people and thereby elevates growth. On the other hand, Bhagwati focussed on the economic growth that enhances GDP which eventually leads to investing in social sector schemes and thus reducing poverty. Sen mentioned that investing in health and education to improve human capabilities would reduce inequality and the growth process will continue. While Bhagwati believed that economic growth might raise inequality initially, however, sustained economic growth would finally augment enough resources for the state to reallocate and alleviate the side effects of the initial inequality (Bhattacharya, 2013). The philosophy of social sector development is in line with Sen (1989) who visualises economic development as an outcome of human welfare first rather than Bhagwati and Panagariya (2013) who failed to achieve its objective in the initial phase of Indian development.

Social Sector Development and the Five Year Plans

Ever since independence, poverty alleviation has been India's top priority amidst the list of various other national agendas. And it has been 50 years since the social objective was to guarantee an adequate standard of living for the population of

India, in other words, to get rid of the perpetuated poverty. Productive employment generation has been the foremost objective for both development planning as well as implementation. Labour, being the main asset for the majority of the poor, and expanding productive employment would result in attaining sustained poverty eradication (Dev, 2000). Components of the social sector development emphasised contributing to human development; thus considered to be a significant factor that plays an indispensable role in economic development (Panchamukhi, 2000).

Table 16 presents the disaggregated plan allocations and actual expenditure on various components of the social sector, that is, education, health, family welfare, housing, urban and regional development, water supply, and rural development by the Indian governments during different plan periods. The expenditure on education has grown significantly during the plan period. The allocation and expenditure incurred on education in 1951–1956 were Rs. 149 crores and Rs. 153 crores, respectively, which have risen to Rs. 2.8 lakh crores and Rs. 3.6 lakh crores, respectively, in the Twelfth Five Year Plan. The percentage share of education allocation and expenditure was 7.2 per cent and 7.8 per cent. The First Five Year Plan increased to 8.6 per cent and 10.2 per cent in the Twelfth Five Year Plan. The table reveals that in the Sixth Five Year Plan, the ratio of education outlay to total plan outlay is the lowest, that is, 2.6 per cent and 2.7 per cent, respectively.

On the other hand, the data reveal that investment in healthcare and family welfare has indicated an increasing trend during the planning era. The allocation and expenditure on medical and public health in 1951–1956 were Rs. 65.2 crores and Rs. 98 crores, respectively, which escalated to Rs. 8.9 thousand crores and Rs. 9.3 thousand crores, respectively, in 2012–2017. The allocation and expenditure of family welfare were Rs. 10 lakhs each which has risen to Rs. 4.2 thousand crores and Rs. 4.9 thousand crores. However, the ratio of health investment to total plan investment indicates the increasing trend of allocations and outlays but at a marginal pace. During the First Five Year Plan, it was 3.2 per cent of allocation and 5 per cent of expenditure which further came up to 2.9 per cent and 4.4 per cent, respectively, in the Twelfth Five Year Plan. On the contrary to the health, family welfare has increased considerably from 0.01 per cent of each to 1.9 per cent and 3.5 per cent, respectively, of the allotted and spent amount during the same period.

Rawat et al. (2008) witnessed that the expenditure incurred on healthcare and family welfare had increased so far, but the health expenditure ratio to total plan investment had registered a declining trend and family welfare increased in the planning era. Both in rural as well as urban areas, the healthcare services were not up to the mark. Due to India's large population and low per capita income, India's position in global health status is quite low (Government of India, 2002).

Other significant components, water supply and sanitation, accounted for Rs. 7.9 crores in outlay and Rs. 11 crores of actual expenditure in the First Five Year Plan and Rs. 8.3 thousand crores and Rs. 8.6 thousand crores, respectively, in the Twelfth Five Year Plan with its proportionate share hovering between the lowest of 0.4 per cent to the highest of 4.2 per cent.

Table 16. Plan-wise Allocations and Actual Outlays Incurred on Components of Social Sector in India.

FYP	Social Services											
	Education, Art, and Culture		Medical and Public Health		Family Welfare		Water Supply and Sanitation		Housing and Urban Development		Welfare of SC, ST, and O	
	Outlays	Actual Exp	Outlays	Actual Exp	Outlays	Actual Exp	Outlays	Actual Exp	Outlays	Actual Exp	Outlays	Ac E
1st	149 (7.2)	153 (7.8)	65.2 (3.2)	98 (5.0)	0.1 (0.0)	0.1 (0.0)	7.9 (0.4)	11 (0.6)	82.5 (4.0)	129 (6.6)	39 (1.9)	29.8 (1.5)
2nd	265.8 (5.5)	273.5 (5.9)	140.8 (2.9)	226 (4.8)	2.3 (0.0)	5 (0.1)	59.1 (1.2)	74 (1.6)	128.2 (2.7)	149v (3.2)	90 (1.9)	83 (1.8)
3rd	589.1 (7.9)	660.8 (7.7)	221.29 (3.0)	225.4 (2.6)	22.4 (0.3)	25 (0.3)	88.2 (1.2)	105.7 (1.2)	119 (1.6)	127.6 (1.5)	114 (1.5)	99.1 (1.2)
Plan Holiday	323 (4.8)	353.6 (5.3)	132.4 (2.0)	140.2 (2.1)	65.9 (1.0)	70.4 (1.1)	91.8 (1.4)	102.7 (1.6)	67.9 (2.9)	73.3 (1.1)	62 (0.9)	68.4 (1.0)
4th	963 (6.1)	905.2 (5.7)	433.5 (2.7)	335.5 (2.1)	315 (1.2)	278 (1.8)	407.3 (2.6)	458.9 (2.9)	237 (1.5)	270.2 (1.7)	142 (0.9)	181.5 (1.2)
5th	1,729.6 (4.5)	1,710 (4.3)	681.7 (1.8)	760.8 (1.9)	497.4 (1.3)	491.8 (1.2)	530.2 (1.4)	591.6 (1.5)	1,106.9 (2.8)	1,150 (2.9)	227.89 (0.6)	226 (0.6)
Rolling Plan	384.5 (3.3)	354.4 (2.9)	268.2 (2.3)	223.1 (1.8)	116.2 (1.0)	118.5 (1.0)	429.5 (3.7)	387.6 (3.2)	301.8 (2.6)	368.8 (3.0)	214.6 (1.8)	247.9 (2.0)
6th	2,523.7 (2.6)	2,918.6 (2.7)	1,821.1 (1.9)	2,214 (2.0)	1,010 (1.0)	1,048 (1.0)	3,922 (4.0)	3,976.1 (3.6)	2,146 (2.2)	2,832.1 (2.6)	1,365 (1.4)	1,48 (1.4)
7th	6,382.6 (3.5)	7,685.5 (3.5)	3,392.89 (1.9)	3,689 (1.7)	3,256.26 (1.8)	3,121.06 (1.4)	6,522.47 (3.6)	7,329.19 (3.4)	4,229.49 (2.3)	4,835.86 (2.2)	1,560 (0.9)	1,22 (0.6)
Annual Plans	4,419.3 (3.2)	4,915.45 (3.7)	1,253.86 (0.9)	1,965.57 (1.5)	1,424 (1.3)	1,805.47 (1.3)	3,426.99 (2.5)	4,080.02 (3.0)	3,059.24 (2.2)	3,032.28 (2.3)	1,596.1 (1.2)	1,56 (1.2)
8th	30,824.7 (4.5)	31,028.0 (4.1)	12,132.99 (1.7)	11,994.8 (1.5)	9,407.45 (1.5)	10,305.8 (1.3)	22,850.74 (3.8)	25,199.6 (3.3)	18,299.19 (2.4)	18,519.48 (2.4)	9,641.11 (1.3)	11,16 (1.7)
9th	53,286.22 (4.6)	59,222.6 (5.8)	20,330.32 (2.2)	28,196.3 (2.8)	13,282.8 (1.6)	19,924.9 (2.0)	35,464.42 (3.6)	46,911.5 (4.4)	43,377.86 (4.1)	37,340.9 (5.2)	154,464 (1.6)	25,05 (2.1)
10th	75,949.96 (4.6)	85,030.5 (8.5)	26,866.95 (2.5)	38,335.4 (2.7)	20,054.9 (1.8)	27,810.9 (2.3)	43,207.34 (3.7)	62,293.8 (4.4)	72,165.54 (5.3)	74,724.2 (7.7)	23,214.67 (1.4)	33,67 (2.3)
11th	154,498.02 (8.2)	199,628.7 (9.4)	50,495.98 (2.7)	59,921.4 (3.2)	25,470.22 (1.7)	41,698.2 (3.1)	62,997.79 (3.1)	81,110.5 (4.0)	157,709.9 (7.8)	190,039,1 (8.8)	39,677.23 (2.1)	51,29 (3.0)
12th	281,601.96 (8.6)	367,270.0 (10.2)	89,086.81 (2.9)	93,196.4 (4.4)	42,983.55 (1.9)	49,590.2 (3.5)	83,224.83 (3.1)	86,626.9 (4.3)	272,264.2 (7.9)	257,155.9 (9,6)	88,397.44 (3.3)	102,3 (4.2)
CV	249.83	239.83	219.76	214.91	192.47	205.58	193.03	191.64	253.69	238.99	234.08	226.4

Sources: Government of India. (various issues-a), *Annual Reports*. New Delhi: Planning Commission.
Government of India. (various issued-b). *Economic Survey*. New Delhi: Ministry of Finance.
Government of India. (various issued-c). *Outlays Budget (Vol. 1)*. New Delhi: Ministry of Finance.

Notes: 1. Labour and employment and social security and welfare have been initiated from the Fifth Five Year Plan onwards.

2. Food the storage and warehousing has been introduced from Seventh Five Year Plan onwards.

3. Other social services include information and publicity, broadcasting, nutrition, and secretariat social services.

4. Figures in parentheses indicate the percentage of total expenditure.

Labour and Employment		Social Security and Welfare		Other Social Services		Economic Services				Total	
						Rural Development		Food Storage and Warehousing			
Outlays	Actual Exp	Outlays	Actual Exp	Outlays	Actual Exp	Outlays	Actual Exp	Outlays	Actual Exp	Outlays	Actual Exp
–	–	–	–	49 (2.4)	55.7 (2.8)	41.9 (2.3)	52.92 (2.7)	–	–	433.9 (21.3)	529.32 (27.0)
–	–	–	–	46.6 (1.0)	44.7 (1.0)	178.34 (3.9)	196.24 (4.2)	–	–	911.14 (19.2)	1,051.44 (22.5)
–	–	–	–	223.7 (3.0)	250.1 (2.9)	1,138.67 (11.2)	1,308.12 (15.3)	–	–	2,685.82 (29.6)	2,801.86 (32.7)
–	–	–	–	115.8 (1.7)	167.8 (2.5)	1,779.8 (17.5)	1,997.0 (13.1)	–	–	2,855.8 (29.6)	2,973.49 (44.9)
39.9 (0.3)	51.1 (0.3)	41.4 (0.3)	69.4 (0.4)	332.3 (2.1)	437.2 (2.8)	2,654.50 (17.2)	2,820.0 (17.8)	–	–	5,565.9 (36.2)	5,807 (36.8)
50.1 (0.1)	52.2 (0.1)	86.2 (0.2)	88.2 (0.2)	958.6 (2.5)	1,078.7 (2.7)	4,123.8 (9.7)	4,252.0 (10.8)	–	–	9,992.4 (24.8)	10,401.3 (26.4)
67.2 (0.6)	89.6 (0.7)	27.2 (0.2)	30.7 (0.3)	342.6 (2.9)	336.5 (2.8)	1,378.12 (11.1)	1,418.0 (11.6)	–	–	3,529.92 (29.6)	3,575.1 (29.4)
183.2 (2.0)	195.3 (0.2)	197.6 (0.2)	205.8 (0.2)	866.4 (0.9)	1,047.4 (1.0)	5,363.73 (5.5)	6,996.8 (6.4)	–	–	19,398.73 (19.9)	22,914.1 (21.0)
249.7 (0.1)	264.95 (0.1)	986.4 (0.5)	1,071.19 (0.5)	4,965.47 (2.8)	5,742.09 (2.6)	8,906.08 (5.0)	5,246.5 (6.9)	89.4 (0.05)	131.01 (0.06)	40,540.81 (22.5)	40,338.03 (23.0)
303.97 (0.2)	257.62 (0.2)	1,373.68 (1.0)	1,202.1 (0.9)	1,026.47 (0.7)	1,080.24 (0.8)	8,744.51 (6.4)	8,291.5 (6.2)	124.7 (0.14)	144.3 (0.11)	26,752.87 (21.9)	28,340.7 (21.2)
2,224.28 (0.4)	1,989.62 (0.4)	7,388.96 (1.3)	7,398.9 (1.1)	6,189.36 (1.2)	7,191.89 (1.0)	52,144.2 (7.9)	53,956.3 (7.7)	1,175.97 (0.10)	1,345.18 (0.07)	1,722,876.5 (26.2)	180,090.88 (24.6)
2,161.97 (0.3)	6,294.8 (0.3)	15,266.19 (1.4)	18,376.22 (1.9)	7,954.64 (1.1)	14,665.9 (1.4)	59,413.62 (7.1)	126,749.5 (8.9)	2,715.27 (0.08)	3,589.99 (0.09)	268,699.6 (27.6)	386,325.63 (29.6)
2,998.54 (0.3)	8,346.93 (0.3)	19,268.01 (1.5)	29,726.26 (2.3)	16,726.74 (1.7)	24,663.3 (3.4)	74,371.31 (8.0)	168,116.28 (9.5)	4,762.48 (0.07)	6,723.08 (0.08)	379,585.1 (30.8)	5,529,465.57 (34.3)
7,852.96 (0.4)	7,467.5 (0.4)	46,910.62 (2.6)	64,525.5 (3.7)	19,956.39 (2.0)	28,046.1 (3.4)	114,083.6 (8.3)	194,193.7 (9.9)	5,986.64 (0.10)	7,060.53 (0.12)	685,439.9 (38.6)	924,986.9 (41.0)
22,952.57 (0.8)	16,462.5 (0.8)	92,623.18 (3.0)	115,032.2 (4.1)	22,239.84 (1.7)	35,503.9 (3.8)	160,857.4 (8.7)	266,327.4 (10.5)	7,170.85 (0.15)	9,228.8 (0.15)	1,163,403.0 (41.95)	13,987,928.0 (45.78)
230.93	213.16	255.70	255.02	227.30	228.31	133.70	196.15	130.20	135.49	233.01	220.77

Panchamukhi (2000) indicated the rising trend of investment outlays for water supply and sanitation from the period of the First Five Year Plan to the Eighth Five Year Plan. India's performance is quite disappointing for the same despite numerous efforts put in by the government for safe and adequate water and sanitation facilities. Only 30 per cent of the population had been drinking safe and potable water and had basic sanitation facilities.

The housing and urban development sector reveals the rising trend both in allocations as well as outlays for the First Five Year Plan to the Eleventh Five Year Plan. The amount allotted for housing and urban development in the First Five Year Plan was Rs. 85.2 crores which has escalated to Rs. 2.7 thousand crores in the Twelfth Five Year Plan with a percentage share of 4.0 per cent to 7.9 per cent, respectively. The investment made on housing and urban development is Rs. 129 crore which further rose to Rs. 2.5 thousand crores during the same planning period. The ratio of this sector to total plan outlay is 6.6 per cent and 9.6 per cent, respectively, in the First and Twelfth Five Year Plans.

Bhat (2005) highlighted that the government had put in several efforts to expand and improve the infrastructure facilities like housing, water supply, and sanitation facilities but failed. As per the 1991 Census report, 30.9 million people resided in semi-pucca houses and 27.4 million people lived in kutcha houses in comparison to 41.6 million people who had pucca houses. The overall shortages had been estimated in housing and infrastructure facilities both in rural areas and urban areas, with approximately 185 lakhs and 140 lakhs dwelling units. respectively. Hence, the government must take cautious steps to promote housing development.

The plan allocation and actual expenditure on the welfare of underprivileged classes have risen marginally from Rs. 39 crores to Rs. 7.7 thousand crores and Rs. 88 thousand crores and Rs. 1 lakh crores, respectively, during the period of the First to Twelfth Five Year Plans with an increase of 2.4 per cent and 3.7 per cent, respectively, in plan periods. Regardless of this planned economic development, a large part of the population especially the Scheduled Castes (SCs), Scheduled Tribes (STs), and Other Backward Classes (OBCs), women, and children still face social and financial exclusion. A new policy or strategy should be framed to remove economic inequalities by stimulating economic activity and providing equality of opportunity simultaneously (Government of India, 2010). It was pointed out that the increase in central government expenditure was partly attained by dropping the distributions by the centre and state plans (Joshi, 2006).

From the Fourth Five Year Plan, two more components were introduced, that is, labour and employment & social security and welfare. The allocation and amount expended for labour and employment was Rs. 39.9 crores and Rs. 51.1 crores in the Fourth Five Year Plan with a percentage of 0.3 per cent of each which is increased to Rs. 25 thousand crores and Rs. 16 thousand crores at a minuscule level with the increase in 0.8 per cent of each of their respective plan outlays. Social security and welfare have shown an increasing trend but at a marginal rate. The allocation and outlay in the Fourth Five Year Plan were Rs. 41.4 crores and Rs. 69.4 crores, respectively, which have increased to Rs. 92 thousand crores and Rs. 1 lakh crores, respectively, in Twelfth Five Year Plan.

The unemployment rate increased from 6.1 per cent in 1993–1994 to 8.3 per cent in 2004–2005 indicating the low growth of the labour force post-reform period. The average annual rise in employment during the pre-reform period was 7.09 million as compared to 6.45 million annual increases during the post-reform period. It would require more effort to transfer the surplus workers to more productive and profitable employment areas in organised as well as unorganised sectors to make this inclusive (Government of India, 2007).

The next component of the social sector is rural development. The plan outlay allocated for rural development from the period of the Sixth Five Year Plan to the Twelfth Five Year Plan has bolstered up to Rs. 1.6 lakh crores from Rs. 5,353.75 crores with the percentage hovering between 5.5 per cent and 8.7 per cent of total plan allocation. The actual outlay incurred on rural development from the First Five Year Plan to the Twelfth Five Year Plan has registered an increasing trend of Rs. 2.6 lakh crores. This sector has witnessed the highest growth in the Fourth Year Plan with 10.5 per cent.

Roy (2014) analysed the rural development initiatives in India since 1951 and mentioned that improvement had been observed in the country's rural sector. From the Third Five Year Plan onwards, the main emphasis was given to agricultural development. Numerous rural development programmes like Applied Nutrition Programme, Intensive Agricultural Area Programme, High Yielding Variety Programme, Drought Prone Area Programme, and Minimum Needs Programme were initiated during the Third and Fourth Five Year Plans. All these programmes facilitated the acceleration of the country's overall development; however, the contribution to alleviating rural poverty had not been noticed. After the Sixth Five Year Plan, all succeeding plans envisaged and emphasised rural employment and rural development (Government of India, 2007).

Food storage and warehousing of the states initiated since the Seventh Five Year Plan. Rs. 89.4 crores and Rs. 131 crores, respectively, have been allotted and utilised in the Seventh Five Year Plan which raised to Rs. 7 thousand crores and Rs. 9 thousand crores, respectively, in the Twelfth Five Year Plan. Shariff et al. (2002a) stated that food storage and warehousing are the responsibilities of the state government, and implemented the distribution of foods at reasonable prices via fair price shops (FPS) for benefitting the downtrodden members of society. However, the public distribution system (PDS) failed as it was only for below-the-poverty-line (BPL) card holders. During the Seventh Five year Plan, an Advisory Committee on PDS headed by the Union Minister introduced targeted public distribution system (TPDS) in 1997. It followed the two-tier subsidised pricing structure to serve the population BPL as well as above the poverty line (APL). Other schemes to support TPDS were also launched by the Government of India like Antyodaya Anna Yojana, Annapoorna Anna Yojana, and Annapurna Yojana to achieve the targets.

The coefficient of variation is found to be the highest in social security and welfare, housing, and urban development followed by that education, the welfare of underprivileged classes, labour and employment, water supply and sanitation, health and family welfare besides other social services both in plan allocations and outlays. Pathak (2005) stated that amidst the different social sector components, education, health and family planning, housing, and urban development were getting high amounts of allocations as well as outlays. The coefficient of variation was observed to be highest in housing and urban development followed by family welfare, education, and health among other social sector components. The distribution and outflows for rural development revealed the growing trend with a notable change during the planning process.

Social Sector and India's Economic Reforms

Panchamukhi (2000) studied the impact of economic reforms on different components of the social sector in India. The impact of economic reforms affected the allocations of the Indian economy's resources distributed to the social sector as the role of government had reduced in the economic activity which influenced the social sector most.

The underlying philosophy of economic reforms was to introduce privatisation in some sectors. In India, the public sector and private sector distribution on social sector development were not very satisfactory and even the allocation ratio of the public–private sector to different components of the social sector was not accessible. The post-economic reforms performance of social sector expenditure till certain years had shown a dip as compared to pre-economic reforms. The different sectors of economic policy influenced the economy differently and integration of social sector planning and economic planning must be ensured. There must be transparency with the data about public and private sector allocation to the different components of the social sector (Jain & Runa, 2014)

Economic reforms of the 1990s opened a new chapter in the socio-economic history of new India. Therefore, many new social and rural development schemes were ushered in to make growth more inclusive such as Prime Minister Rozgar Yojana, Prime Minister Employment Generation Programme, National Rural Health Mission, Swarnajayanti Gram Swarozgar Yojana, Mahatma Gandhi National Rural Employment Guarantee Act, National Old Age Pension Scheme, National Family Benefit Scheme, National Maternity Benefit Scheme, Annapurna Scheme, Indira Gandhi National Widow Pension Scheme, Indira Gandhi National Disability Pension Scheme, etc.

Table 17 elucidates yearly allocations and actual expenditure incurred on components of the social sector since economic reforms which have shown the rising trend reflecting the higher priority given to the indicators of human development. The amount allocated and actual outlays for education is Rs. 6 thousand crores and Rs. 5 thousand crores approximately in the year 1991 which have significantly come up to Rs. 75 thousand crores and Rs. 87 thousand crores approximately in the year 2015–2016 at an average rate of 11.51 per cent and 12.71 per cent. In other words, allocations and actual expenditure for education have registered an increasing trend of 7.5 per cent and 8.7 per cent during the same period. It had been seen that the public expenditure on elementary education, secondary education, higher and university education, and technical education had indicated an increasing trend of four times approximately from the year 1991 to the year 2008. After the implementation of the Revised National Policy on Education (1992), the education sector had given much-needed outcomes (Government of India, 1997). De and Endow (2008) also studied the expenditure incurred on education and stated that the education sector had shown splendid results by growing at a rate of 13.5 per cent for the period from 1990–1991 to 2003–2004. The main reason for this increase was because the revision of pay scales in the public sector.

Medical and public health and family welfare have increased from approximately Rs. 2.6 thousand crores and Rs. 1.6 thousand crores in the year 1991 to Rs. 26 thousand crores and Rs. 11 thousand crores at an average rate of 9.99 per cent and 7.95 per cent, respectively, in the year 2015 for the approved share. The actual outlay for the same also increased but at a marginal pace with Rs. 22 thousand crores and Rs.11 thousand crores at an average rate of 10.34 per cent and 8.32 per cent during the same period. Chopra (2008) observed a negligible upward trend in health expenditure from 0.8 per cent of GDP in 1980–1981 to 0.92 per cent in 1989–1990 which further reduced to 0.76 per cent in 1997–1998. The study suggested taking needed action as spending on the health sector had been quite low. The National Health Policy (2002) and Common Minimum Programme (CMP) focussed on the need of attaining the required level of good health among the masses of India. Public expenditure on health at least has to increase to 2 or 3 per cent of GDP.

The ratio of allocations and outlays for water supply and sanitation to the total allocation and total expenditure have shown an increasing trend from the year 1991 to the year 2000 that is 3.5 per cent to 4.0 per cent for both and afterward the decreasing trend has been observed from 2001 to 2013 of nearly 1 per cent in both while amount invested in this component has indicated the rising trend of Rs. 10 thousand crores approximately from 1991–1992 to 2015–2016 at an average growth rate of 6.5 per cent. Kumar and Das (2014) studied that India failed to achieve the norms related to safe drinking water and sanitation facilities. The majority of India's rural and slum population faced problems due to a lack of basic sanitation facilities, unsafe and non-potable water, and unhygienic conditions. India's 70 per cent population was exposed to waterborne and vector-borne diseases. Almost 1.2 million children under five years old suffer from diarrhoea every year because of non-potable water and lack of basic sanitation. Potable water supply and basic sanitation facilities are the prerequisites as they would help to reduce the child and mother mortality rates and combat other chronic diseases.

Housing and urban development also disclosed an upward trend for both allocation and actual outlays of Rs. 4 thousand crores to Rs. 22 thousand crores for an allocated amount at an average growth rate of 14.22 per cent. The actual amount spent on the same for the period was Rs. 3 thousand crores in 1991–1992 and Rs. 19 thousand crores in 2015–2016 at average growth rate of 15.85 per cent. Housing is one of the basic requirements of humans. Other facilities in the micro-environment of housing are also required like the type of dwelling unit, drinking water, sanitation, hygiene, etc. to raise the overall quality of life. In India, about 65.8 per cent of households in rural areas and 93.6 per cent of households in urban areas resided in their own houses with pucca structures (Government of India, 2014).

Table 17.   Yearly Allocations and Actual Expenditure Incurred on Components of Social Sector in India Since Economic Reforms.

Years	Social Services											
	Education, Art & Culture		Medical & Public Health		Family Welfare		Water Supply & Sanitation		Housing & Urban Development		Welfare of SC, ST, and C	
	Outlays	Actual Exp	Outlays	Actual Exp	Outlays	Actual Exp	Outlays	Actual Exp	Outlays	Actual Exp	Outlays	Ac E
1991–1992	6,489.24 (4.0)	6,312.29 (4.0)	2,651.22 (1.6)	2,168.24 (1.4)	1,675.04 (1.0)	2,288.43 (1.6)	5,623.04 (3.5)	5,423.05 (3.5)	3,909.85 (2.4)	3,924.25 (2.1)	1,991.44 (1.2)	1,92 (1.3)
1992–1993	6,153.33 (3.7)	668.42 (4.0)	2,623.65 (1.6)	2,495.47 (1.7)	2,140.01 (1.3)	2,272.29 (1.4)	4,511.25 (2.7)	5,696.00 (3.1)	3,788.97 (2.3)	4,264.15 (2.0)	1,907.53 (1.1)	2,02 (1.3)
1993–1994	7,445.06 (4.0)	7,147.58 (4.0)	3,031.75 (1.6)	2,630.29 (1.5)	2,373.55 (1.3)	2,453.20 (1.5)	5,503.93 (2.9)	6,082.73 (3.1)	4,286.42 (2.3)	4,313.03 (2.4)	2,240.50 (1.2)	2,28 (1.4)
1994–1995	8,179.54 (4.3)	7,920.66 (4.0)	3,095.06 (1.6)	2,866.41 (1.7)	2,433.05 (1.3)	2,866.71 (1.7)	6,105.61 (3.2)	6,546.13 (3.3)	4,575.26 (2.4)	4,540.26 (2.1)	2,345.73 (1.2)	3,17 (1.9)
1995–1996	9,046.11 (4.5)	9,331.31 (5.0)	3,382.54 (1.7)	4,002.61 (1.8)	2,460.79 (1.2)	2,713.64 (1.6)	6,729.94 (3.4)	6,874.20 (3.5)	5,648.54 (2.8)	5,401.68 (2.7)	3,148.09 (1.6)	3,67 (2.2)
1996–1997	12,236.06 (5.8)	9,908.93 (5.6)	4,174.93 (2.0)	4,440.88 (1.9)	2,214.73 (1.1)	3,072.26 (1.5)	7,270.57 (3.4)	7,734.38 (3.8)	8,284.47 (3.9)	6,132.83 (3.3)	3,499.01 (1.7)	4,42 (2.0)
1997–1998	11,958.52 (5.7)	10,792.99 (6.1)	4,395.86 (2.1)	4,960.39 (2.1)	2,478.24 (1.2)	3,468.49 (1.4)	8,068.96 (3.8)	8,557.99 (4.1)	9,674.99 (4.6)	6,847.35 (3.9)	3,586.92 (1.7)	5,22 (1.8)
1998–1999	12,796.63 (5.5)	12,139.85 (6.4)	4,736.92 (2.0)	5,784.24 (3.6)	3,120.61 (1.3)	3,936.82 (1.5)	8,728.76 (3.7)	9,305.74 (5.2)	9,409.95 (4.0)	7,476.47 (3.9)	4,043.48 (1.7)	4,81 (2.5)
1999–2000	13,685.09 (5.9)	13,147.31 (6.2)	5,265.44 (2.3)	6,335.19 (2.2)	3,547.16 (1.5)	4,606.83 (1.8)	9,129.81 (3.9)	10,637.46 (4.4)	11,119.17 (4.8)	8,001.21 (3.9)	3,894.54 (1.7)	5,03 (2.1)
2000–2001	14,845.97 (6.2)	13,233.53 (6.3)	5,932.10 (2.5)	6,675.62 (2,1)	4,136.92 (1.7)	4,839.92 (1.7)	9,536.89 (4.0)	10,675.89 (4.0)	13,173.75 (5.5)	8,883.01 (3.6)	3,921.47 (1.6)	5,55 (1.5)
2001–2002	15,592.78 (6.0)	13,456.03 (6.2)	6,365.79 (2.4)	7,018.94 (2.4)	4,394.55 (1.7)	5,114.31 (1.9)	9,454.06 (3.6)	11,993.11 (3.5)	13,707.08 (5.3)	11,993.11 (6.4)	3,754.72 (1.4)	6,09 (1.4)
2002–2003	15,109.67 (5.7)	13,650.10 (6.0)	5,629.45 (2.1)	7,215.94 (2.1)	4,864.49 (1.8)	5,432.78 (1.8)	9,998.00 (3.7)	12,250.31 (3.8)	15,478.14 (5.8)	12,250.38 (6.8)	4,814.82 (1.8)	6,55 (1.8)
2003–2004	16,103.03 (5.9)	15,014.86 (6.3)	6,448.56 (2.4)	7,916.06 (2.1)	4,692.38 (1.7)	5,473.47 (1.9)	10,523.10 (3.9)	12,794.38 (4.0)	16,353.79 (6.0)	13,254.54 (6.8)	5,220.90 (1.9)	6,97 (1.9)
2004–2005	18,503.54 (6.4)	17,543.05 (7.5)	6,048.02 (2.1)	8,282.60 (2.3)	4,950.00 (1.7)	5,770.00 (1.8)	10,838.66 (3.8)	13,157.80 (3.7)	17,465.60 (6.1)	14,123.15 (7.4)	5,884.13 (2.0)	7,36 (2.1)
2005–2006	26,233.71 (7.6)	25,366.56 (10.7)	8,740.92 (2.5)	7,921.84 (3.3)	5,547.53 (1.6)	6,020.82 (2.5)	11,847.27 (3.4)	12,098.25 (5.1)	22,868.01 (6.6)	25,538.57 (7.7)	7,294.74 (2.1)	6,68 (2.8)
2006–2007	31,421.50 (7.9)	29,785.03 (10.7)	10,423.99 (2.6)	9,314.58 (3.3)	6,636.16 (1.7)	7,015.27 (2.5)	13,169.09 (3.3)	13,940.55 (5.0)	26,916.26 (6.8)	30,396.81 (7.9)	8,069.14 (2.0)	7,57 (2.7)
2007–2008	31,867.82 (6.7)	33,699.28 (11.0)	10,934.06 (2.3)	10,548.40 (3,4)	5,461.12 (1.1)	7,896.23 (2.6)	14,224.94 (3.0)	15,572.50 (5.1)	32,158.24 (6.8)	34,700.79 (8.1)	8,376.4 2 (1.8)	8,37 (2.7)
2008–2009	39,140.17 (7.3)	38,174.07 (7.7)	12,780.95 (2.4)	11,839.60 (2.4)	6,997.78 (1.3)	8,461.22 (1.7)	15,873.97 (3.0)	17,133.30 (3.5)	40,842.38 (7.6)	41,431.45 (8.3)	10,220.37 (1.9)	10,0 (2.0)
2009–2010	37,091.81 (6.3)	42,436.79 (8.0)	12,516.82 (2.1)	13,227.59 (2.5)	6,444.61 (1.1)	9,089.41 (1.7)	16,346.30 (2.8)	17,463.84 (3.3)	42,485.77 (7.2)	40,725.50 (7.7)	10,255.40 (1.7)	10,8 (2.0)

						Economic Services				Total	
Labour & Employment		Social Security & Welfare		Other Social Services		Rural Development		Food Storage & Warehousing			
Outlays	Actual Exp	Outlays	Actual Exp	Outlays	Actual Exp	Outlays	Actual Exp	Outlays	Actual Exp	Outlays	Actual Exp
548.16 (0.3)	393.48 (0.2)	1,706.60 (1.1)	1,635.53 (1.0)	1,321.06 (1.4)	1,461.24 (0.8)	9,934.66 (6.14)	10,262.25 (6.40)	246.29 (0.15)	252.79 (0.10)	36,096.61 (22.94)	36,046.81 (22.40)
342.00 (0.2)	383.19 (0.2)	1,752.90 (1.1)	1,620.16 (1.0)	1,320.96 (0.8)	1,554.98 (1.2)	10,298.90 (6.20)	10,466.19 (6.99)	283.81 (0.10)	280.84 (0.11)	35,123.31 (21.9)	37,688.84 (22.94)
646.65 (0.3)	458.29 (0.2)	1,780.40 (1.0)	1,663.03 (1.0)	1,530.02 (0.8)	1,656.68 (0.8)	11,564.25 (6.18)	13,144.88 (7.99)	265.93 (0.08)	306.07 (0.09)	40,668.45 (21.68)	42,144.92 (23.99)
556.56 (0.3)	518.92 (0.2)	1,842.31 (1.0)	1,918.33 (1.1)	1,575.15 (0.8)	1,955.11 (1.7)	14,678.86 (7.69)	14,831.56 (8.88)	282.03 (0.07)	335.67 (0.06)	45,669.15 (23.84)	47,474.77 (26.68)
679.06 (0.3)	629.46 (0.3)	2,012.47 (1.0)	2,197.33 (1.3)	1,763.66 (0.9)	2,024.44 (1.0)	15,600.21 (7.79)	15,513.68 (9.28)	344.22 (0.07)	423.16 (0.05)	50,815.63 (25.28)	52,782.35 (28.74)
724.37 (0.3)	709.75 (0.2)	3,632.82 (1.7)	2,742.35 (0.9)	1,955.64 (0.9)	2,348.42 (1.0)	15,932.07 (7.56)	18,602.18 (8.45)	439.32 (0.08)	462.21 (0.07)	60,363.98 (28.50)	60,575.03 (28.80)
647.20 (0.3)	865.68 (0.2)	3,481.20 (1.6)	3,183.85 (0.6)	1,790.30 (0.8)	2,600.41 (0.9)	15,113.68 (7.16)	23,730.54 (7.81)	492.75 (0.08)	598.36 (0.08)	61,688.63 (29.05)	70,834.96 (29.02)
562.13 (0.2)	1,306.66 (0.7)	3,754.11 (1.6)	3,476.78 (1.6)	1,870.10 (0.8)	2,874.25 (0.8)	14,181.33 (6.09)	26,534.20 (7.25)	595.69 (0.06)	713.34 (0.02)	63,799.7 (27. 18)	78,622.31 (33.48)
480.46 (0.2)	1,637.73 (0.2)	3,860.83 (1.7)	4,153.04 (1.8)	1,967.93 (0.8)	3,280.99 (1.2)	14,610.44 (6.26)	282,003.39 (7.02)	739.44 (0.07)	819.84 (0.07)	68,300.31 (29.00)	85,855.73 (31.02)
472.19 (0.2)	1,744.99 (0.2)	4,170.05 (1.7)	4,820.65 (1.8)	2,326.07 (1.0)	3,561.87 (1.1)	15,508.18 (6.49)	29,679.14 (6.30)	887.35 (0.09)	995.74 (0.09)	74,910.96 (31.06)	90,697.71 (27.65)
484.21 (0.2)	1,951.38 (0.2)	4,854.88 (1.9)	5,136.13 (2.1)	3,105.31 (2.3)	3,931.53 (1.3)	15,305.96 (5.87)	32,305.74 (7.64)	954.77 (0.06)	1,097.37 (0.10)	77,974.10 (30.69)	98,688.76 (32.69)
596.30 (0.2)	2,245.87 (0.2)	3,853.39 (1.4)	5,576.25 (1.6)	3,448.45 (2.8)	4,855.26 (3.1)	16,976.95 (6.36)	34,005.67 (9.40)	1,000.43 (0.08)	1,134.75 (0.10)	81,770.09 (31.86)	104,140.9 (36.60)
931.78 (0.3)	1,550.74 (0.2)	4,480.48 (1.7)	6,041.62 (1.7)	4,245.46 (3.0)	5,270.77 (3.1)	16,798.54 (6.20)	373,222.42 (9.22)	1,164.09 (0.07)	1,555.79 (0.04)	86,962.12 (33.24)	113,167.4 (37.16)
617.84 (0.2)	1,722.16 (0.2)	4,465.97 (1.6)	6,246.75 (1.6)	4,354.67 (3.0)	5,526.56 (3.5)	17,634.16 (6.13)	18,584.55 (7.05)	1,225.93 (0.04)	1,621.95 (0.05)	91,988.52 (33.10)	120,840.2 (37.34)
852.62 (0.2)	875.60 (0.4)	6,468.17 (1.9)	6,725.40 (1.9)	4,677.70 (3.5)	5,079.20 (3.8)	22,961.66 (6.62)	24,997.93 (10.54)	1,372.03 (0.06)	1,317.88 (0.09)	118,864.37 (36.13)	122,628.54 (46.46)
1,106.93 (0.3)	1,102.73 (0.4)	7,871.67 (2.0)	8.766.32 (2.0)	4,383.06 (3.5)	5,245.08 (3.1)	27,692.98 (6.96)	30,227.01 (10.82)	1,399.15 (0.08)	1,388.23 (0.10)	139,089.92 (37.05)	144,660.95 (47.22)
1,738.64 (0.4)	1,304.02 (0.4)	9,312.75 (2.0)	10,574.70 (3.4)	4,385.35 (2.9)	5,448.31 (2.7)	26,732.44 (5.63)	34,859.7 (11.35)	1,446.40 (0.05)	1,450.57 (0.11)	146,638.17 (32.60)	164,324.59 (48.57)
1,735.63 (0.3)	1,687.70 (0.3)	11,143.93 (2.1)	12,627.43 (2.6)	4,674.90 (3.1)	5,644.93 (1.8)	29,016.99 (5.41)	40,297.45 (8.18)	1,444.95 (0.06)	1,409.48 (0.08)	173,872.03 (34.44)	188,789.71 (38.63)
1,640.71 (0.3)	1,509.14 (0.3)	11,393.74 (1.9)	15,258.23 (2.9)	5,004.06 (3.4)	5,649.56 (1.7)	28,395.80 (4.83)	43,334.69 (8.17)	14,100.05 (0.10)	1,413.63 (0.08)	172,985.07 (31.87)	200,926.27 (38.37)

(Continued)

Table 17.   (*Continued*)

Years	Social Services											
	Education, Art & Culture		Medical & Public Health		Family Welfare		Water Supply & Sanitation		Housing & Urban Development		Welfare of SC, ST, and O▮	
	Outlays	Actual Exp	Outlays	Actual Exp	Outlays	Actual Exp	Outlays	Actual Exp	Outlays	Actual Exp	Outlays	Actu Ex
2010–2011	46,398.50 (7.4)	55,533.53 (9.9)	14,264.15 (2.3)	14,991.20 (2.7)	6,567.29 (1.0)	9,236.01 (1.6)	16,552.62 (2.6)	17,000.32 (3.0)	42,223.49 (6.7)	42,784.53 (7.6)	10,825.04 (1.7)	14,44▮ (2.6)
2011–2012	58,761.22 (8.7)	61,980.75 (10.6)	18,763.53 (2.6)	15,816.11 (2.7)	9,273.73 (1.4)	9,551.65 (1.6)	18,406.10 (2.7)	17,324.41 (2.6)	47,279.53 (7.0)	47,397.88 (7.1)	15,345.30 (2.3)	16,79▮ (2.9)
2012–2013	66,170.55 (9.0)	67,292.89 (11.2)	20,736.29 (2.8)	16,005.31 (3.3)	9,857.04 (1.3)	9,168.82 (1.9)	19,291.09 (2.6)	16,046.60 (2.5)	56,424.43 (7.7)	44,311.24 (7.4)	18,140.41 (2.5)	19,23▮ (3.3)
2013–2014	67,697.83 (9.4)	72,365.98 (11.8)	21,953.91 (3.1)	18,430.24 (3.5)	10,497.51 (1.2)	99,722.9.75 (1.7)	19,785.0 (2.6)	16,390.12 (2.8)	57,276 .49 (8.0)	51,257.39 (7.7)	19,783.20 (2.8)	20,56▮ (3.5)
2014–2015	72,161.03 (10.2)	78,073.24 (12.1)	23,644.46 (3.5)	20,263.85 (3.7)	11,023.20 (1.8)	9,912.9 (1.9)	21,550.21 (2.8)	17,846.60 (3.0)	74,714. 51 (8.6)	56,511.74 (8.0)	23,838.00 (3.0)	21,32▮ (3.7)
2015–2016	75,572.36 (11.5)	87,557.3 (12.7)	26,752.0 (3.9)	22,681.14 (4.0)	11,606.01 (1.8)	11,234.1 (2.0)	22,598.53 (2.9)	19,018.98 (3.1)	83,849.17 (9.3)	62,677.69 (8.2)	26,635.10 (3.2)	24,41▮ (3.9)
CGR	11.35	12.63	9.99	10.34	7.95	8.32	6.55	6.81	14.22	15.49	10.35	10.33
CV	74.83	82.24	66.12	65.59	49.46	53.25	40.49	43.56	79.31	79.87	69.50	75.73

Source: 1. Government of India. (various issued-a), *Annual Reports*. New Delhi: Planning Commission.

2. Government of India. (various issued-b), *Economic Survey*. New Delhi: Ministry of Finance.

3. Government of India. (various issued-c), *Expenditure Budget (Vol. 1)*. New Delhi: Ministry of Finance.

Notes: 1. Other social services include information and publicity, broadcasting, nutrition, and secretariat social services.

2. Figures in parentheses indicate the percentage of total expenditure.

The welfare of underprivileged classes also highlights the rising trend for the same period both for allotted and actual outlays with the rise of Rs. 80 thousand crores and Rs. 63 thousand crores, respectively, at an average growth rate of 10.67 per cent each. The social problems in marginalised classes still prevailed in India even though it was foretold in the year 1950 that untouchability had been removed in India but it still prevailed. Marginalised sections could be protected from atrocities and the promotion of these classes could be enhanced by the systematic formulation of policies and programmes (Sangeeth, 2016).

Labour and employment have increased but at a marginal pace. Both the allocated and expended amount for the development of this component has shown a growing trend from 1991–1992 to 2015–2016. The allocation and actual outlay registered an increase of Rs. 22 thousand crores and 24 thousand crores approximately with an average growth rate of 8.73 and 10.48 per cent, respectively, for the period 1990–1991 to 2015–2016. Numerous schemes were launched by the Government of India to create productive employment opportunities. The government initiated many activities organising entrepreneurship development, self-help

						Economic Services				Total	
Labour & Employment		Social Security & Welfare		Other Social Services		Rural Development		Food Storage & Warehousing			
Outlays	Actual Exp	Outlays	Actual Exp	Outlays	Actual Exp	Outlays	Actual Exp	Outlays	Actual Exp	Outlays	Actual Exp
2,737.08	1,863.89	15,060.20	17,298.78	5,892.58	6,058.19	29,938.41	45,474.51	1,485.24	1,598.23	191,944.59	226,285.34
(0.4)	(0.3)	(2.4)	(3.1)	(3.5)	(2.0)	(4.74)	(8.11)	(0.10)	(0.11)	(32.82)	(41.14)
2,641.61	2,231.49	19,360.55	19,753.00	5,280.90	6,233.47	37,265.21	48,251.23	1,542.34	1,711.34	243,920.01	242,144.56
(0.4)	(0.4)	(2.9)	(3.4)	(4.0)	(2.2)	(5.00)	(7.20)	(0.11)	(0.12)	(36.38)	(40.84)
3,000.32	2,787.50	22,377.56	21,094.41	4,561.39	6,928.8.81	32,206.31	44,741.35	1,631.87	1,732.13	265,397.24	249,372.87
(0.6)	(0.4)	(3.1)	(3.3)	(4.0)	(2.3)	(5.76)	(7.4)	(0.17)	(0.11)	(37.58)	(40.62)
4,158.52	3,147.53	22,394.59	22,921.81	5,416.05	7,172.13	36,306.74	52,133.34	1,711.42	1,813.19	266,981.25	275,919.07
(0.5)	(0.4)	(3.0)	(3.2)	(4.2)	(2.5)	(5.58)	(7.90)	(0.21)	(0.14)	(38.97)	(45.14)
6,717.71	3,708.75	23,411.37	24,370.44	6,018.51	7,424.60	39,125.10	57,884.8	1,810.95	1,897.08	300,015.27	299,223.71
(0.6)	(0.5)	(3.0)	(3.3)	(4.4)	(2.9)	(6.80)	(8.10)	(0.23)	(0.17)	(40.21)	(47.37)
8,076.41	4,587.34	24,439.66	26,793.14	6,243.99	7,744.45	43,219.23	63,316.9	2,016.61	2,074.98	331,009.11	332,097.80
(0.8)	(0. 6)	(3.2)	(3.5)	(4.5)	(3.3)	(7.00)	(8.30)	(0.25)	(0.20)	(42.96)	(49.8)
8.73	10.48	12.45	14.91	17.67	13.50	6.36	7.76	7.90	9.45	10.25	10.77
83.42	80.93	86.03	93.64	96.56	75.07	47.65	53.31	76.22	75.32	67.02	67.46

groups, and other training programmes to cultivate more employment opportunities. Creating employment opportunities and engagement of the deprived and marginal segments would lead to the elimination of poverty and inequalities. Regardless of such efforts, India has failed to achieve the desired results to reduce poverty by generating more employment opportunities.

The allocation and investment made for social security and welfare have also increased from Rs. 17 hundred crores and Rs. 14 hundred crores to Rs. 6.2 thousand crores and Rs. 7.7 thousand crores, respectively, at an average growth rate of 12.25 per cent and 14.91 per cent. Rao (2002) stated that the benefits related to social security must improve the capabilities of the population, so that the people should have basic facilities to shun unnecessary morbidity and mortality. Thus, social security provides benefits related to people either via public or collective arrangements to protect them against poor living conditions. Social security measures include provident funds/gratuity, old age, survivor, widow and disability pension, medical care of all sorts, and protection from all kinds of risks (Chadha & Chadda, 2018).

Rural development has also highlighted the rising trend of allocations and expenditure from 1991–1992 to 2015–2016. The amount which is allocated and used for the development of the rural sector is Rs 9 thousand crores approximately of each which has spiralled up to Rs. 43 thousand crores and Rs. 63 thousand crores, respectively. The percentage of rural development allocation and expenditure on total expenditure out of total central government expenditure is indicating that there is an increasing trend but at a marginal pace from 6.14 per cent in the year 1991–1992 to 7.00 per cent in the year 2015–2016 for allocation while giving the increasing trend for the outlays from 6.40 per cent in the year 1991–1992 to 11.35 per cent in the year 2007–2008 and which further declined to 8.30 per cent in the year 2015–2016 during 25 years since economic reforms.

Since 1950, the government introduced several new schemes and programmes for rural development yet, they did not attain the expected outcomes. Many rural development projects and programmes failed because of sluggish implementation of the planning. The main reasons were lack of micro-level planning, absence of appropriate rural development policy, lack of coordination by the agencies, and fewer people's participation did not yield the desired results. Proper planning along with coordinated efforts from people and agencies is essential for rural development (Patel, 2010).

Food storage and warehousing are revealing the increasing trend for both allocations as well as outlays for the same period. The amount which is assigned for this component is Rs. 2 thousand crores in the year 2015–2016 which has risen from Rs. 1 hundred crores in the year 1991–1992 at an average growth rate of 7.90 per cent. The amount utilised for the same component is Rs. 1 hundred crores in the year 1991–1992 and Rs. 2 thousand crores in the year 2015–2016 at an average growth of 9.45 per cent. The government initiated a PDS wherein people belonging to lower groups get food at reasonable rates through a FPS. It indicated the increasing trend for food storage and warehousing. However, the low-income groups were not benefitted properly. There must be a properly structured identification format that must be followed to find out the meaningfully targeted poor and destitute people (Bhat et al., 2005).

In the table, it has also been observed that allocations are more than actual outlays as the actual expenditure might sometimes fall short of expected allocations. The coefficient of variation is found to be highest in social security and welfare, education, labour, and employment, housing, and urban development followed by the welfare of underprivileged classes, water supply and sanitation, health, and family welfare both in plan allocations and outlays. Sarma (2005) stated that there had been seen shortages in funds distributed by the government as compared to the allocations in the case of urban employment and poverty alleviation, rural development, family welfare, and social equity. As actual utilisation of funds by these concerned departments in 2004–2005 was 21 per cent, 7 per cent, 4 per cent, and 9 per cent, respectively, lower than the allocation for that year. Hence, mere allocation of funds in the budget is not sufficient but the concerned departments must be fully equipped and accountable to use the funds effectively.

Maheshwari (2012) studied the social sector expenditure in India from the year of economic reforms in 1991 till the year 2010 and depicted that expenditure on the social sector was stagnant over the post-reform period. It was noted that the expenditure should be stimulated to exacerbate human development. It is necessary to have an effective monitoring system to check the outcomes implemented by social sector development programmes to achieve the desired targets set in the plans and streamline expenditures.

Table 18 reveals the allocation pattern used for the development of the social sector by all states and union territories (UTs) of India from 1991–1992 to 2013–2014. States like Maharashtra, Gujarat, Tamil Nadu, Karnataka, and Andhra Pradesh have the highest allocation of Rs. 15,253 crores, Rs. 12,987 crores, Rs. 11,586 crores, Rs. 11,570 crores, and Rs. 11,245 crores, respectively, in the year 2012–2013 which was Rs. 797 crore, Rs. 706 crores, Rs. 605 crores, Rs. 848 crores and Rs. 532 crores in the year 1991–1992 which highlight the increasing trend. States like Arunachal Pradesh, Nagaland, Manipur, Tripura, and Sikkim indicate the lower distribution of allotted amounts of Rs. 368 crores, Rs. 453 crores, Rs. 673 crores, Rs. 721 crores, and Rs. 738 crores, respectively, in the year 2013–2014 and Rs. 78 crores, Rs. 84 crores, Rs. 91 crores, Rs. 115 crores and Rs. 57 crores in the year 1991–1992, respectively, comparative to other states. Among the Union Territories, Delhi shows a significant upward trend from Rs. 754 crores in 1991–1992 to Rs. 6,704 crores in 2013–2014. The coefficient of variation is found to be highest in Andhra Pradesh, Uttar Pradesh, and Haryana, followed by Gujarat, Goa, and Rajasthan while Mizoram, Nagaland, Himachal Pradesh, and Arunachal Pradesh have resulted in contradicting manner.

Chhattisgarh's social allocation ratio is 51.1 per cent in 2013–2014 which has crossed 40 per cent, the level of benchmark which is recommended by UNDP. Jharkhand, Meghalaya, Rajasthan, and West Bengal also have social allocation ratios of more than 40 per cent which are 47.3 per cent, 41.0 per cent, 42.8 per cent, 41.1 per cent, 42.9 per cent, and 42.6 per cent, respectively, in the year 2013–2014. Tripura, Punjab, Manipur, Jammu and Kashmir, and Nagaland have a social allocation ratio of 20 per cent, 29.1 per cent 31.7 per cent, 32.5 per cent, and 33.4 per cent, respectively, in the same year. As observed from the table, Punjab, Goa, Himachal Pradesh, Gujarat, Tripura, Uttar Pradesh, and Nagaland have not maintained that level during the entire period. However, this table provides a clear view of allocations of the social sector of states and UTs, perhaps, it may not disclose the true picture. The reason is that if the small economy of the state with a large population spent more percentage of the state's domestic products on the social sector, it certainly would not mean that the state had disbursed more. Nonetheless, the per capita expenditure had risen in all Indian states yet in some states the main components of the social sector like education, housing, health, and potable water remained the same or less. Hence, it had been quite clear that although the trend of budgetary allocations for the social sector had increased still it did not give satisfactorily improving results for attainment in the terms of healthcare and education (Goswami & Bezbaruah, 2011).

Sudhakar and Mose (2008) emphasised the budgetary expenditure pattern of social services and economic services of 26 states of India from the period of

Table 18.   State-wise Allocations on Social Sector Since Economic Reforms (Rs. Crore).

States	1991–1992	1992–1993	1993–1994	1994–1995	1995–1996	1996–1997	1997–1998	1998–1999	1999–2000	2000–2001	2001–2002	2002–2003	2003–2004
Andhra Pradesh	532 (33)	613 (34)	697 (36)	1,073 (42)	1,193 (38)	1,470 (36)	1,849 (37)	1,884 (37)	2,103 (33)	2,187 (36)	2,741 (34)	2,921 (33)	3,662 (33)
Arunachal Pradesh	78 (32)	102 (35)	113 (34)	126 (33)	128 (33)	137 (35)	172 (35)	198 (34)	217 (35)	263 (29)	211 (32)	234 (32)	232 (28)
Assam	471 (28)	576 (30)	515 (31)	639 (36)	682 (33)	667 (34)	697 (34)	681 (35)	727 (36)	769 (35)	732 (36)	813 (36)	938 (35)
Bihar	1,252 (45)	1,398 (42)	1,473 (45)	1,577 (42)	1,658 (42)	1,731 (42)	1,853 (41)	2,431 (38)	2,849 (38)	3,027 (33)	3,381 (33)	3,073 (34)	3,143 (33)
Chhattisgarh	–	–	–	–	–	–	–	–	–	–	968 (50)	1,035 (47)	1,120 (45)
Goa	91 (37)	101 (39)	122 (38)	136 (38)	162 (37)	181 (30)	179 (28)	186 (30)	192 (30)	207 (26)	292 (25)	350 (26)	415 (29)
Gujarat	706 (31)	772 (31)	843 (33)	769 (32)	841 (34)	1,046 (36)	1,252 (33)	1,537 (33)	1,790 (32)	1,826 (32)	1,993 (31)	2,344 (33)	2,456 (33)
Haryana	488 (24)	550 (25)	595 (26)	676 (25)	681 (36)	755 (24)	793 (25)	704 (28)	798 (32)	817 (30)	929 (29)	1,074 (28)	1,172 (31)
Himachal Pradesh	223 (21)	251 (39)	322 (37)	398 (36)	373 (38)	444 (38)	495 (37)	521 (40)	581 (37)	631 (36)	681 (34)	694 (31)	742 (30)
Jammu and Kashmir	273 (32)	338 (26)	360 (34)	358 (32)	314 (35)	400 (35)	432 (34)	587 (29)	601 (26)	747 (27)	823 (29)	993 (29)	1,023 (29)
Jharkhand	–	–	–	–	–	–	–	–	–	–	1,727 (48)	1,904 (50)	1,320 (45)
Karnataka	848 (37)	900 (38)	985 (38)	1,025 (36)	1,658 (35)	1,710 (40)	2,050 (32)	2,361 (35)	3,441 (34)	4,534 (35)	4,842 (33)	5,299 (33)	6,557 (35)
Kerala	391 (39)	424 (42)	441 (39)	557 (43)	618 (40)	918 (40)	942 (40)	976 (39)	1,109 (40)	1,197 (36)	1,477 (35)	1,594 (37)	1,791 (37)
Madhya Pradesh	897 (35)	956 (37)	947 (39)	1,077 (40)	1,373 (40)	1,683 (41)	1,937 (42)	2,527 (40)	2,810 (39)	2,877 (40)	3,439 (37)	3,664 (38)	4,020 (36)
Maharashtra	797 (37)	800 (38)	927 (38)	1,362 (33)	1,724 (34)	1,855 (35)	3,202 (35)	2,585 (36)	3,755 (37)	3,189 (37)	3,380 (36)	4,215 (35)	4,548 (32)
Manipur	91 (32)	124 (30)	147 (31)	161 (34)	165 (37)	180 (37)	189 (37)	211 (36)	251 (35)	255 (33)	351 (28)	385 (27)	396 (28)
Meghalaya	119 (36)	130 (35)	160 (35)	189 (36)	198 (36)	238 (39)	216 (39)	288 (39)	314 (40)	338 (41)	390 (41)	502 (36)	578 (37)
Mizoram	117 (40)	126 (40)	153 (41)	173 (40)	200 (41)	212 (42)	239 (38)	292 (42)	343 (43)	320 (40)	379 (41)	406 (41)	442 (36)
Nagaland	84 (27)	110 (27)	150 (30)	154 (32)	181 (33)	182 (33)	179 (32)	224 (27)	269 (33)	299 (31)	364 (27)	353 (29)	370 (28)
Orissa	406 (37)	559 (38)	668 (37)	742 (38)	843 (40)	938 (39)	1,113 (39)	1,310 (39)	1,492 (46)	1,747 (44)	1,864 (39)	2,188 (38)	2,467 (34)
Punjab	488 (21)	681 (24)	469 (24)	595 (21)	629 (25)	690 (19)	657 (23)	699 (26)	658 (24)	735 (28)	765 (23)	801 (17)	831 (18)

2004–2005	2005–2006	2006–2007	2007–2008	2008–2009	2009–2010	2010–2011	2011–2012	2012–2013	2013–2014	2014–2015	2015–2016	CV
3,919 (30)	4,265 (30)	5,507 (34)	6,284 (34)	6,759 (33)	8,927 (34)	8,831 (34)	1,000 (36)	1,087 (40)	1,124 (38)	1,188 (38)	1,265 (39)	87.05
272 (32)	225 (31)	249 (32)	321 (32)	320 (31)	350 (33)	342 (29)	343 (33)	353 (33)	368 (34)	389 (34)	432 (35)	38.78
1,097 (35)	1,238 (34)	1,415 (35)	1,608 (37)	1,792 (38)	1,951 (38)	2,040 (39)	2,177 (39)	2,035 (38)	2,125 (39)	2,237 (38)	2,595 (39)	52.04
3,434 (34)	3,524 (35)	3,796 (37)	4,014 (35)	4,375 (40)	5,354 (35)	6,338 (38)	6,408 (39)	6,783 (38)	6,954 (38)	7,083 (38)	7,954 (38)	50.90
1,544 (38)	1,935 (39)	2,295 (43)	2,707 (46)	2,947 (47)	3,587 (50)	4,255 (53)	5,022 (51)	5,895 (49)	6,012 (50)	6,495 (49)	6,628 (51)	58.65
470 (32)	518 (32)	543 (32)	626 (31)	686 (33)	798 (32)	880 (34)	1,010 (36)	1,124 (38)	1,294 (37)	1,324 (38)	1,393 (37)	77.58
2,844 (33)	3,273 (33)	3,666 (33)	4,068 (34)	4,953 (35)	6,609 (36)	7,571 (36)	9,681 (37)	10,029 (37)	12,987 (38)	13,291 (37)	13,875 (38)	78.45
1,287 (24)	1,675 (28)	1,810 (28)	2,018 (21)	2,497 (22)	3,742 (26)	3,605 (30)	4,343 (30)	5,267 (35)	5,126 (38)	5,267 (35)	5,826 (38)	83.74
753 (29)	701 (32)	763 (33)	812 (36)	873 (36)	948 (36)	928 (38)	984 (35)	1,034 (36)	921 (37)	1,134 (36)	983 (37)	37.39
1,196 (29)	1,226 (30)	1,044 (32)	1,321 (31)	1,518 (31)	1,493 (30)	1,604 (30)	1,830 (31)	1,948 (31)	2,010 (33)	1,848 (31)	2,103 (33)	47.15
2,127 (44)	2,156 (46)	2,392 (48)	2,984 (48)	3,270 (48)	3,428 (47)	3,545 (49)	3,967 (46)	4,029 (47)	4,322 (47)	4,293 (47)	4,623 (47)	33.42
7,063 (35)	8,449 (37)	8,895 (38)	9,526 (40)	9,886 (38)	8,851 (40)	8,803 (40)	9,541 (38)	10,642 (38)	11,570 (39)	14,642 (38)	15,170 (39)	66.11
2,061 (36)	2,387 (36)	2,691 (26)	3,215 (31)	4,239 (33)	4,660 (33)	5,432 (34)	5,242 (33)	4,932 (36)	6,338 (38)	5,932 (36)	6,138 (38)	69.50
4,508 (36)	4,854 (37)	5,416 (38)	5,267 (38)	6,622 (38)	7,887 (40)	7,417 (41)	7,153 (41)	8,007 (39)	8,158 (40)	8,107 (39)	8,581 (40)	62.26
3,540 (30)	5,566 (33)	5,886 (37)	9,350 (34)	11,712 (36)	11,896 (41)	12,560 (40)	13,489 (41)	14,809 (40)	15,253 (40)	15,509 (40)	15,853 (40)	62.90
410 (31)	441 (34)	507 (31)	584 (32)	516 (32)	591 (32)	605 (31)	649 (30)	623 (30)	673 (32)	698 (30)	721 (32)	52.40
565 (37)	570 (37)	640 (38)	741 (37)	767 (36)	873 (38)	839 (37)	983 (40)	991 (40)	1,023 (41)	991 (40)	1,023 (41)	59.56
462 (36)	509 (36)	512 (35)	547 (37)	522 (41)	551 (41)	536 (39)	560 (40)	598 (40)	640 (40)	600 (40)	640 (40)	33.30
315 (28)	379 (30)	385 (30)	344 (30)	367 (28)	344 (27)	329 (29)	409 (26)	414 (29)	453 (33)	446 (29)	469 (33)	36.99
2,636 (34)	3,246 (35)	3,889 (31)	3,065 (36)	3,122 (41)	3,210 (41)	4,360 (42)	4,598 (43)	5,386 (40)	6,127 (41)	5,420 (40)	6,127 (41)	63.82
942 (18)	1,054 (19)	1,724 (19)	1,887 (19)	1,730 (23)	1,990 (23)	2,525 (23)	3,747 (28)	3,520 (29)	4,706 (29)	3,555 (29)	4,750 (29)	55.38

(Continued)

Table 18.   (*Continued*)

States	1991–1992	1992–1993	1993–1994	1994–1995	1995–1996	1996–1997	1997–1998	1998–1999	1999–2000	2000–2001	2001–2002	2002–2003	2003–2004
Rajasthan	123	215	398	544	625	768	971	1,439	1,412	1,405	1,866	2,036	2,393
	(34)	(37)	(38)	(38)	(35)	(36)	(38)	(40)	(39)	(41)	(40)	(38)	(38)
Sikkim	57	56	61	73	81	90	101	151	166	188	254	245	259
	(32)	(33)	(34)	(27)	(26)	(25)	(25)	(27)	(27)	(26)	(26)	(23)	(24)
Tamil Nadu	605	798	931	972	1,444	1,559	1,735	1,921	2,339	2,985	3,433	3,929	4,251
	(35)	(40)	(40)	(39)	(39)	(40)	(38)	(41)	(39)	(40)	(37)	(37)	(35)
Tripura	115	133	170	216	227	264	286	261	324	383	429	517	594
	(12)	(14)	(11)	(11)	(11)	(12)	(14)	(13)	(13)	(13)	(13)	(16)	(12)
Uttar Pradesh	2,041	1,934	1,995	2,189	2,549	4,505	3,218	2,848	2,556	3,041	2,478	2,436	2,523
	(33)	(35)	(33)	(29)	(31)	(33)	(34)	(34)	(33)	(33)	(33)	(32)	(29)
Uttarakhand	–	–	–	–	–	–	–	–	–	–	355	720	1,190
											(33)	(34)	(34)
West Bengal	856	1,115	1,202	1,500	1,652	1,852	2,092	2,824	2,716	2,747	3,323	3,827	4,097
	(43)	(42)	(42)	(42)	(40)	(38)	(39)	(39)	(41)	(39)	(37)	(40)	(33)
A&N Islands	30.0	34.9	34.6	42.7	45.7	51.4	73.5	89.2	105.1	108.1	132.1	145.7	163.9
	(31)	(32)	(32)	(35)	(34)	(36)	(40)	(41)	(41)	(43)	(43)	(44)	(43)
Chandigarh	154.3	154.5	157.0	188.8	180.5	196.6	206.7	237.2	246.0	254.0	265.0	273.0	287.0
	(35)	(33)	(32)	(33)	(34)	(34)	(40)	(40)	(39)	(40)	(42)	(40)	(41)
D&N Haveli	5.8	5.6	5.7	6.4	7.4	7.7	8.7	10.4	12.2	14.0	17.5	23.4	23.1
	(18)	(17)	(17)	(17)	(18)	(20)	(19)	(20)	(20)	(19)	(19)	(19)	(19)
Daman & Diu	20.4	23.2	25.2	24.9	31.0	40.3	43.5	51.1	56.1	69.0	74.3	87.4	91.2
	(17)	(17)	(16)	(16)	(17)	(17)	(17)	(17)	(17)	(17)	(16)	(16)	(17)
Delhi	754	847	1,031	1,282	1,434	1,968	1,480	1,603	1,937	2,446	2,792	2,601	2,561
	(41)	(43)	(45)	(44)	(46)	(47)	(47)	(46)	(45)	(43)	(40)	(38)	(40)
Lakshadweep	5.9	5.4	5.7	6.4	6.3	8.0	9.1	10.5	11.2	11.7	15.8	16.1	19.7
	(17)	(17)	(16)	(16)	(17)	(17)	(17)	(17)	(18)	(16)	(16)	(16)	(17)
Puducherry	74.1	57.8	64.7	70.2	61.2	86.6	111.3	138.2	163.4	178.7	193.7	240.5	307.4
	(15)	(16)	(15)	(16)	(16)	(16)	(16)	(16)	(17)	(18)	(18)	(18)	(19)

Source: 1. Government of India. (various issued-a), *Annual Reports*. New Delhi: Planning Commission.

2. Government of India. (various issued-b), *Economic Survey*. New Delhi: Ministry of Finance.

3. Government of India. (various issued-c), *Expenditure Budget (Vol. 1)*. New Delhi: Ministry of Finance.

Notes: 1. NA is not available.

2. Figures in parentheses indicate the percentage of total expenditure.

1986–1987 to 1995–1996. The expenditure proportion of the social sector had gone up from 39.24 per cent in 1991–1992 to 40.16 per cent in 1994–1995. Thus, the trend of different components of social sector development for government budgetary expenditure had risen significantly in the post-reform period.

It was apparent that social sector development was now attaining prominence among the different states of India in the last two decades. The size of the population along with the financial and fiscal conditions of the states decided the

2004–2005	2005–2006	2006–2007	2007–2008	2008–2009	2009–2010	2010–2011	2011–2012	2012–2013	2013–2014	2014–2015	2015–2016	CV
2,783	3,291	3,912	4,324	4,697	5,953	6,377	7,224	7,730	8,032	7,760	8,073	76.30
(36)	(41)	(40)	(39)	(43)	(44)	(43)	(42)	(43)	(43)	(43)	(43)	
314	348	406	479	501	547	589	611	663	738	672	767	71.83
(26)	(23)	(24)	(26)	(27)	(28)	(32)	(36)	(37)	(38)	(37)	(38)	
4,550	5,145	6,210	6,654	8,153	8,862	9,618	9,190	9,662	11,586	9,680	11,570	63.15
(39)	(39)	(34)	(36)	(39)	(39)	(40)	(38)	(39)	(39)	(39)	(39)	
539	573	635	673	676	696	689	674	663	721	680	750	37.01
(15)	(14)	(15)	(18)	(19)	(19)	(19)	(20)	(20)	(20)	(20)	(20)	
3,987	3,836	4,842	8,973	10,567	12,658	13,004	14,929	16,713	17,435	16,780	17,450	84.68
(29)	(33)	(33)	(34)	(38)	(39)	(37)	(38)	(39)	(39)	(39)	(39)	
1,347	1,674	1,708	1,894	2,027	2,327	2,781	3,226	3,726	3,679	3,770	3,690	51.61
(32)	(32)	(32)	(32)	(34)	(36)	(36)	(36)	(36)	(37)	(36)	(37)	
4,991	5,180	6,626	9,338	9,623	9,581	8,463	9,008	9,732	10,445	9,750	10,485	79.60
(37)	(38)	(38)	(35)	(37)	(41)	(42)	(43)	(42)	(43)	(42)	(43)	
194.6	204.3	242.7	274.0	282.8	297.2	317.0	365.0	473.6	538.3	490.4	548.7	63.97
(40)	(37)	(38)	(39)	(38)	(40)	(40)	(42)	(42)	(43)	(42)	(43)	
294.0	274.4	320.3	354.0	369.0	372.0	366.0	382.0	395.1	472.5	405.9	486.4	39.59
(41)	(41)	(40)	(38)	(37)	(36)	(39)	(41)	(41)	(42)	(41)	(42)	
43.2	64.4	72.2	77.3	80.3	92.3	98.4	109.2	125.8	146.8	152.5	1,476.8	93.24
(19)	(18)	(18)	(19)	(20)	(21)	(22)	(22)	(24)	(25)	(24)	(25)	
97.6	107.0	112.0	120.0	125.0	129.0	131.0	136.0	140.1	146.0	160.4	156.7	83.41
(17)	(18)	(17)	(18)	(18)	(18)	(19)	(19)	(20)	(20)	(20)	(20)	
2,204	2,723	2,361	2,195	2,609	2,407	3,844	4,429	5,452	6,704	5,556	6,756	58.84
(38)	(41)	(40)	(42)	(43)	(43)	(46)	(47)	(48)	(50)	(48)	(50)	
24.3	37.1	41.9	56.2	59.5	73.8	79.7	113.8	123.0	144.9	144.1	156.8	86.3
(16)	(17)	(16)	(17)	(17)	(17)	(18)	(19)	(19)	(19)	(19)	(19)	
472.1	419.0	467.5	582.2	596.9	597.2	674.4	820.3	1,037.6	1,145.0	1,047.2	1,170.5	84.0
(20)	(20)	(20)	(20)	(20)	(22)	(23)	(24)	(25)	(26)	(25)	(26)	

efficiency and efficacy of investment in the social sector. It had been observed that the population with a smaller size has a more developed attitude and good governance, which could achieve better results for promoting human development and attaining a better status in the social sector. This could be seen in states like Himachal Pradesh, Meghalaya, Sikkim, Puducherry, and Uttarakhand had achieved the desired results of social sector development. On the contrary, states like Bihar, Punjab, West Bengal, Kerala, Jharkhand, and Orissa had not attained the expected outcomes. The state/UT government must ensure the regularity of funds to improve the status of the social sector and with efficient fiscal and effective financial management in tandem with good governance that eventually leads to removing inequalities from India. Social sector is necessitated to remove the regional as well as caste disparities and satisfy the welfare needs of the masses (Nayak & Mishra, 2014). The macro-level planning needs a coordinated role that is played by the centre and state governments to provide better guidance for planning, regulation, commitment, and participation of the local community at the micro-planning level (Government of India, 1985).

Table 19 indicates the pattern of the social sector expenditure of all states and UTs of India from 1991–1992 to 2014–2015. The higher proportion of expenditure is shown in the states of Uttar Pradesh, Andhra Pradesh, and Maharashtra followed by Tamil Nadu and Karnataka of Rs. 16,609.13, Rs. 14,205 crores, Rs. 12,963 crores, Rs. 10,944.59 crores, and Rs. 10,325.9 crores, respectively, in the year 2012–2013 which was Rs. 2,180.87 crores, Rs. 801.29 crores, Rs. 1,980.17 crores, Rs. 1,528 crores and Rs. 984.50 crores in the year 1991–1992 which highlight the increasing trend. States like Sikkim, Manipur, Mizoram, Meghalaya, Nagaland, and Goa indicate a lower share of expended money of Rs. 68.52 crores, Rs. 104.51 crores, Rs.127.90, Rs. 136.53 crores, Rs. 127.90 crores and Rs. 150.04 crores, respectively, in the year 1991–1992 to Rs. 699.06 crores, Rs. 585.37 crores, Rs. 446.98 crores, Rs. 850.32 crores, Rs. 377.84 crores and Rs. 1,381.88 crores in the year 2012–2013, respectively, comparative to other states. Among the Union Territories, Delhi shows a significant upward trend from Rs. 1,027.95 crores in 1991–1992 to Rs. 5,706 crores in 2012–2013. Chandigarh and Puducherry also depict an upward trend of Rs. 239 crores and Rs. 682 crores, respectively. The coefficient of variation is found to be highest in Andhra Pradesh, Haryana, Uttar Pradesh West Bengal, Goa, and Gujarat which implies more allotment towards the improvement of the Social Sector while states like Mizoram, Nagaland, Himachal Pradesh, and Arunachal Pradesh indicate the contradictory outcome.

Chhattisgarh's social allocation ratio is 51.6 per cent in 2011–2012 which has crossed the 40 per cent level of the benchmark which is recommended by UNDP. Bihar, Haryana, Jharkhand, Maharashtra, Orissa, Rajasthan, and West Bengal also have social allocation ratios of more than 40 per cent which are 40.1 per cent, 40.9 per cent, 41.2 per cent, 41.1 per cent, 42.9 per cent, 42.6 percent, and 42.5 per cent, respectively. Punjab, Kerala, Madhya Pradesh, and Karnataka have a social allocation ratio of 27.1 per cent, 34.8 per cent, 33.6 per cent, and 37.8 per cent, respectively, in 2011–2012. As observed from the table, Andhra Pradesh, Kerala, Bihar, Goa, Madhya Pradesh, and Jharkhand have not maintained that level during the entire period. Madhya Pradesh has indicated some noticeable fluctuations. It spent 40.1 per cent of its total expenditure on the social sector in 1991–1992, then increased and reached a peak value of 43.1 per cent in 1998–1999, came down to 28.0 per cent in 2003–2004, and later registered an increase with a value of 33.6 per cent. Under special category states, only two states Tripura and Uttarakhand have crossed the recommended level of social allocation ratio, that is, 41.7 per cent and 45.5 per cent, respectively, in the year 2011–2012. Assam, Jammu and Kashmir, Mizoram, Nagaland, and Sikkim have 37.0 per cent, 29.3

per cent, 36.6 per cent, 24.9 per cent, and 36.8 per cent, respectively, in 2011–2012 of the total expenditure on the social sector. Himachal Pradesh with the lowest share, that is, 21.1 per cent in 1991–1992 registered remarkable improvement and spent 34.6 per cent in 2011–2012 when all states' average was 38.7 per cent. Delhi is spending 50 per cent on social sector expenditure out of its total expenditure.

Sudhakar and Mose (2005) pointed out that, the funds allotted for the development of different components of the social sector for the period of 10 years, that is, from 1986–1987 to 1995–1996 had registered an increasing trend. The proportion of total budgetary amount out of total budgetary on social sector development had risen since the economic reforms in the case of the central government. During this period, attention was given to rural development and the welfare of SC, ST, and OBC while social security schemes and food subsidies were completely ignored by the central government.

Tsujita (2005) examined the social sector expenditure in 15 Indian states from 1980–1981 to 1999–2000 and mentioned that the real per capita social sector expenditure decreased because of poor fiscal conditions. The main responsibility to manage finances for social services lay with state governments under the guidance of the central government. It had been seen that the pattern of social services and economic services fluctuated significantly from state to state. Social Sector expenditure had indicated the reducing trends in various Indian states since the economic reforms because of meeting the increasing fiscal deficit in every fiscal year. Tilak (1995) stated that the private sector expenditure on the social sector is more compared to public sector expenditure on the social sector. But the effect of privatisation did not reach the downtrodden levels. So, the state government should come up with a better delivery mechanism for the needy people of India.

Mercy (2007) studied the share of the social sector in total expenditure of 15 states from 1980–1981 to 2003–2004. The study concluded that the social sector expenditure of states was low if compared with UNDP recommended ratios. The expenditure of the social sector in states like Kerala and Punjab had registered a continuously decreasing from 45 per cent to 25.9 per cent and 31.8 per cent to 16.6 per cent, respectively, for the same period. This is because the presence of significant disparities had been found in terms of education, health, and infrastructure among the high-income, middle-income, and low-income states. Setting up basic infrastructure is more important. The overall social sector expenditure is ineffective in Indian states as the gap period has been widening for the fiscal deficits. Hence, filling up the fiscal deficit required to achieve human development and inclusiveness in India (Kaur et al., 2013).

The expenditure incurred for social sector development from economic reforms to the year 2000 was low as compared to the proportion of the social sector spent earlier by the Indian government. There has been a paradigm shift to basic minimum needs programmes from wage employment programmes like housing, water, road connectivity, etc. Poor governance and the failure of the delivery system led to the failure of many good schemes started for infrastructure and human capabilities. The effectiveness of numerous schemes related to social sector development, employment generation, and poverty eradication had been poor (Mooij & Dev, 2004).

Table 19. State-wise Expenditure on Social Sector Since Economic Reforms.

States	1991–1992	1992–1993	1993–1994	1994–1995	1995–1996	1996–1997	1997–1998	1998–1999	1999–2000	2000–2001	2001–2002	2002–2003
Andhra Pradesh	801.29 (40)	781.92 (41)	1,004.83 (37)	1,078.30 (34)	1,317.87 (39)	1,620.65 (39)	1,553.46 (38)	1,943.34 (41)	1,883.19 (39)	1,029.77 (36)	2,322.38 (35)	2,712.8 (33)
Arunachal Pradesh	159.92 (31)	157.05 (34)	166.69 (34)	177.00 (32)	204.10 (33)	263.40 (36)	278.98 (34)	217.51 (33)	210.78 (34)	244.65 (27)	281.73 (33)	273.10 (31)
Assam	503.97 (40)	635.70 (36)	751.12 (39)	754.25 (39)	7,055.67 (41)	7,034.65 (40)	7,036.45 (38)	942.97 (36)	913.78 (37)	1,006.07 (40)	1,077.63 (36)	975.03 (36)
Bihar	1,362.00 (45)	1,445.33 (41)	1,376.96 (41)	1,254.40 (41)	1,435.06 (40)	1,721.05 (43)	1,740.22 (43)	1,259.93 (44)	1,220.93 (43)	1,023.70 (44)	1,620.09 (39)	1,526.2 (36)
Chhattisgarh	–	–	–	–	–	–	–	–	–	–	928.99 (51)	1,119.6 (43)
Goa	150.04 (39)	121.68 (39)	130.12 (39)	132.03 (37)	138.50 (27)	145.42 (31)	156.29 (28)	138.67 (29)	134.38 (29)	154.16 (26)	210.45 (23)	306.31 (26)
Gujarat	939.01 (34)	1,841.36 (31)	1,338.29 (34)	1,252.80 (35)	1,419.81 (34)	1,396.59 (32)	2,363.67 (33)	2,289.06 (35)	2,218.20 (35)	3,193.35 (36)	3,314.41 (35)	3,760.2 (30)
Haryana	623.59 (29)	863.67 (32)	664.59 (27)	674.23 (19)	762.36 (28)	790.32 (21)	725.99 (23)	755.17 (29)	731.80 (31)	936.03 (37)	1,044.51 (34)	889.00 (27)
Himachal Pradesh	310.27 (21)	370.89 (40)	381.54 (37)	397.71 (37)	447.57 (38)	547.90 (38)	602.98 (36)	822.64 (37)	797.18 (36)	937.32 (37)	1,048.04 (34)	1,070.4 (30)
Jammu and Kashmir	553.30 (32)	642.38 (38)	530.72 (35)	523.02 (31)	546.67 (34)	608.35 (35)	653.69 (33)	795.61 (26)	788.72 (24)	658.41 (27)	716.73 (29)	712.22 (29)
Jharkhand	–	–	–	–	–	–	–	–	–	–	1,618.69 (47)	1,573.3 (50)
Karnataka	984.50 (37)	1,679.00 (36)	1,852.94 (37)	1,902.73 (39)	1,893.29 (38)	2,519.18 (38)	2,143.84 (39)	2,317.50 (39)	2,245.77 (38)	2,932.90 (38)	3,612.16 (35)	3,036.7 (31)
Kerala	529.19 (40)	654.34 (41)	493.66 (40)	514.43 (40)	540.25 (39)	943.00 (41)	816.92 (43)	669.01 (44)	648.30 (42)	522.99 (40)	586.61 (38)	910.97 (37)
Madhya Pradesh	1,418.08 (40)	2,230.46 (39)	1,256.37 (40)	1,432.22 (41)	1,738.48 (42)	1,995.43 (40)	2,335.10 (39)	2,079.46 (43)	2,015.09 (41)	2,159.53 (42)	2,006.05 (35)	2,295.3 (38)
Maharashtra	1,980.17 (38)	2,479.13 (40)	1,928.57 (39)	2,135.67 (34)	2,887.47 (39)	4,620.99 (37)	3,502.36 (38)	4,708.31 (37)	4,562.57 (34)	3,748.03 (37)	3,849.02 (37)	4,535.4 (33)
Manipur	104.51 (35)	201.44 (24)	115.50 (33)	181.29 (36)	160.30 (38)	181.67 (38)	177.41 (37)	189.88 (35)	184.00 (34)	255.47 (33)	216.25 (26)	199.56 (26)
Meghalaya	136.53 (38)	156.01 (36)	163.64 (35)	152.04 (37)	158.93 (37)	214.10 (40)	191.01 (40)	168.34 (39)	163.13 (42)	246.43 (41)	224.03 (41)	216.30 (36)
Mizoram	127.90 (42)	142.27 (41)	150.86 (41)	155.10 (40)	146.45 (41)	198.20 (42)	160.02 (37)	186.95 (42)	185.24 (44)	264.67 (39)	272.55 (41)	286.88 (40)
Nagaland	131.92 (28)	150.87 (26)	155.42 (29)	147.67 (33)	167.80 (35)	199.22 (32)	191.66 (30)	193.48 (28)	185.08 (32)	170.68 (32)	189.59 (27)	208.41 (30))
Orissa	577.36 (36)	630.23 (38)	590.73 (39)	788.85 (37)	938.36 (39)	1,429.36 (39)	1,161.52 (38)	1,263.09 (38)	1,223.99 (48)	1,342.11 (37)	926.65 (34)	778.52 (32)
Punjab	571.93 (22)	961.79 (25)	714.04 (26)	796.59 (21)	763.56 (25)	940.30 (16)	1,013.65 (23)	1,142.72 (28)	1,107.35 (23)	1,066.00 (28)	1,149.91 (24)	1,013.2 (17)
Rajasthan	99.92 (35)	81.65 (38)	92.82 (38)	1,266.33 (39)	1,668.59 (36)	1,894.26 (39)	1,611.21 (37)	1,891.92 (42)	1,833.36 (39)	2,230.52 (42)	2,480.59 (41)	2,121.1 (37)

2003–04	2004–2005	2005–2006	2006–2007	2007–2008	2008–2009	2009–2010	2010–2011	2011–2012	2012–2013	2013–2014	2014–2015	CV
4,276.60 (33)	4,450.62 (29)	4,254.13 (31)	6,257.14 (33)	10,541.00 (33)	15,211.51 (35)	10,083.76 (36)	11,062.43 (38)	12,632.91 (39)	14,205.52 (40)	12,645.72 (39)	14,227.52 (40)	96.14
267.74 (28)	259.44 (31)	243.75 (30)	268.88 (30)	214.11 (31)	165.70 (30)	208.88 (34)	428.79 (28)	300.16 (30)	385.01 (32)	321.21 (30)	405.01 (32)	28.12
879.10 (35)	907.23 (32)	760.67 (37)	1,078.06 (39)	951.70 (40)	1,375.15 (39)	1,787.44 (37)	2,452.40 (40)	2,078.51 (39)	2,193.13 (37)	2,088.41 (39)	2,198.13 (37)	58.6
1,526.63 (37)	1,793.39 (35)	2,140.16 (38)	3,163.97 (41)	2,907.89 (44)	4,251.61 (44)	5,216.75 (42)	5,533.38 (38)	5,861.96 (39)	6,673.59 (40)	5,871.96 (39)	6,693.59 (40)	69.11
1,258.84 (41)	1,677.55 (36)	2,008.53 (38)	3,144.55 (44)	3,177.85 (48)	4,170.59 (47)	4,938.02 (50)	4,928.95 (51)	5,600.44 (51)	6,341.38 (52)	5,653.44 (51)	6,361.38 (52)	57.88
335.58 (28)	390.38 (31)	426.96 (31)	505.90 (32)	551.74 (32)	626.85 (32)	681.35 (33)	702.74 (34)	934.94 (33)	1,381.88 (33)	944.94 (33)	1,396.88 (33)	84.73
3,204.40 (27)	3,730.87 (29)	4,352.03 (32)	4,469.19 (33)	6,122.15 (35)	7,571.98 (35)	8,245.41 (39)	9,718.64 (40)	10,385.63 (39)	12,867.34 (38)	10,396.31 (39)	12,877.34 (38)	77.09
945.20 (19)	1,079.57 (24)	1,506.65 (33)	1,570.04 (29)	2,383.15 (33)	2,772.66 (37)	3,858.87 (41)	5,588.29 (40)	5,016.56 (40)	5,414.89 (41)	5,046.56 (40)	5,434.89 (41)	91.64
683.14 (29)	765.04 (29)	779.23 (30)	851.92 (33)	864.45 (35)	733.00 (37)	750.40 (35)	862.67 (36)	771.07 (35)	821.06 (34)	793.07 (35)	841.06 (34)	30.70
788.17 (28)	995.77 (28)	1,114.73 (45)	1,006.84 (31)	1,114.77 (30)	1,002.19 (30)	1,322.79 (31)	1,550.67 (30)	1,513.53 (29)	1,989.99 (29)	1,551.53 (29)	1,999.99 (29)	42.55
1,616.52 (44)	2,085.81 (44)	2,217.11 (45)	2,290.49 (47)	2,622.38 (44)	3,107.00 (48)	3,270.73 (44)	3,482.75 (46)	4,308.56 (43)	4,124.89 (41)	4,328.56 (43)	4,143.89 (41)	35.61
3,762.07 (28)	3,797.32 (29)	4,205.28 (33)	4,770.12 (33)	6,635.21 (37)	9,638.06 (39)	10,024.03 (40)	9,909.94 (40)	9,785.38 (38)	10,325.90 (37)	9,798.38 (38)	10,425.90 (37)	71.12
2,244.32 (30)	2,039.89 (36)	2,822.77 (37)	3,035.54 (31)	1,893.36 (31)	2,102.55 (33)	2,614.72 (37)	2,848.44 (33)	2,707.38 (34)	2,975.56 (35)	2,727.38 (34)	2,987.56 (35)	66.53
2,440.96 (28)	2,890.66 (29)	3,372.26 (33)	3,977.78 (33)	4,549.49 (37)	4,730.30 (35)	5,887.82 (39)	6,021.17 (38)	6,773.59 (35)	7,613.73 (33)	6,787.59 (35)	7,642.73 (33)	58.07
4,810.24 (31)	3,540.08 (28)	5,340.93 (35)	5,308.12 (37)	7,951.99 (37)	9,184.85 (37)	11,688.47 (40)	12,387.87 (41)	13,113.95 (41)	12,963.98 (42)	13,141.95 (41)	12,983.98 (42)	63.93
261.77 (26)	420.13 (34)	430.07 (34)	353.64 (29)	281.72 (32)	340.76 (33)	340.74 (33)	467.87 (32)	660.04 (34)	585.37 (36)	690.04 (34)	598.37 (36)	51.83
238.31 (36)	312.64 (36)	303.95 (38)	317.29 (38)	351.38 (38)	398.62 (36)	309.09 (37)	440.52 (37)	634.48 (39)	850.32 (40)	6,365.48 (39)	860.32 (40)	59.90
246.13 (36)	254.21 (36)	281.93 (33)	289.16 (35)	302.34 (37)	413.06 (40)	445.16 (42)	332.94 (39)	358.89 (37)	446.98 (37)	378.89 (37)	476.98 (37)	38.36
225.36 (27)	220.52 (27)	243.04 (29)	265.05 (30)	233.99 (30)	335.83 (28)	341.65 (26)	369.22 (28)	323.31 (27)	377.84 (25)	343.31 (27)	387.84 (25)	32.88
882.10 (28)	859.32 (29)	1,061.58 (34)	1,052.49 (32)	1,527.38 (36)	1,927.95 (42)	2,042.32 (41)	2,306.48 (42)	3,169.16 (42)	3,519.88 (43)	3,179.16 (42)	3,529.88 (43)	58.04
971.28 (17)	1,051.71 (18)	1,106.10 (20)	917.20 (18)	1,648.50 (19)	1,651.84 (24)	2,136.27 (23)	2,133.75 (23)	2,864.82 (25)	3,328.51 (27)	2,894.82 (25)	3,348.51 (27)	53.57
2,278.06 (36)	2,847.25 (34)	3,069.89 (40)	3,165.37 (40)	3,217.76 (39)	4,030.93 (45)	5,048.67 (44)	5,231.92 (42)	6,968.68 (42)	8,220.32 (43)	6,989.68 (42)	8,243.32 (43)	74.41

(Continued)

Table 19.   (*Continued*)

States	1991–1992	1992–1993	1993–1994	1994–1995	1995–1996	1996–1997	1997–1998	1998–1999	1999–2000	2000–2001	2001–2002	2002–2003
Sikkim	68.52 (32)	117.28 (32)	74.70 (34)	101.01 (17)	94.04 (15)	139.58 (13)	143.68 (13)	161.21 (16)	156.22 (15)	128.87 (27)	159.16 (17)	194.74 (16)
Tamil Nadu	1,528.00 (36)	1,484.30 (40)	1,800.57 (42)	1,772.25 (40)	2,006.69 (41)	2,558.91 (40)	2,357.39 (38)	2,524.07 (41)	2,445.94 (39)	3,123.88 (39)	3,171.91 (37)	3,027.4 (32)
Tripura	188.39 (12)	217.49 (13)	223.80 (12)	183.69 (10)	235.96 (12	268.54 (13)	325.58 (15)	300.96 (13)	291.64 (12)	326.04 (14)	333.18 (13)	419.37 (16)
Uttar Pradesh	2,180.87 (34)	2,076.28 (34)	1,973.82 (32)	2,235.58 (29)	2,633.49 (31)	4,157.05 (33)	3,327.18 (34)	2,840.48 (33)	2,752.56 (34)	3,198.41 (33)	2,047.88 (32)	2,429.3 (31)
Uttarakhand	–	–	–	–	–	–	–	–	–	–	525.50 (33)	488.74 (34)
West Bengal	1,015.89 (44)	974.29 (41)	714.12 (42)	945.44 (41)	1,144.39 (39)	1,477.06 (38)	1,886.45 (38)	1,051.56 (39)	1,032.30 (41)	1,909.25 (36)	2,192.54 (34)	1,552.1 (31)
A&N Islands	51.21 (32)	54.43 (33)	56.52 (30)	67.38 (35)	103.24 (32)	123.17 (35)	130.49 (41)	141.53 (41)	140.78 (40)	130.74 (42)	163.36 (43)	168.93 (43)
Chandigarh	105.65 (35)	103.36 (32)	114.68 (31)	118.11 (32)	122.04 (31)	136.56 (35)	126.52 (40)	139.32 (40)	138.78 (39)	143.03 (40)	140.57 (42)	136.91 (41)
D&N Haveli	12.90 (18)	10.01 (16)	12.02 (16)	15.09 (18)	17.42 (19)	23.39 (21)	20.06 (20)	21.45 (19)	22.02 (19)	20.05 (18)	18.45 (17)	21.26 (18)
Daman & Diu	12.30 (18)	10.01 (16)	9.64 (15)	11.47 (16)	14.18 (17)	14.00 (17)	16.19 (18)	15.44 (17)	17.27 (17)	11.71 (15)	11.85 (15)	12.56 (15)
Delhi	1,027.95 (18)	935.64 (46)	980.87 (48)	1,416.78 (48)	1,526.58 (46)	1,748.93 (49)	1,550.59 (49)	1,669.59 (45)	1,740.60 (42)	1,956.66 (41)	2,234.47 (43)	2,259.9 (44)
Lakshadweep	11.96 (17)	10.20 (16)	11.34 (16)	12.15 (16)	12.37 (16)	13.45 (16)	16.18 (18)	16.05 (17)	17.01 (17)	18.35 (18)	20.96 (18)	20.90 (18)
Puducherry	81.56 (15)	69.07 (15)	77.45 (14)	81.24 (15)	102.91 (15)	111.17 (16)	120.89 (16)	143.16 (16)	142.40 (16)	198.89 (18)	191.43 (18)	238.95 (19)

Source: 1. Government of India. (various issued-a), *Annual Reports*. New Delhi: Planning Commission.

2. Government of India. (various issued-b), *Economic Survey*. New Delhi: Ministry of Finance.

3. Government of India. (various issued-c), *Expenditure Budget (Vol. 1)*. New Delhi: Ministry of Finance.

Notes: 1. NA is not available.

2. Figures in parentheses indicate the percentage of total expenditure.

Dev and Mooij (2004) observed that there existed a pattern of underspending of allocated funds on social services as well as economic services. India could not achieve the targeted growth. However, numerous schemes were launched to eradicate poverty yet the results revealed that states were not able to use funds efficiently. Poor implementation of schemes, absence of appropriate infrastructure, misuse of resources, corruption, and unintentional delays worsen the situation. The high share of spending contributed towards revenue expenditure as compared to capital outlays. Revenue expenditure took more than 95 per cent of overall social sector expenditure by the late 1990s. There is no proper format to monitor the utilisation of the allocated funds in different sectors and schemes.

2003–04	2004–2005	2005–2006	2006–2007	2007–2008	2008–2009	2009–2010	2010–2011	2011–2012	2012–2013	2013–2014	2014–2015	CV
227.65 (28)	254.86 (22)	256.76 (23)	261.87 (24)	307.78 (24)	347.57 (27)	456.61 (29)	415.57 (31)	461.39 (31)	699.06 (32)	471.39 (31)	730.06 (32)	66.26
4,019.62 (34)	4,448.20 (33)	4,407.25 (37)	5,218.97 (33)	6,861.64 (36)	6,584.45 (38)	7,085.50 (40)	7,645.29 (40)	8,927.89 (39)	10,944.59 (38)	8,945.89 (39)	10,956.59 (38)	62.26
305.61 (13)	406.67 (14)	360.14 (14)	417.21 (15)	440.62 (16)	547.02 (18)	637.79 (19)	521.98 (18)	621.76 (18)	541.89 (19)	641.76 (18)	561.89 (19)	36.99
2,523.19 (29)	3,539.87 (29)	3,858.36 (34)	4,487.42 (32)	9,673.22 (34)	11,510.67 (38)	12,953.83 (39)	13,056.04 (38)	14,926.29 (38)	16,609.13 (39)	14,946.29 (38)	16,629.13 (39)	85.54
412.90 (33)	850.26 (32)	993.16 (31)	1,784.66 (32)	1,948.28 (31)	1,778.95 (35)	1,698.78 (36)	1,835.31 (36)	2,042.77 (37)	2,459.95 (37)	2,056.77 (37)	2,489.95 (37)	50.20
1,465.42 (33)	2,027.24 (39)	2,582.06 (38)	2,566.12 (39)	4,325.66 (35)	4,913.38 (36)	6,138.60 (41)	6,981.23 (42)	8,468.24 (43)	8,330.52 (43)	8,488.24 (43)	8,350.52 (43)	85.59
170.74 (43)	159.95 (36)	247.75 (37)	273.29 (39)	192.96 (41)	195.21 (40)	243.13 (41)	271.08 (42)	367.72 (43)	407.54 (44)	372.72 (43)	417.54 (44)	54.30
133.81 (40)	144.38 (40)	139.34 (40)	157.00 (40)	169.43 (36)	193.83 (36)	205.84 (35)	260.01 (37)	355.42 (39)	344.65 (43)	365.42 (39)	356.65 (43)	42.16
22.26 (18)	25.53 (19)	24.86 (17)	25.16 (16)	27.50 (16)	55.11 (20)	59.95 (20)	76.73 (22)	96.34 (23)	132.68 (24)	100.34 (23)	145.68 (24)	90.01
17.69 (16)	18.70 (17)	22.74 (17)	21.02 (15)	21.22 (15)	39.91 (17)	43.22 (17)	48.95 (18)	83.79 (18)	109.61 (19)	93.79 (18)	123.61 (19)	95.94
2,330.28 (46)	2,492.49 (44)	2,709.82 (41)	2,895.71 (42)	4,080.23 (41)	4,317.66 (42)	4,289.07 (42)	4,383.02 (43)	5,288.20 (44)	5,706.19 (45)	5,298.20 (44)	5,721.19 (45)	54.54
19.47 (17)	21.23 (17)	18.63 (17)	40.32 (18)	28.36 (18)	52.24 (19)	69.66 (19)	47.86 (19)	68.26 (19)	102.97 (19)	78.26 (19)	123.97 (19)	82.33
278.57 (19)	355.59 (19)	450.60 (19)	598.62 (20)	754.37 (20)	884.01 (20)	924.09 (21)	1,012.47 (22)	1,005.00 (23)	1,063.10 (24)	1,026.00 (23)	1,093.10 (24)	90.12

The underutilisation was reflected while evaluating the budget allocations, releases, and utilisation rates due to the lack of a proper financial management information system (Shariff et al., 2002b). Hence, there is a need for better plans for the utilisation of funds out of allocations.

Human welfare is an essential element of the economic development of a modern economy. That is why, since independence, the social welfare of the masses has become both the tool and objective of Indian economic policy. At independence, India inherited a fast-growing population, food deprivation, rampant poverty, ignorance and illiteracy of the masses, and an overall unbalanced and decadent socio-economic antecedent of eastern society. Nevertheless, the planners were conscious of the reality that unless the fruits of economic growth percolate down to the lowest runs of society, real development and welfare are meaningless. The introduction of the stabilisation and structural adjustment programme (SAP)/ economic reforms was to mend the crisis related to more fiscal deficit, growing balance of payments deficit, escalating inflation, low forex reserves, etc. (Joshi, 2006). The attempts that had been made to reconcile these crises were even met with success also. The concept of liberalisation, privatisation, and globalisation was related to the implementation of several policy measures in more concrete and discrete terms as the objective of development could be achieved (Panchamukhi, 2000). The structural shifts within Indian planning ranging from 'development with stability' to 'development with social equity' to 'strengthening with growth' and lastly to 'neo-liberal development' is noticeable (Pandey, 2011).

The basic objective and intent of providing developmental programmes are to help the downtrodden sectors including the underprivileged and deprived sections. The government policies and programmes are directed towards bringing weaker sections to the mainstream, yet it seems that this lowest ring lag behind. It must create an adequate livelihood and decent employment opportunities for the excluded ones. To remove poverty and for equal distribution of income among the masses, the government must invest in social sector development to make growth inclusive. This can be done by accumulating the indicators like education, health, water supply and sanitation, housing and urban development, rural development, and labour and employment. This expenditure incurred on social sector development will generate more opportunities for employment for the deprived classes.

The government's social sector policy of 'providing approach' must be shifted to an 'entitlement-based approach' to promote social sector development effectively in India. The use of technology and delivery mechanisms would empower the grass root level that finally contributes significantly to the end. Transparency and accountability must be ensured in the delivery mechanism. This will happen only when local government and Panchayati Raj Institutions (PRIs) work jointly as they are more answerable than the central government. This beneficiary-oriented social sector approach uses Aadhar numbers to check duplications and also the eligibility of the beneficiaries (Goswami & Bezbaruah, 2011).

The whole ground of the policy framework which has been astutely designed by policymakers for inclusive growth must be monitored for effective implementation. The identification of the real beneficiaries is very significant as it will help to reach the right beneficiaries and also make sure that all qualified beneficiaries would be covered. The various measures adopted by the government, to reduce the likelihood of corruption, need to create stronger mechanisms to identify the loopholes. The components of the social sector are education, health, water supply, sanitation, rural development, etc., associated with human development in adjunct to the value system of the economy like values of freedom, removal of gender discrimination, and self-sufficiency. Any improvement within the social sector may start a little growth as it is imperative for development (Jain & Runa, 2014).

Chapter 6

Construction of India's Index of Growth Inclusivity

India's development policy has continued to prioritise inclusive growth, and the growth of the social sector supports this goal. Inclusive growth and social sector development are mutually reinforcing. The attainment of inclusive growth is sparked by social sector development, whereas social sector development is the direct consequence of inclusive growth. With the aim of eliminating hunger and poverty and elevating the poorer segment of society, the focus has been placed on the expansion of the schooling, healthcare, and rural sectors since the independence of India (Chadda & Chadha, 2020a). According to India's policy, social welfare must be strengthened and broadened, and more Indians should partake in the country's economic growth (Government of India, 2012a). As a result, measures that promote employment generation, equality, poverty reduction, and eventually inclusive growth took precedence. The priority must be on disseminating the rewards to underprivileged communities, primarily scheduled tribes (ST) and scheduled castes (SC), minorities, and the disabled (Chadda & Chadha, 2020b).

Suryanarayana (2013) stated that economic growth is perceived from two angles, either using the conventional approach or the current approach. The conventional approach, on one hand, focussed on measuring the economic performance of a country by quantifying the outcome of economic activity in terms of percentage changes. But this analysis would overlook the distribution of justice to the poor masses. Hence, the conventional approach could be misleading. The current approach, on the other hand, hinges on the welfare measure which emphasises on universal adoption of programmes to reduce the incidence of poverty and food insecurity. But this approach also had limitations manifesting in conventional measures of consumption and poverty after income generation. A minor improvement in the betterment of lower rungs of society would indicate inclusiveness in economic activity. The objective of inclusive growth is the upliftment of the socially and economically deprived sectors in the mainstream economy by ensuring more employment opportunities for them.

Ali (2007) emphasised inclusive growth via the equalisation of opportunities for pro-poor growth. Pro-poor growth is implicit in the reduction of inequalities

Social Sector Development and Inclusive Growth in India, 125–138
Copyright © 2023 by Ishu Chadda
Published under exclusive license by Emerald Publishing Limited
doi:10.1108/978-1-83753-186-820231007

and the eradication of poverty in lower sects of society. Equalising opportunities indicated that the benefits generated from the economic growth would percolate across the population including the deprived sections. Reducing economic and political inequality from the perspective of poor people would improve equitable access to opportunities, public goods, and services and catalyse an inclusive growth process.

Inclusive growth incorporates the concept of equity, equal opportunity, security in the market, and more employment opportunities as fundamental constituents of economic growth. The eradication of poverty could be delayed by rising levels of inequality, which could also impede the progress of economic development. A combination of growth-oriented policies with participative development policies would be for the dispersion of benefits to all the sectors including the marginalised sections. Everyone who took part in the growth process should be included in the actual growth, both in regard to making contributions and decisions to drive the overall progress. So, it has been related to broad-based or people-oriented growth. Participation without sharing the benefit would make the growth unfair, and sharing of benefits without participation would result in rising inequality (Nayak et al., 2010).

Inclusive growth would benefit many people. The absolute definition considered the pro-poor growth with increased income for the poor, while the relative definition linked the growth with the increase in income proportionately among the poor, which is accompanied by declining inequality. If inclusive growth is related to absolute poverty, it merely reduces poverty but raises disparities. Subsequently, there would be no inclusive growth. Nevertheless, inclusive growth in relative terms emphasised on inclusion of the rich, middle-income group, the near-poor, and the destitute and poor in partaking of the rewards of growth. This type of growth indicates shared, sustainable, and inclusive prosperity (Klasen, 2010).

The concept of inclusive growth is defined as growth in which all the members of society participated and contributed equally. The most direct way to achieve inclusive growth is to bring the objective of full employment to the top of the policy agenda (Felipe, 2012).

The four main dimensions of inclusive growth include 'growth, productive employment, and economic infrastructure, income poverty and equity, human capabilities and social protection'. The concept of inclusive growth has been associated with socially perceived deprivation concerning human needs (McKinley, 2010). These essential human needs include adequate nourishment, decent clothes, reasonable shelter, avoidable diseases, education, and participation in economic activity (Puri & Mishra, 2013).

The policies that promoted equality of opportunities would ensure long-run growth by enabling the poor and participation of the deprived sections in the development process. The pursuit of equality is defined here in terms of equality of opportunities rather than the redistribution of income. The equality of opportunities would result in having equal chances of acquiring assets of adequate quality irrespective of the identification of individuals, whether belonging to a different caste, gender, or class. To make this possible, the challenge of rapid growth along with making growth inclusive has to be followed positively (World Bank, 2006).

Hirway (2011) defined inclusive growth as a broad-based growth process in which eradication of poverty, new job prospects, and reduction of urban–rural inequalities, as well among different socio-economic groups. Increasing opportunities for the excluded and deprived groups, as contributors but not as beneficiaries in the process of growth would indicate inclusiveness. This process of inclusiveness could not be achieved in the short run. Inclusive growth could be achieved in the long run which has comprised the expansion of productive employment and redistribution policies.

Palanivel (2011) suggested that the main areas that need to be improved include, education and the healthcare services through policy intervention and increasing public spending as well as ensuring facilitating good quality of social services and expansion of more employment opportunities for the poor. In addition to the poverty reduction strategy, a long-term strategic framework should be followed for social development which must emphasise empowering the meagre group for equal access and opportunities. The policymakers must ensure that the benefits must be trickled down to everyone.

Kuroda (2006) stated that policies and strategies must be framed to improve the quality of infrastructure, especially in rural areas. The creation of farm and non-farm employment opportunities and equitable redistribution policy in rural and urban areas must ensure the development process is more inclusive in India. Bolt (2004) highlighted the role of agriculture and the rural economy to make growth more inclusive. One-third of the population lives in rural areas and depends upon rural-based activities for earnings. This study laid stress on the acceleration of agriculture and rural development. The right incentives, improved technology, well-functioning markets, high-value products, employment incomes, non-farm commodities, and infrastructure connectivity would provide the base for value addition. Femando (2008) focussed on the rural infrastructure which is associated with the good accessibility of markets and basic services to rural people and influences rural economic growth and more income opportunities. The physical infrastructure deficiencies present in rural areas need to be improved so that better access could be provided for the basic services to make life better.

The policymakers and planners of India favoured the new approach of faster growth with inclusivity and renounced its traditional policy of high investment and growth. India pledged its support to sustainable growth in the economy in order to enhance the quality of life for people while also striving to strengthen their overall economy. Widespread expansion is necessary for the destitute and disadvantaged social groups to participate in it.

A composite score of inclusive growth is required to be generated firstly in order to gauge the extent and aspects of India's social sector development, both in terms of their monetary and physical accomplishments. The composite index of inclusive growth was derived using the principal component analysis approach, as outlined in the chapter on database and methodology.

Constructing Composite Index of India's Inclusive Growth

The inclusive development index was suggested by the World Economic Forum as a measure of prosperity (Chadda & Chadha, 2020b). *A scoring system and a* weighted system are used to establish a composite indicator of inclusive growth. The statistics and analysis use the years 1985–2016 as their frame of reference.

Ramos et al. (2013) mentioned that the elimination of poverty, fair opportunities for job prospects, and economic and social involvement in the developmental process are the three elements that make up the notion of inclusive growth. An additional set of variables that represent these three aspects of inclusive growth is used to create the inclusive growth index (Chadha & Chadda, 2020a).

1. *The elimination of destitution and poverty, exemplified by (i) absolute and abject poverty; and (ii) disparities in income.*
2. *Fair opportunities for employment options are suggested by (i) the proportion of men and women who participate in the labour force; (ii) Mahatma Gandhi National Rural Employment Guarantee Act's (MGNREGA) employment creation programme; and (iii) the percentage of the workforce that belongs to the SC and ST classifications.*
3. *Evidence of increasing economic and social inclusion is shown by (i) the index of gender parity; (ii) the gender balance in Parliament; (iii) the overall enrolment for the reserved group; and (iv) the political representation by reserved classes.*

By delivering welfare benefits and boosting economic activities simultaneously, an inclusive and sustainable agenda would accomplish two major purposes, namely increasing employment and eliminating economic disparities. The galloping population and labour force of the country has resulted in a higher unemployment rate. The primary goal of inclusive growth is the eradication of poverty by ensuring equality of opportunity for all underprivileged groups of society and by eliminating their economic and social exclusion (Government of India, 2012a).

To achieve this, employment would act as a link between economic growth and poverty reduction. Thus, the strategy implemented from the Sixth Five-Year Plan consisted of special programmes intended to enhance prospects for productive work and to ensure that everyone had access to the basic necessities, particularly in unorganised sectors and rural areas (Gangopadhyay et al., 2009). Inclusive growth envisions participative growth along with benefit sharing more fairly (Organization for Economic Cooperation and Development (OECD), 2013).

The intent of compiling these several indicators into a single indicator that clearly reflected the collection of data is to generate an inclusive growth index for India from the years 1985 to 2016 by using the procedure outlined above. By doing so, the data are condensed from a complicated and multilayered frame into a single score (Chadda & Chadha, 2020b). A strong correlation has existed among the mentioned variables of inclusive growth. Hence, to overcome the problem of multicollinearity as well as selection bias, using principal component analysis, this study created a comprehensive index of inclusive growth (Chadda & Chadha, 2020b).

In order to eliminate duplicates or redundancies from the collection of associated variables, the principal component analysis method is employed. Instead of discussing the variables, emphasis is placed on explaining their covariance structure in this method (Chadda & Chadha, 2020b). The very first step is to check the normalisation of data so that there must be no presence of outliers in the data set. The findings and interpretations of the component analyses can be impacted by outliers. Correlations may be significantly affected by outliers or data that are noticeably lower or higher than the rest of the data set, which will lead to inaccurate results (Krishnan, 2010).

The descriptive statistical analysis of the variables displaying the lowest, highest, mean, standard deviation, kurtosis, and skewness are presented in Table 20. The value of skewness and kurtosis must lie between -1 and 1 and -2 and 2, respectively. These were checked using SPSS software by adopting the procedure of histogram and the box plot of the distribution of scores (Krishnan, 2010; Leech et al., 2014). No outliers were detected in the present data set so the next step is to standardise the data.

After data normalisation, the variables' descriptive statistical analysis is described in Table 21. Pradhan and Puttuswamaiah (2005) mentioned that to prevent the impact of a single variable on the major components, the data set for each variable was normalised. After standardisation, the variables had a mean of 0 and a variation of 1 (Chadda & Chadha, 2020a).

The subsequent part entails evaluating the partial correlations using the Kaiser–Meyer–Olkin (KMO) measure as well as the coefficient correlations through Bartlett's sphericity test to determine the strength of the association between the variables. The value of KMO is shown to be 0.829 in Table 22. Bartlett's test of sphericity results in a level of statistical significance at 0.000, a number small enough to rule out the null hypothesis, signifying a satisfactory measure (Chadda & Chadha, 2020a).

According to Field (2005), KMO scores above 0.5 are considered adequate, values between 0.5 and 0.7 are considered medium, values with both 0.7 and 0.8 are regarded as good, values with 0.8 and 0.9 are considered excellent, and values beyond 0.9 are considered fantastic. Factor analysis is necessary since Bartlett's test is extremely significant ($p<0.001$).

Leech et al. (2014) mentioned that the distribution of the variation among its potential components was described by the total variance. The first two main components for the current data set described more than 80 per cent of the variation (Chadda & Chadha, 2020a).

The first principal component, which reports for 73.243 per cent of the variation, and the second principal component, which accounts for 10.943 per cent of the variation, are projected in Table 23. This highlights the significance of principal components and advises the development of the inclusive growth index (Chadda & Chadha, 2020a).

Scree plot (Fig. 1) demonstrates graphically the relationship between the Eigenvalues from the principal components (OECD, 2008). The association between the components and the particular variables is shown in the initial matrix. As a result of the factors' high correlation with other variables, it tends to produce factors that can be deciphered. This particular matrix in which values of components arrived before rotation is quite difficult to interpret.

In the initial matrix of Table 24, it appears that the gender parity index and gross enrolment ratio of SC have the same value and do not indicate the high loading for the first component. Therefore, through rotation, this initial factor matrix is transformed from a complex to a simple one which is the matrix that

Table 20.   Descriptive Statistics of the Variables.

S. No.	Variables	Minimum	Maximum	Mean	Standard Deviation	Skewness	Kurtosis
1	Absolute and abject poverty	19.20	45.30	28.89	7.34	0.507	−0.844
2	Disparities in income	0.3031	0.3590	0.330	0.135	0.234	−0.717
3	The proportion of men and women who participate in the labour force	33.73	44.27	39.81	3.59	−0.841	−0.944
4	MGNREGA's employment creation programme	9,050	28,160	7,304.16	10,230.1	0.883	−0.949
5	The percentage of the workforce that belongs to the SC and ST classifications	22.29	24.48	23.21	0.50	0.102	0.670
6	The index of gender parity	1.88	3.05	2.4	0.37	0.320	−1.217
7	Gender balance in Parliament	7.3	12	8.93	1.46	0.704	−0.662
8	Overall enrolment for the reserved groups	111.20	190.6	144.46	28.12	0.565	−1.347
9	Political representation of reserved classes	20.74	22.68	21.88	0.41	−0.548	1.831

Source: Author's own calculations using IBM SPSS Statistics 21.

Table 21. Descriptive Statistics of the Variables After Standardisation of Data.

S. No.	Variables	Minimum	Maximum	Mean	Standard Deviation
1	Absolute and abject poverty	−1.32	2.23	0.00	1.00
2	Disparities in income	−1.82	1.84	0.00	1.00
3	The proportion of men and women who participate in the labour force	−1.69	1.24	0.00	1.00
4	MGNREGA's employment creation programme	−0.71	2.04	0.00	1.00
5	The percentage of the workforce that belongs to the SC and ST classifications	−1.82	2.52	0.00	1.00
6	The index of gender parity	−1.39	1.74	0.00	1.00
7	Gender balance in Parliament	−1.11	2.09	0.00	1.00
8	Overall enrolment for the reserved groups	−1.18	1.64	0.00	1.00
9	Political representation of reserved classes	−2.78	1.92	0.00	1.00

Source: Chadha and Chadda (2020a).

Table 22.   KMO Measure of Sampling Adequacy and Bartlett's Test of Sphericity.

KMO Measure of Sampling Adequacy	Bartlett's Test of Sphericity		
	Chi-Square	Df	Sig.
0.829	330.625	45	0.000

Source: Chadha and Chadda (2020a).

Table 23.   Principal Components, Eigen Values, and Total Variance.

Component	Initial Eigenvalues		
	Total	Percentage of Variance	Cumulative Percentage
1	**7.324**	**73.243**	**73.243**
2	**1.094**	**10.943**	**84.125**
3	0.590	5.900	90.085
4	0.384	3.845	93.930
5	0.329	3.292	97.222
6	0.136	1.361	98.583
7	0.069	0.691	99.274
8	0.041	0.406	99.680
9	0.032	0.321	100.00

Source: Chadha and Chadda (2020a).

Note: Bold Values indicate the two components were extracted and further used for the construction of Index.

contains all the loadings of those <0.3 for each component. Rotation does not affect the commonalities and the percentage of total variance explained. The rotation is called orthogonal rotation and in the present study, the varimax procedure for rotation has been employed, which helps to minimise the number of variables with high loadings and makes it easier to interpret (Malhotra et al., 2006).

Table 25 described that the plot of component loadings in the rotated component matrix is explained by the high component loadings for these variables, namely 'MGNREGA's employment creation programme', 'The overall enrolment for the reserved group', 'The gender balance in Parliament', 'disparities in income', and 'The index of gender parity'. However, 'MGNREGA's employment creation programme' has the highest and most positive loading on the first component. The first component of 'the percentage of the workforce that belongs to the SC and ST classifications' has a loading close to zero, however, the second component has a large loading (Chadha & Chadda, 2020a).

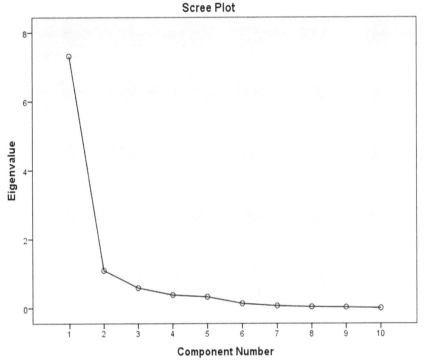

Fig. 1.   Scree Plot of Components.

Estimated Results

Component scores were estimated and saved as variables to be used in generating the index score. The component score coefficients of the two retrieved components were weighted according to the proportion of these percentages, and a non-standardised index was constructed for them. A standardised index was created in order to facilitate an easy understanding of the values of the index because it can be positive or negative as a result of the construction process (Krishnan, 2010).

The Indian economy lagged in development despite observing an upward pattern in gross domestic product (GDP) during previous plan periods. Many groups, particularly ST, SC, and minorities were not included in the benefits of the development. The issue of gender equality is still very much present. Earlier plans have shown a lack of inclusion (Government of India, 2008b).

The composite measure of inclusiveness of India's growth is shown in Table 26. An unstandardised measure of inclusive growth shows declining inclusivity until 2007. While the maximum value is 1.588 in the years 2009–2010, the non-standardised index indicates a positive value ranging from 0.433 to 1.267 over the years 2008–2015. The standardised inclusivity index of growth first displays an upward trend until 2009, at which point it returns to a downward trend. The

Table 24.   Initial Matrix: Values of Components Loadings Before Rotation.

Components	Variables	Component 1	Component 2
1	Absolute and abject poverty	−0.729	−0.439
2	Disparities in income	**0.808**	−0.253
3	The proportion of men and women who participate in the labour force	−0.896	0.247
4	MGNREGA's employment creation programme	**0.908**	−0.308
5	The percentage of the workforce that belongs to the SC and ST classifications	**0.414**	**0.779**
6	The index of gender parity	**0.973**	0.099
7	Gender balance in Parliament	**0.935**	−0.012
8	Overall enrolment for the reserved groups	**0.973**	−0.100
9	Political representation of reserved classes	**0.810**	0.211

Source: Author's Calculation using IBM SPSS Statistics 21.

Notes: 1. Principal component analysis used extraction method.

2. Two components were extracted.

3. Bold Values indicate all the loadings of those <0.3 for each component

data reveal that India's inclusivity trend growth rate is slowing down (Chadha & Chadda, 2020a).

Although the number of people living in poverty has dropped, the rate of poverty decline had not soared in tandem with GDP growth. There had been a rapid widening of the wealth gap. A slow but consistent improvement had been seen in the parameters of human growth. Although there has been an improvement in overall employment, the labour force has expanded even faster, which has raised the unemployment rate. Despite the country's recent strong growth, income disparity has increased as well. Education levels and health status vary greatly between demographic groups. It is important to overcome the opportunity gaps that exist between various social categories as they impede the development of inclusivity. By empowering more people, equalising chances will increase their access to benefits and strengthen their livelihood options (Chadha & Chadda, 2020a).

Table 25.   Varimax Rotated Matrix: Values of Components Loadings After Rotation.

Components	Variables	Component 1	Component 2
1	Absolute and abject poverty	−0.461	−0.715
2	Disparities in income	**0.837**	0.128
3	The proportion of men and women who participate in the labour force	−0.913	−0.173
4	MGNREGA's employment creation programme	**0.951**	0.123
5	The percentage of the workforce that belongs to the SC and ST classifications	0.029	**0.882**
6	The index of gender parity	**0.830**	**0.517**
7	Gender balance in Parliament	**0.845**	**0.401**
8	Overall enrolment for the reserved groups	**0.917**	**0.339**
9	Political representation of reserved classes	**0.635**	**0.546**

Sources: Chadha and Chadda (2020a, 2020b).

Note: Bold values indicate the high component loadings for the mentioned variables.

In 2004–2005, the index of inclusive growth of India increased. With the implementation of policies like Antyodaya Anna Yojana (AAY, 2000), Sampoorna Grameen Rojgar Yojana (2001) National Rural Health Mission (NRHM, 2005), and MGNREGA (2005), there has been some improvement in the growth phase. AAY was initiated in 2000 to ensure food security across the country. Therefore, the goals of this programme were to eradicate hunger in India and enhance the public distribution system (PDS) in order to assist the most vulnerable populations in both rural and urban regions (Government of India, 2000).

To follow the approach of inclusive growth, MGNREGA proved to be a very effective programme. It covered social protection, livelihood security, and democratic empowerment. It was a programme driven by demand, meaning that when wage earners expressed a need for work, it created jobs (Government of India, 2012a). It provided a legal guarantee of wage employment. In particular, vulnerable communities were the target of the National Rural Health Mission (NRHM),

Table 26.   Composite Index of India's Inclusive Growth.

Years	Component Scores		Inclusive Growth Index	
	Component 1	**Component 2**	**Non-standardised Index**	**Standardised Index**
1985–1986	−0.297	−1.989	−0.517	0.160
1986–1987	−3.067	−2.053	−0.534	0.154
1987–1988	−0.316	−2.120	−0.551	0.147
1988–1989	−0.326	−2.188	−0.569	0.139
1989–1990	−0.337	−2.256	−0.586	0.132
1990–1991	−0.347	−2.323	−0.604	0.125
1991–1992	−0.240	−1.825	−0.447	0.189
1992–1993	−0.515	−1.333	−0.623	0.119
1993–1994	−0.795	−1.246	−0.855	0.026
1994–1995	−0.907	−0.407	−0.843	0.031
1995–1996	−0.717	−0.654	−0.709	0.084
1996–1997	−0.877	−0.377	−0.813	0.043
1997–1998	−0.965	−0.594	−0.918	0.001
1998–1999	−0.673	−0.173	−0.609	0.124
1999–2000	−0.627	0.376	−0.498	0.169
2000–2001	−0.265	−0.642	−0.314	0.242
2001–2002	−1.023	1.015	−0.759	0.064
2002–2003	−0.783	0.419	−0.627	0.117
2003–2004	−0.898	1.293	−0.613	0.122
2004–2005	−0.097	−0.304	−0.124	0.318
2005–2006	−0.466	0.814	−0.300	0.248
2006–2007	−0.610	2.252	−0.239	0.272
2007–2008	0.426	0.476	0.433	0.540
2008–2009	1.321	−0.966	1.025	0.776
2009–2010	2.044	−1.475	1.588	1.001
2010–2011	1.441	0.304	1.295	0.884
2011–2012	1.311	0.506	1.208	0.849
2012–2013	1.286	0.572	1.194	0.844
2013–2014	1.329	0.939	1.280	0.878
2014–2015	1.301	1.031	1.267	0.873
2015–2016	1.670	1.409	1.637	1.020

Source: Chadha and Chadda (2020a).

which aimed to provide rural populations with equal, inexpensive healthcare services. The Government of India reported that NRHM increased institutional deliveries, increased full immunisation rates, established Rogi Kalyan Samitis, hired and trained Accredited Social Health Activists (ASHAs), established Village Health Committees, established village health and nutrition days, provided mobile medical units, and co-located Ayurveda, Yoga, Naturopathy, Unani, Siddha, and Siddhi practices (Sharma, 2014). Appropriate measures must be considered for implementation and governance issues with the launch of multiple programmes to support inclusivity (Chadha & Chadda, 2020a).

However, despite the fact that the level of chronic poverty has been steadily and slowly declining, sizable portions of the population continue to live below the national and international poverty levels. A sizeable portion of the workforce was working in the unorganised sector, typically in low-wage, low-productivity employment. India had minimal access to basic services. The inclusiveness of growth can be demonstrated by promoting equitable access to its benefits through solid fiscal and monetary policy and the successful deployment of economic measures. All levels of government would need to participate in the efforts. In order for social expenditure to be effective, it must reach the poorest people, as rising inequality and rising unemployment cannot be addressed by social spending alone (OECD, 2012).

Palanivel and Unal (2010) mentioned that the inclusivity of growth would be strengthened and expanded when poverty will be abolished. This theory states that when markets where the poor work is more accessible, with improved living conditions for the poor, including better housing and related amenities, as well as lower costs for items that the poor must pay, then growth becomes inclusive. Since independence, there have not been any explicitly pro-poor and broad-based policies because the concentration has been on pro-growth policies and initiatives to address and eliminate poverty by trickling down. Though, this path of economic growth resulted in significant and rising inequalities, which made it difficult to eradicate poverty and, in turn, slowed the process of economic development. Therefore, the benefits of growth policies must result in additional opportunities for productive employment and increased earnings for the poor. As a result, the development strategy needs to be more broad-based, sustainable, democratic, equitable, and people-centric. Since the majority of people consumed public goods more frequently, increasing social spending might elevate their standard of living. Consequently, social sector expenditure assures that the socioeconomically disadvantaged groups in the country have access to essential requirements like quality healthcare and education, increased employment opportunities, and improved infrastructure, all of which will eventually result in sustainable inclusive development (Chadha & Chadda, 2020b).

To provide the basic amenities to the people, there is a need to increase the people's participation, decentralisation of planning, the extension of irrigation facilities, better-equipped facilities, and improvement in the techniques of cultivation. Several efforts have been put by the Government of India into programmes and projects for the development of households. The empowerment of the rural poor, the development of skills and knowledge, the empowerment of women and children, the creation of community-based programmes, the creation of more fruitful employment opportunities, the eradication of pervasive poverty, the improvement of literacy and health services, and the availability of safe and potable water are just a few of the measures that have been taken to raise the standard of living of the least privileged. The main focus of these schemes and programmes is to improve in quality of life of vulnerable and poor people in society.

Inclusive growth envisions participative growth along with benefit sharing more fairly. India must make sure that the advantages of growth are felt by all societal groups. By delivering social security benefits and boosting economic activity simultaneously, an inclusive growth policy must ensure two broader aims, namely increasing employment and the elimination of economic inequities. The faster pace of population growth and labour force expansion has contributed to the rising unemployment rate. The primary focus of inclusive growth is on reducing poverty by including opportunity equality and, in addition, minimising the economic and social exclusion of all marginalised segments of society (Chadha & Chadda, 2020b). Along with assessing important government programmes, inclusive development also includes social and financial inclusion, as well as major aspects including the eradication of poverty, creation of productive jobs, improved health, access to education, social protection, and social welfare (Government of India, 2012a).

Chapter 7

Social Sector Development and Inclusive Growth in India: A Quantitative Analysis

The eradication of poverty and the creation of jobs has been the main agenda of the development policy of India as discussed in the previous chapters. India has adamantly believed since its independence for its progress phenomenon to be inclusive so that everyone, even at the downtrodden level, can participate in the process of development. Hunger, disease, and poverty would all be eradicated as a result of this process of development, which would also reduce social inequality. Growth had to be inclusive, sustainable, and broadly based in order to accomplish this. Employment creation and participation did not diminish even when India anchored its development policy on Nehruvian principles comprising significant investment, intensive industrialisation, import substitution, and indigenisation of goods and services (Balkrishnan, 2013).

Fukuda-Parr (2023) mentioned that India wanted to include people in its development strategy by making it primarily focussed on them. The poorest of the poor have been put at the forefront of measures to remove monopolies, prohibit the accumulation of economic power, promote socio-economic equality, and promote participatory development. The shortcomings of the trickle-down theory made India more determined to boost inclusive growth. Sen's strategy led to the social sector's development by being given importance to enhancing the capabilities and capacities of the populace.

In order to boost the chances of equal economic involvement and thereby strengthen inclusivity, social sector development placed a strong emphasis on creating more opportunities for decent living in both rural and urban areas. Because it places a strong emphasis on human welfare and development, the approach to growth policy's social sector facilitates inclusive growth.

Inclusionary growth and the expansion of the social sector work in tandem. The conditions of the underprivileged and disadvantaged groups in society would improve if more funds were spent on the social sector. The less advantaged groups would be given the opportunity to participate equally in social prosperity by increasing their income and gaining equal access to work and productive activities. Poverty, inequality, deprivation, and diseases would all be lessened by

Social Sector Development and Inclusive Growth in India, 139–185
Copyright © 2023 by Ishu Chadda
Published under exclusive license by Emerald Publishing Limited
doi:10.1108/978-1-83753-186-820231008

the development of the social sector. Inclusionary and sustainable development would be facilitated by that (Chadha & Chadda, 2020a).

In keeping with this goal, the Eleventh Five Year Plan established new goals for reviving agricultural dynamism and developing adequate infrastructure facilities in remote areas. It also placed a strong emphasis on implementing programmes to enhance the social standard of the weaker sections and to increase their access to economic prospects for the socio-economic empowerment of the masses. The eradication of severe poverty, illiteracy, diseases, and discrimination is also possible only by improved access to healthcare and education. Even though multifaceted inclusive growth may be challenging to attain in a diverse country like India, it is nevertheless a required objective of the country's economic policy (Chadha & Chadda, 2020a).

Gupta (2014) stated that the concept of inclusive growth is not new in India. India had implemented policies that focussed on a socialistic society based on social fairness, self-sufficiency, and the eradication of hunger and poverty. But later on, India emphasised economic growth, spontaneously eventuating its inclusiveness. It was previously found that the rates of maternal mortality rates, infant mortality rates, education, and literacy rates had all declined, although at a slow rate. Rural development in India is regarded as essential for inclusive and equitable growth. In order to reduce poverty, the Indian government runs a number of programmes, and at the macro-level, which would prove to be significant for the Indian economy to make growth inclusive. No doubt, economic growth manifests equality in income redistribution but the slowdown of the Indian economy portrays no such evidence.

The social sector development programmes, both for rural as well as urban India, like better employment prospects and other facilities were facilitated by the Rajiv Awas Yojana (RAY), Integrated Child Development Programme (ICDS), Sarva Shiksha Abhiyaan (SSA), Mid-Day Meal (MDM), Total Sanitation Campaign (TSC), National Rural Drinking Water Programme (NRDWP), Accelerated Irrigation Benefit Programme (AIBP), National Rural Employment Guarantee Programme (NREGP), National Rural Health Mission (NRHM), Pradhan Mantri Gram Sadak Yojna (PMGSY). However, despite such efforts, India needs to focus on more concrete policies so that the desired results of inclusiveness and equality would be achieved.

The Government of India (2013) defined inclusiveness as poverty reduction, socio-economic participation of marginal classes, regional balance, and reducing inequality and empowerment. As a result, inclusivity comprises involvement and empowerment in addition to ensuring that there is a broad distribution of benefits or economic opportunities. The participatory democratic system has been built so that people actively demand benefits and opportunities. The objective of inclusiveness is the reduction of poverty with a focus on promoting productive employment and the upliftment of deprived sections. The goal of stronger and more inclusive growth should be pursued with steady advancement; this requires the growth of infrastructure, institutional capacity, and human capability.

Thorat and Dubey (2013) explained that inclusive growth in India is presumed to take place when there has been a positive increase in income as well as non-income dimensions. However, all growth scenarios were not inclusive. This study examined the changes in poverty incidence and monthly per capita expenditure and revealed that some groups benefitted more than others from the poverty reduction strategies. The inequalities had also been to affect the poverty eradication process unfavourably since the concept of equality of opportunities had been missing. The benefits of growth were not evenly distributed. In the earlier years, a lot of efforts were on structural changes to promote growth. Inclusiveness and distributional issues were treated as secondary matters. There must be a proper recognition of distributional matters to make growth inclusive which further is significant for both long-term growth and macro-economic stability. An inclusive growth process would comprise the improvement factors related to three perspectives of the macro-economy namely production, income generation, and income distribution (Mello & Dutz, 2012).

Naqvi (2015) emphasised an overarching vision of the inclusive growth strategy to focus on increasing the wealth of nations accordingly, making improvements in the quality of distributive justice and elimination of poverty possible. The inclusive growth strategy is aimed at growth, distribution, and poverty reduction simultaneously. With the reduction of poverty, equity had to be enforced through redistributive policies on both economic and moral grounds. The principle of equality of opportunity should be the focus of the government since it would ensure that everyone has an equal chance to benefit from economic growth.

Social Sector Development as Catalyst of Inclusive Growth in India

The social sector is concerned with the sub-segments like basic facilities and amenities, education, health, employment, livelihood, skill development, as well as social security measures that directly deal with human welfare. Inclusive growth is related to poverty reduction, employment generation, and equitable access to the opportunity for every section of the society. Social sector development is a process and the outcome is inclusive growth.

Contribution of Development of the Social Sector and Inclusivity of Growth

India's development policy has always placed a high priority on inclusive growth. Being a multifaceted notion, inclusive growth is complicated to accomplish. It resulted in a lower incidence of poverty and better employment opportunities with an improvement in the welfare of marginalised sections including women.

Social and economic services are both encompassed by the social sector. Education, family welfare, water supply and sanitation, housing and urban development, the welfare of underprivileged classes, labour and employment, social security and welfare, and other social services are all included under the heading 'social services'. The heading 'economic services', on the other hand, deals with rural development, food storage, and food warehousing. All of this spending in the social sector is directed towards achieving a larger goal of increasing social opportunities and raising population-wide social indicators for health, nutrition, and education (Dev & Mooij, 2004).

In keeping with the aim of the research, this study will examine the outcomes and achievements of various social sector development components in India with the inclusivity of economic expansion, the proclaimed theme of India's new policy (Chadha & Chadda, 2020a). Backward stepwise multiple regression analysis is used to regress several chosen elements of the Indian social sector on the inclusive growth index as a dependent variable after creating a composite index of inclusive growth. For this purpose, two models are constructed. By using log differences of independent and dependent variables, both models were prepared. The years 1985–2016 are used as a time frame for both the data and the empirical analysis. The construction of the first model takes into account the costs associated with varied social sector component spending, whereas the construction of the second model is by selecting the physical achievements of the components of social sectors. In order to measure inclusive growth, Anand et al. (2013) built a model that included indices of economic growth as independent variables and took the log differences of both the independent and dependent variables.

Model 1: Relationship Between Government Spending on Social Sector and Inclusive Growth (Regression Analysis)

The first model explores how spending on various social sector elements affects the composite indicator of inclusive growth in India (LDIIG). Log differences of both the explanatory and response variables are used to create the model in this case. To eliminate the issue of heteroscedasticity and complexity while framing the model, natural log transformations of the variables are preferred. By compressing the scale, the formerly ten-fold difference between the values in which variables are measured is reduced to a two-fold difference (Gujarati, 2003).

SPSS has been used to run the regression estimations. The developed model is displayed below:

$$\text{LDY*} = a + b_1\,\text{LD}(X^*) + U_t$$

Here, $\text{LDY*} = \text{LD}\,(Y_{i,t} - Y_{i,t-1})$, a is a constant, and b_1 is the regression coefficient.

$$\text{LD}\,(X)^* = \text{LD}(X_{i,t} - X_{i,t-1})$$

Here, LD is the natural logarithm with differences and U_t is the white noise disturbance term.

Components of Social Sector as Independent Variables.   Once an inclusive growth composite index has been created, this study would regress the different components of the social sector with this composite index to assess the relative contribution of social sector components towards achieving the proclaimed objective of inclusive growth. As explained, the following explanatory variables have been selected namely The percentage of total government spending that goes on education, sports, the arts, and culture (LDED); the proportion of total government spending that goes towards healthcare, public health, and family welfare (LDHFW); the amount spent on water supply and sanitation relative to total government spending (LDWSS); the proportion of total government spending that goes towards housing and urban development (LDHUD); the percentage of total government spending allocated to spending on the welfare of underprivileged groups (LDWPC); the proportion of labour and employment spending to total government spending (LDLE); the amount spent on social security and welfare relative to total government spending (LDSSW); rural development expenditures as a percentage of overall government spending (LDRD); and the amount spent on food storage and warehousing relative to total government spending (LDFSW). All these expenditures are taken as a proportion of total central government expenditure.

After finalizing the variables of the model, the very next step is to check the assumptions of the data which are normality, heteroscedasticity, and multicollinearity. All the variables must be of normal distribution. If the data are not normally distributed, then transformation is needed. The data should be free from heteroscedasticity. This means if the model missed any important variable, then heteroscedasticity will occur. The last assumption is that these variables should not be correlated with each other.

The model is displayed below:

$$LDIIG_1{}^* = a + b_{11}\,LDED^* + b_{12}\,LDHFW^* + b_{13}\,LDWSS^* + b_{14}\,LDHUD^*$$
$$+ b_{15}\,LDWPC^* + b_{16}LDLE^* + b_{17}LDSSW^* + b_{18}\,LDRD^*$$
$$+ b_{19}\,LDFSW^* + U_{1t}$$

Here, LDIIG is the index of inclusive growth; LDED, the percentage of total government spending that goes on education, sports, the arts, and culture; LDHFW, the proportion of total government spending that goes towards healthcare, public health, and family welfare; LDWSS, the amount spent on water supply and sanitation relative to total government spending; LDHUD, the proportion of total government spending that goes towards housing and urban development; LDWPC, the percentage of total government spending allocated to spending on the welfare of underprivileged groups; LDLE, the proportion of labour and employment spending to total government spending; LDSSW, the amount spent on social security and welfare relative to total government spending; LDRD, the rural development expenditures as a percentage of overall government spending; and LDFSW, the amount spent on food storage and warehousing relative to total government spending. a is a constant; $b_{11}, b_{12}, b_{13}, b_{14}, b_{15}, b_{16}, b_{17}, b_{18}$, and b_{19} are the regression coefficients; and U_t is the white-noise disturbance term.

The backward approach of multiple stepwise regressions is employed here. It is the method where firstly all the variables of the model have entered then the variables which do not contribute significantly to the model are subsequently removed one by one resulting in the final model.

All of the variables are put in the first model, as shown in Table 27. The insignificant variables are then gradually eliminated, leaving three variables that are substantial enough to be included in the model. Here, spending on rural development (LDRD), social security, and welfare (LDSSW), as well as spending on the welfare of the less-privileged groups (LDWPC), all contribute to India's inclusive growth in the given model (Chadha & Chadda, 2020a).

The values of R, R^2, and adjusted R^2 are listed in Table 28. The significance of the correlation between the outcomes and the predictors is explained by R. R^2 denotes the extent of variation in the outcome that the predictors can explain. There are seven models in the table. The model's fitness is implied by the adjusted R^2. R^2 and adjusted R^2 would both have values that are identical or fairly similar to one another.

The individual expenditures made on the social sector's identified components are used as an explanatory variable in Model 1. This model's variability is addressed by R^2, which is equal to 0.674, and the association between both

Table 27.   Variable Entered/Removed as Per Backward Elimination Method in Model 1.

Model	Variables Entered	Variables Removed	Method
1	LDED, LDHFW, LDWSS, LDHUD, LDWPC, LDLE, LDSSW, LDRD, LDFSW		Enter
2		LDHUD	Backward (criterion: probability of F-to-remove ≥ 0.100)
3		LDHFW	Backward (criterion: probability of F-to-remove ≥ 0.100)
4		LDED	Backward (criterion: probability of F-to-remove ≥ 0.100)
5		LDSSW	Backward (criterion: probability of F-to-remove ≥ 0.100)
6		LDWSS	Backward (criterion: probability of F-to-remove ≥ 0.100)
7		LDLE	Backward (criterion: probability of F-to-remove ≥ 0.100)

Source: Chadha and Chadda (2020a).

the constituents of social sector development and inclusivity is obtained to be 0.821, or 82.1 per cent. The component, that is, expense incurred on housing and development (LDHUD) was deleted from Model 2, however, R and R^2 stayed unaltered, while adjusted R^2 climbed to 0.555 per cent. Similarly, three variables with the values of R, R^2, and adjusted R^2 were input to make up the final model, that is, model 7, which accounts for 79.9 per cent, 63.8 per cent, and 59.8 per cent of the variation in the dependent variable, named inclusiveness. The absence of autocorrelation in the residuals is one of the fundamental premises behind regression. The ideal range for the Durbin–Watson (DW) test is 1.5–2.5. The variables are not autocorrelated in this instance because the DW score is 2.081, as displayed in Table 28 (Chadha & Chadda, 2020a).

Table 29 explains the analysis of the variance (ANOVA). ANOVA tests whether the model fits or not. This indicates that compared to using the mean, the model significantly outperforms the mean in predicting the outcome. A better prediction as a result of model fitting is shown by the F ratio.

The value of F will be more than 1 if the prediction accuracy that is improved to fit the regression is significantly higher than the model's own accuracy. The F ratio in this instance is 4.825 in the first model and rises to 15.845 in the seventh, which is statistically impossible to occur by coincidence. In comparison to the preceding six models, model seventh is relatively better. Additionally, the p-value is very significant.

The coefficients in Table 30 that correspond to the model's parameters are the next consequence of the current model. By applying the t-statistic, the b-value may be used to determine whether or not the predictor contributed significantly to the model. It also has an accompanying standard error that explains whether the value differs or not. As a result, the predictor is significantly impacting the model if the t-test corresponding to the b-value is significant.

The findings of the backward elimination stepwise regression are presented in Table 30. The b-values and p-values of the variables are displayed together. It outlines the three components that make a significant contribution namely, the amount expended on social security and welfare (LDSSW) contributes positively

Table 28.   Summary of Model 1.

Model	R	R^2	Adjusted R^2	Std. Error of the Estimate	DW
1	0.821	0.674	0.534	0.984	2.081
2	0.821	0.674	0.555	0.962	
3	0.820	0.672	0.573	0.942	
4	0.819	0.671	0.588	0.925	
5	0.815	0.664	0.597	0.915	
6	0.811	0.658	0.606	0.905	
7	0.799	0.638	0.598	0.914	

Source: Chadha and Chadda (2020a).

Table 29.   ANOVA Test of Model 1.

Model		Sum of Squares	Df	Mean Square	*F*	Sig.
1	Regression	42.058	9	4.673	4.825	0.001
	Residual	20.340	21	0.969		
	Total	62.398	30			
2	Regression	42.030	8	5.254	5.675	0.001
	Residual	20.368	22	0.926		
	Total	62.398	30			
3	Regression	41.953	7	5.993	6.742	0.000
	Residual	20.445	23	0.889		
	Total	62.398	30			
4	Regression	41.844	6	6.974	8.143	0.000
	Residual	20.554	24	0.856		
	Total	62.398	30			
5	Regression	41.423	5	8.285	9.874	0.000
	Residual	20.975	25	0.839		
	Total	62.398	30			
6	Regression	41.076	4	10.269	12.522	0.000
	Residual	21.322	26	0.820		
	Total	62.398	30			
7	Regression	39.795	3	13.265	15.845	0.000
	Residual	22.604	27	0.837		
	Total	62.398	30			

Source: Chadha and Chadda (2020a).

to the improvement of inclusiveness (LDIIG) while investment made on the welfare of the marginalised class (LDWPC) and rural development (LDRD) have shown negative *b*-values (Chadha & Chadda, 2020a).

According to the *b*-values of these variables, an increase of one unit spent on rural development (LDRD) and on the welfare of marginalised classes (LDWPC) will result in a fall in the inclusivity of 2.032 units and 0.30 units, respectively. Ironically, the data show a decrease in inclusiveness despite an increase in welfare spending on rural development (LDRD) and the welfare of marginalised groups (LDWPC). Fan et al. (2000) stated that this is because of the presence of leakages and corrupt practices and also a lack of awareness and education, preventing the benefits from reaching the ground level, and leaving many of the intended poor beneficiaries without these benefits (Thorat & Dubey, 2013). Because of this,

Table 30. Results of Stepwise Regression – Backward Elimination Method of Model 1.

Variables	Steps						
	1	2	3	4	5	6	7
Constant	2.827	3.019	3.118	4.612	5.388	5.234	4.179
LDED	0.272	0.236	0.167	—	—	—	—
	(0.652)	(0.668)	(0.730)				
LDHFW	−0.089	−0.090	—	—	—	—	—
	(0.783)	(0.775)					
LDWSS	−0.064	−0.071	−0.095	−0.833	−0.082	—	—
	(0.731)	(0.689)	(0.532)	(0.413)	(0.526)		
LDHUD	−0.067	—	—	—	—	—	—
	(0.867)						
LDWPC*	**−2.164***	**−2.142***	**−2.079***	**−4.319***	**−1.951***	**−1.954***	**−2.032***
	(0.001)	**(0.001)**	**(0.000)**	**(0.000)**	**(0.000)**	**(0.000)**	**(0.000)**
LDLE	0.116	0.118	0.119	1.119	0.154	0.157	—
	(0.473)	(0.454)	(0.439)	(0.274)	(0.237)	(0.222)	
LDSSW*	**2.650***	**2.597***	**2.542***	**5.180***	**2.513***	**2.523***	**2.646***
	(0.003)	**(0.001)**	**(0.001)**	**(0.000)**	**(0.000)**	**(0.000)**	**(0.000)**
LDRD*	**−0.256**	**−0.256**	**−0.275**	**−1.899**	**−0.284**	**−0.322**	**−0.302***
	(0.181)	**(0.171)**	**(0.171)**	**(0.070)**	**(0.073)**	**(0.028)**	**(0.038)**
LDFSW	−0.115	−0.104	−0.110	−0.701	—	—	—
	(0.521)	(0.523)	(0.523)	(0.490)			

Source: Chadda and Chadda (2020a).

Notes: 1. Figures in parenthesis are *p*-values.

2. *signify that the coefficient is significant at a 5 per cent and the bold values represent that these variables are significant to inclusive growth in the present model.

inclusivity is resisted even as spending on the welfare of underprivileged groups and rural development is rising. Additionally, an increase in social security and welfare (LDSSW) spending by one unit will result in an increase in the inclusiveness of 2.646 units, or more than two times as much inclusiveness (Chadha & Chadda, 2020a).

Collinearity statistics point out the problem of multicollinearity with the help of two measures which are the tolerance level and variation inflation factor (VIF). The tolerance level is $(1-R^2)$. A rule of thumb is that tolerance is less than 0.10 indicating multicollinearity. If the value of VIF is less than 5, then multicollinearity is not serious, if it goes beyond 5, then it is substantial, and a value of more than 10 a quite serious. The condition index must be less than 15 as the rule of thumb (O'Brien, 2007).

Table 31 displays that this model's tolerance values of 0.362 $(1-R^2)$ and 2.762 (1/tolerance limit) imply that multicollinearity is not an issue. There is no multicollinearity in the final model, as shown by the fact that even the values of the condition index are less than 15 (Chadha & Chadda, 2020a).

The unstandardised coefficients shown in Table 32 are deployed in the regression model. The model is explained below:

$$LDIIG_1 = 4.179 + 6.003 \, (LDSSW) - 2.528 \, (LDRD) - 4.726(LDWPC)$$

Inferences from Model 1.   Even though untouchability was formally abolished in India, the model's findings are supported and reinforced by the evidence that social isolation among Dalits is still widespread (Sangeeth, 2016). Panda (2016) emphasised that despite several efforts by the government, 170–200 million Scheduled Castes (SCs)/Scheduled Tribes (STs) – representing 17 per cent of India's population – remain at the bottom of the caste system. Without proper work and educational prospects, many SCs/STs had been living in severe poverty. Because of prejudice and violence, their vulnerability is further highlighted. Under the programmes and policies for the welfare of the marginalised class, only a small proportion of this class receives benefits. The total programmes and schemes for the SC and ST had been scaled back in 2016 from 294 to 256 and 307 to 261, respectively. A total of Rs. 91,863 crores were set aside for SC or 16.6 per cent of the total budget, however, only 4.62 per cent of that money was actually

Table 31.   Collinearity Statistics and Diagnostics of Entered Variables in Model 1.

Variables Entered	Collinearity Statistics		Collinearity Diagnostics	
	Tolerance Level	VIF	Eigen Value	Condition Index
LDWPC	0.831	1.203	1.367	1.000
LDSSW	0.763	1.310	1.010	1.163
LDRD	0.660	1.516	0.624	1.480

Source: Chadha and Chadda (2020a).

Table 32.   Coefficients – Final Model 1.

Model	Unstandardised Coefficients		Standardised Coefficients	*t*-Value	Sig.
	Beta	**Std. Error**	**Beta**		
Constant	4.179	2.305		1.813	0.081
LDWPC	−4.726	1.028	−2.032	−4.596	0.000
LDSSW	6.003	1.006	2.646	5.965	0.000
LDRD	−2.528	1.161	−0.302	−2.177	0.038

Source: Chadha and Chadda (2020a).

spent. Likewise, only 2.32 per cent of Rs. 47,276 crores, or 13.76 per cent, that was allocated during 2015–2016 was dispersed (Chadha & Chadda, 2020a; Divakar, 2017). Thus, increasing expenditure on the welfare of marginalised sections (LDWPC) did not promote inclusive growth in India.

In India, inclusive development is strongly correlated with social security and welfare spending (LDSSW) in the present model. Shivangi (2017) mentioned that there is proof that the programme is benefiting the people who were expected to get it. In the post office and bank accounts, about 76 per cent of beneficiaries received their pension payments. Three new programmes were introduced at the same time in 2015 at 115 different locations across the nation. In a very short amount of time, these programmes, which were primarily directed at India's unorganised sector, reached 10 crore individuals (Chadha & Chadda, 2020a).

A negative and strong association exists between inclusive growth and the funds utilised for rural development (LDRD). Additionally, it was explained by Fan et al. (2000) and Jha and Acharya (2011) that a notable decrease was observed in the amount spent in India on the development of the rural economy. Rural development funding was distributed at a rate of 10.9 per cent in the early 1990s, but in 2016 it was cut to 8 per cent. Because state governments were forced to cut their spending on rural development in order to close the budget deficit, the neoliberal economic framework made the situation considerably worse. The efficacy of programmes specifically created for rural development in reducing rural poverty was little. This limited the effects of rural development (Chadha & Chadda, 2020a).

Central government expenditure as well as state government expenditure incurred on social services and economic services with the purpose of development in India, had augmented in the last decade; yet India's social sector accomplishments are not satisfactory enough and should be subjected to improvement. The government has made various efforts to improve the welfare of disadvantaged groups, yet they still face social and economic marginalisation. Since the disadvantaged sections were denied equitable access to jobs and income-generating opportunities, the existence of disparities hampered the elimination of poverty. All population segments must have equal access to the key components of an inclusive society, including the reduction of poverty, creation of productive jobs,

improved healthcare, opportunities for education, social welfare, and welfare programmes (Chadha & Chadda, 2020a; Mukhopadhaya & Saha, 2005; Shukla &
Mishra, 2013; Thorat & Dubey, 2013).

So, welfare nations like India focus their socio-economic strategy on the
concept of 'development with equity'. Government spending on social sector
development is necessary to make growth inclusive and end poverty and income
redistribution to the populace (Chadha & Chadda, 2020b). Strengthening the
social sector will result in the enhancement of inclusiveness as the social sector
will be pivotal in promoting inclusive growth in India.

Model 1: Nexus Among the Inclusive Growth and the Government Spending on the Different Components of the Social Sector (Auto Regressive Lag Model)

The next part of the study is to examine the association between the index of
inclusiveness and government spending on various social sector components.
This model is based on Kolawole's idea (2016), which looked at the nexus between
government finances and Nigeria's economic growth from 1995 to 2016. Since log
transformation might lessen the issue of heteroscedasticity, all of these series were
converted into a log form:

$$\text{LDIIG}_1 = a + b_{11}\,\text{LDFSW} + b_{12}\,\text{LDRD} + b_{13}\,\text{LDSSW} + b_{14}\,\text{LDLE}$$
$$+ b_{15}\,\text{LDHUD} + b_{16}\,\text{LDWPC} + b_{17}\,\text{LDWSS} + b_{18}\,\text{LDHFW}$$
$$+ b_{19}\,\text{LDED} + U_{1t}$$

Unit Root Tests.   Gujarati (2003) mentioned that data must be analysed to
determine whether each time series is stationary. The stationary of the data is
examined in the current study using the Phillips–Perron (PP) and Augmented
Dickey–Fuller (ADF) tests. The time series assumed that the null hypothesis must
have the unit root present in the series, which was demonstrated by the ADF
and PP tests as being non-stationary. The time series is stationary would be the
alternate hypothesis. When the mean and variance of a series remain constant
throughout time, it is referred to as stationary (Chadha & Chadda, 2020b).

Each time series, with the exception of the two-time series, is determined to
be stationary at the first difference expressly integrated of order one $I(1)$, according to Table 33, which shows that each time series is non-stationary at level $I(0)$.
Water supply and sanitation spending (LDWSS) and investment in the welfare of
the marginalised class (LDWPC) are integrated at $I(0)$. The ADF test suggests
that the time series LDWPC integrated at $I(0)$, but the PP test shows that this
series integrated at order 1. Due to the PP test's robustness, this series is stationary
at $I(1)$ (Chadha & Chadda, 2020b).

**Autoregressive Distributed Lag (ARDL) Model/Bound Testing Approach to
Cointegration.**   An alternative co-integration test is available in the literature and
is better suitable if the variables are integrated with different orders. This test is
called the bounds cointegration test or ARDL model. Pesaran and Shin (1999)
and Pesaran et al. (2001) invented the ARDL cointegration method. The ARDL

Table 33.   Unit Root Test Results of Model 1.

Variables	ADF		PP		Result of ADF and PP		Order of Integration
	At Level	At First Difference	At Level	At First Difference	At Level	At First Difference	
LDIIG	-2.403 (0.150)	-5.370* (0.002)	-2.403 (0.150)	-12.234* (0.000)	Do not reject	Reject null hypothesis	I(1)
LDED	-0.040 (0.947)	-4.906* (0.000)	0.402 (0.979)	-5.336* (0.000)	Do not reject	Reject null hypothesis	I(1)
LDHFW	-1.918 (0.319)	-6.518* (0.000)	-1.761 (0.391)	-9.615* (0.000)	Do not reject	Reject null hypothesis	I(1)
LDWSS	-3.305* (0.024)	—	-8.601* (0.000)	—	Reject null hypothesis	—	I(0)
LDHUD	-0.9164 (0.768)	-5.830* (0.000)	-0.9164 (0.768)	-5.830* (0.000)	Do not reject	Reject null hypothesis	I(1)
LDWPC	-3.578* (0.012)	—	-8.601 (0.08)	-9.568* (0.000)	Do not reject	Reject null hypothesis	I(1)
LDLE	-2.280 (0.184)	-4.201* (0.002)	-2.229 (0.180)	-4.088* (0.003)	Do not reject	Reject null hypothesis	I(1)
LDSSW	-2.718 (0.08)	-5.557* (0.000)	-4.305 (0.08)	-5.643* (0.000)	Do not reject	Reject null hypothesis	I(1)
LDRD	-2.778 (0.07)	-5.955* (0.000)	-2.601 (0.103)	-11.154* (0.000)	Do not reject	Reject null hypothesis	I(1)
LDFSW	-2.665 (0.091)	-5.458* (0.000)	-2.633 (0.097)	-6.528* (0.000)	Do not reject	Reject null hypothesis	I(1)

Source: Chadha and Chadda (2020b).

Note: All these values show test statistics and the probability of test statistics is in parentheses.

model has been found to be the most effective in creating long-term relationships between independent and dependent variables when the variables are not integrated in the same order.

ARDL can be applied to small and finite data. The ARDL technique is relatively important and useful. Kolawole (2016) referred that by using the ARDL technique, it is possible to estimate the short-run and long-run metrics of the model simultaneously. The Wald test, Breusch–Godfrey serial correlation LM test, Breusch–Pagan–Godfrey heteroskedasticity test, Jarque–Bera (JB) normality test, Ramsey RESET test, and lag length selection criteria defined by vector autoregressive (VAR) are the diagnostic tests that must be performed prior to using ARDL (Chadha & Chadda, 2020b).

The empirical models for estimating used in the following respecifications aim to determine the kind, size, and direction of the relationship between inclusive growth and the investment made on the various social sectoral components in India.

Accordingly,

$$\text{LDIIG}_t = f(\text{LDFSW, LDRD, LDSSW, LDWPC, LDLE, LDHUD, LDWSS,}$$
$$\text{LDHFW, LDED})$$

$$\text{LDIIG}_t = \beta_{10} + \beta_{11}\,\text{LDFSW} + \beta_{12}\,\text{LDRD} + \beta_{13}\,\text{LDSSW} + \beta_{14}\,\text{LDWPC} + \beta_{15}$$
$$\text{LDLE} + \beta_{16}\,\text{LDHUD} + \beta_{17}\,\text{LDWSS} + \beta_{18}\,\text{LDHFW} + \beta_{19}\,\text{LDED} + \varepsilon_{1t}$$

By a priori expectation, $\beta_{11},\ldots,\beta_{19} > 0$.

According to Nkoro and Uko (2016), the model must be free of non-normality, autocorrelation, and heteroskedasticity in order to meet the required lag length conditions. The standard normal variance of the error term is therefore suggested for the model. Consequently, in order to choose the right model for the long term, it is required to identify the optimal lag length employing VAR lag length order selection criteria.

For the ARDL model displayed in Table 34, the Akaike information criterion (AIC) and the Schwarz Bayesian criterion both yield an optimal lag of 1. Schwarz criterion (SC) therefore chooses the selected model based on the ARDL (1,0,1,1,1,1,1,1,1,1) with a maximum latency of 1. The cointegration procedure employs the ARDL-bound testing approach. Firstly, both the dependent and independent variables must be compared to perform the ARDL bound testing approach (Chadha & Chadda, 2020b).

Diagnostic Tests.   The Breusch–Godfrey serial correlation LM test, Wald test, JB normality test, heteroskedasticity test by Breusch–Pagan–Godfrey, and Ramsey RESET test must be performed first before using ARDL (Kolawole, 2016).

Wald Test (F-statistic).   Wald test is used to determine the significance of the bound test's parameters (*F*-statistic). The null hypothesis of no cointegration between the variables is presented below. The ARDL bound testing is performed on the Wald test (*F*-statistic), in which the asymptotic distributions are non-standard.

Table 34.   VAR Lag Order Selection Criteria of Model 1.

Sample: 1985–2016				Included observations: 30		
Lag	Log	Likelihood ratio (LR)	FPE	AIC	SC	Hannan–Quinn Criterion
0	−35.83272	NA*	1.422573*	3.160877	3.632358	3.308539
1	−35.30138	0.659584	1.484694	3.193199*	3.711828*	3.355627*
2	−35.18054	0.141682	1.597957	3.253830	3.819608	3.431025

Source: Chadha and Chadda (2020a).

Note: *indicates lag order selected by the criterion.

Null hypothesis $(H_0) = C(1) = C(2) = C(3) = C(4) = C(5) = C(6) = C(7) = C(9)$
$= C(10)=0$

Alternate hypothesis $(H_1) = C(1) \neq C(2) \neq C(3) \neq C(4) \neq C(5) \neq C(6) \neq C(7) \neq C(9)$
$\neq C(10) \neq 0$

Pesaran et al. (1996) explained that the cointegration test requires two sets of critical values. The upper critical bound explains that there is cointegration based on the assumption that all the variables are $I(1)$ while the lower critical bound suggests that all the variables in the model are $I(0)$, which implies that there is no cointegration. At the 95 per cent level, 2.365–3.513 was the pertinent critical value for the upper bound. There is no long-term association between the dependent variable and the independent variables of the model, according to this, if the F-statistic is between these levels (Chadha & Chadda, 2020b).

The null hypothesis, according to which there is no long-run association between the variables, is rejected and is supported by the estimated F-statistic of 4.157, as shown in Table 35. A long-run association between the variables has existed, according to the results of the F-bound test. The findings demonstrate that the model is significant and that the underlying ARDL regression is well-fitted (Chadha & Chadda, 2020b).

Breusch–Godfrey Serial Correlation LM Test.   The Breusch-Godfrey serial correlation LM test, which denies the prevalence of collinearity in the residual, is

Table 35.   Wald Test of Model 1.

Test Statistic	Value	Df	Probability
F-statistic	4.157732	(10,19)	0.0037
χ^2	41.57732	10	0.0000

Source: Chadha and Chadda (2020b).

Null hypothesis: $C(1)=C(2)=C(3)=C(4)=C(5)=C(6)=C(7)=C(9)=C(10)=0$.

the next diagnostic procedure. According to the defined order of lag, there is no serial relationship, based on the model's null hypothesis. This means that there is no autocorrelation if the model is unable to reject the null hypothesis up to the lag value (Kolawole, 2016).

The p-value in Table 36 is more than 0.05 up to the predefined lag of 1, which was chosen by the VAR technique, hence the hypothesis could not be rejected. As a result, the current model lacks autocorrelation (Chadha & Chadda, 2020a).

Breusch–Pagan–Godfrey Test. Here, the Breusch–Pagan–Godfrey test is employed to assess the model's heteroskedasticity. The presence of homoskedasticity in the series is the null hypothesis for this test. As a result, the model's residuals do not exhibit heteroskedasticity if this test fails to reject the null hypothesis (Kolawole, 2016).

Breusch–Pagan–Heteroskedasticity Godfrey's test results are presented in Table 37. The model's null hypothesis is that the variables have a homoskedastic distribution. The heteroskedasticity test's conclusion supported the notion that the model's residuals are not heteroscedastic. Given that the p-values are greater than 0.05, the model includes homoscedasticity (Chadha & Chadda, 2020a).

Ramsey RESET Test. Testing for specification flaws and model linearity is done by using the Ramsey RESET approach. Furthermore, this test also

Table 36.   Breusch–Godfrey Serial Correlation LM Test of Model 1.

F-statistic	0.998469	Prob. $F(1,20)$	0.3296
Obs*R^2	1.474038	Prob. $\chi^2(1)$	0.2247

Test equation:

Dependent variable:RESID

Method: Least squares

Included observation:30

Presample missing value lagged residuals set to zero

Variable	Coefficient	Std. Error	t-Stats (Prob.)
RESID-1	−0.304355	0.304588	−0.99923(0.3296)
R^2	0.047550	Mean dependent var	−1.15E−16
Adjusted R^2	−0.428676	Standard Deviation (S.D.) dependent var	0.829734
Standard Error (S. E.) of regression	0.991758	AIC	3.092747
Sum squared resid	19.67168	SC	3.601582
Log likelihood	−36.93759	Hannan–Quinn criterion	3.258615
F-statistic	0.099847	DW statistic	2.043279
Prob(F-statistic)	0.999661		

Source: Chadha and Chadda (2020a).

Table 37.   Heteroskedasticity Test: Breusch–Pagan–Godfrey of Model 1.

F-statistic	1.492487	Prob. $F(9,21)$	0.2145
Obs*R^2	12.09338	Prob. $\chi^2(9)$	0.2081
Scaled explained SS	27.95779	Prob. $\chi^2 9)$	0.0010

Test equation:

Dependent variable:RESID$^{\wedge}2$

Method:Least squares

Included observation: 30

R^2	0.390109	Mean dependent var	0.666250
Adjusted R^2	0.128727	S.D. dependent var	2.149773
S.E. of regression	2.006641	AIC	4.486498
Sum squared resid	84.55879	SC	4.949075
Log likelihood	−59.54072	Hannan–Quinn criterion	4.637287
F-statistic	1.492487	DW statistic	2.502738
Prob(F-statistic)	0.214529		

Source: Chadha and Chadda (2020a).

showed that the model is well defined by accepting the null hypothesis. There is no need to reject the null hypothesis, according to the RESET F-statistic, which has a p-value of 0.3925. The model's functional form is thus accurately stated (Chadha & Chadda, 2020b; E Views 10, 2017).

The test statistic was not significantly different from zero at the 5 per cent level, as indicated in Table 38, indicating the absence of specification error.

JB Test.   The JB test assumes that the residuals are not normally distributed, which is the null hypothesis of the residuals.

Table 38.   Ramsey RESET Test of Model 1.

Specification: LDIIG₁ C LDED-1 LDHFW-1 LDWSS-1 LDHUD-1 LDWPC-1 LDLE-1 LDSSW-1 LDRD-1 LDFSW-1

Omitted variables: Squares of fitted values

	Value	Df	Probability
t-Statistic	0.873958	20	0.3925
F-statistic	0.763802	(1,20)	0.3925
Likelihood ratio	1.161846	1	0.2811

Source: Chadha and Chadda (2020a).

The null hypothesis is rejected since the *p*-value is greater than the assumed level of significance, as shown in Fig. 2 by the values of the JB test and the *p*-value of 0.5120 and 0.7741. The residuals, therefore, follow a normal distribution. The JB normality test shouldn't be significant if the residuals are uniformly distributed, and the histogram should be bell-shaped (E Views 10, 2017).

The proposed model is shown to be well-specified, normally distributed, has no heteroscedasticity, and is free from collinearity as per the results of diagnostic testing (Chadha & Chadda, 2020a, 2020b).

Inferences of ARDL Results.   The variables that significantly contributed to the model are presented in Table 39. Investments made by Indian government in welfare for marginalised class (LDWPC), housing and urban development (LDHUD), education (LDED), water supply and sanitation (LDWSS), food storage and warehousing' (LDFSW), and social security and welfare (LDSSW) show the significant contributions for the coefficient estimates of the long-run association between growth inclusiveness and social sector development. The proposed model is believed to fit data well at a 5 per cent significance level, according to the *F*-value statistics.

Estimated Short-run and Long-run Coefficients.   The next stage of ARDL is estimating the long-run coefficients of the model. The following formulation of the ARDL equation represents it as a general VAR model of order k in Z_t, where Z_t is a column vector:

$$
\begin{aligned}
\Delta\left(\text{LDIIG}_{1t}\right) = {} & \beta_{10} + \beta_{11}\,\text{LDFSW}_{t-1} + \beta_{12}\,\text{LDRD}_{t-1} + \beta_{13}\,\text{LDSSW}_{t-1} \\
& + \beta_{14}\,\text{LDWPC}_{t-1} + \beta_{15}\,\text{LDLE}_{t-1} + \beta_{16}\,\text{LDHUD}_{t-1} + \beta_{17}\,\text{LDWSS}_{t-1} \\
& + \beta_{18}\,\text{LDHFW}_{t-1} + \beta_{19}\,\text{LDED}_{t-1} + \sum_{j=1}^{k}\beta_{11j}\,\Delta(\text{LDFSW}_{t-1}) \\
& + \sum_{j=1}^{k}\beta_{12j}\,\Delta(\text{LDRD}_{t-1}) + \sum_{j=1}^{k}\beta_{13j}\,\Delta(\text{LDSSW}_{t-1}) \\
& + \sum_{j=1}^{k}\beta_{14j}\,\Delta(\text{LDWPC}_{t-1}) + \sum_{j=1}^{k}\beta_{15j}\,\Delta(\text{LDLE}_{t-1}) \\
& + \sum_{j=1}^{k}\beta_{16j}\,\Delta(\text{LDHUD}_{t-1}) + \sum_{j=1}^{k}\beta_{17j}\,\Delta(\text{LDWSS}_{t-1}) \\
& + \sum_{j=1}^{k}\beta_{18j}\,\Delta(\text{LDHFW}_{t-1}) + \sum_{j=1}^{k}\beta_{19j}\,\Delta(\text{LDED}_{t-1}) + \varepsilon_{1t}
\end{aligned}
$$

where the drift component is represented by the β_{10} and the white noise residual by ε_t, the first difference operator by Δ.

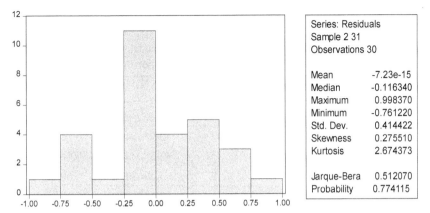

Fig. 2. Normality Test of Model 1. *Source*: Chadha and Chadda (2020a).

Table 40 presents the findings of the long-term association. Spending on water supply and sanitation (LDWSS), education (LDED), and social security and welfare (LDSSW) are variables that are highly associated with inclusiveness, while outlay for housing and development (LDHUD), the welfare of marginalised classes (LDWPC), rural development (LDRD), and food storage and warehousing (LDFSW) are all variables that are found to be negatively related with inclusive growth index. However, the present model does not take into account the expenditures related to labour and employment (LDLE) and public health and family welfare (LDHFW). No association has been found between these variables with inclusivity.

Generating an error correction model variant of the ARDL model stated below yields the function's short-run dynamic parameters:

$$\Delta\left(\text{LDIIG}_{1t}\right) = \sum_{j=1}^{k}\beta_{11j}\,\Delta(\text{LDFSW}_{t-1}) + \sum_{j=1}^{k}\beta_{12j}\,\Delta(\text{LDRD}_{t-1})$$

$$+ \sum_{j=1}^{k}\beta_{13j}\,\Delta(\text{LDSSW}_{t-1}) + \sum_{j=1}^{k}\beta_{14j}\,\Delta(\text{LDWPC}_{t-1})$$

$$+ \sum_{j=1}^{k}\beta_{15j}\,\Delta(\text{LDLE}_{t-1}) + \sum_{j=1}^{k}\beta_{16j}\,\Delta(\text{LDHUD}_{t-1})$$

$$+ \sum_{j=1}^{k}\beta_{17j}\,\Delta(\text{LDWSS}_{t-1}) + \sum_{j=1}^{k}\beta_{18j}\,\Delta(\text{LDHFW}_{t-1})$$

$$+ \sum_{j=1}^{k}\beta_{19j}\,\Delta(\text{LDED}_{t-1}) + \lambda\text{ECT}_{t-1} + \varepsilon_{1t}$$

Table 39.   ARDL Estimates of Model 1.

Model dependent variable is LDIIG

Maximum lags: 1 (Automatic selection by Schwarz Information Criterion)

Selected model: ARDL (1,0,1,1,1,1,1,1,1,1)

Variable	Coefficient	Std. Error	t-Statistic	Prob.
C	−22.26153	7.583947	−2.935349	0.0136
LDIIG-1	0.693411	0.291247	−2.380837	0.0364
LDED*	**11.87008**	**3.414573**	**3.476301**	**0.0052**
LDHFW-1	−3.220027	2.003251	−1.607400	0.1363
LDWSS-1	−4.103541	2.002758	2.048945	0.0510
LDHUD-1*	**−3.487989**	**1..451017**	**−2.403823**	**0.0350**
LDWPC-1*	**−14.30674**	**5.322711**	**−2.687867**	**0.0211**
LDLE-1	1.280770	1.423617	0.899659	0.3876
LDSSW-1*	**17.22862**	**3.336912**	**5.163041**	**0.0003**
LDRD-1*	**−7.411436**	**2.523605**	**−2.936844**	**0.0135**
LDFSW-1*	**−1.103485**	**0.855645**	**−1.289653**	**0.0136**
R^2	0.920159	Mean dependent var		−1.697556
Adjusted R^2	0.789509	S.D. dependent var		1.466659
S.E. of regression	0.672892	AIC		2.308902
Sum squared resid	4.980625	SC		3.196327
Log likelihood	−15.63353	Hannan–Quinn criterion		2.592797
F-statistic	7.042961	DW statistic		2.478961
Prob(F-statistic)	0.001046			

Source: Author's calculation using E VIEWS 10.

Note: *indicates significance of 5 per cent level and the bold values represent that these variables are significant to inclusive growth in the present model.

where λ is the speed of adjustment parameter and ECT is the residual obtained from the above equation.

In accordance with the model's long-run estimates, Table 41 depicts the Estimated error correction mechanism (ECM) results. The dynamic adjustment of all variables is indicated by the short-run coefficients. The spending on labour and employment (LDLE), rural development (LDRD), and food storage and warehousing (LDFSW) have short-run coefficients that are statically significant,

Table 40.   Estimated Long-run Coefficients Using the ARDL Approach of Model 1.

Selected model: ARDL(1,0,1,1,1,1,1,1,1,1)			Dependent variable is LDIIG	
Regressor	**Coefficient**	**Std.Error**	***t*-Statistic**	**Prob**
C	−13.14597	4.331124	−3.035232	0.0113
LDED*	**7.009568**	**1.581388**	**4.43250**	**0.0010**
LDHFW	−3.067318	1.779179	−1.724007	0.1127
LDWSS*	**3.226867**	**1.206817**	**2.673866**	**0.0216**
LDHUD*	**−2.956197**	**0.926919**	**−3.189272**	**0.0086**
LDWPC*	**−8.337210**	**0.871428**	**−9.567292**	**0.0000**
LDLE*	**−1.610020**	**0.749189**	**−2.149015**	**0.0547**
LDSSW*	**9.377670**	**1.241062**	**7.556169**	**0.0000**
LDRD	−1.535984	1.072954	−1.431546	0.1801
LDFSW*	**−2.373608**	**0.564727**	**−4.203111**	**0.0015**

Source: Chadha and Chadda (2020b).

Note: *indicates significance of 5 per cent level and the bold values represent that these variables are significant to inclusive growth in the present model.

with only the outlay incurred on rural development (LDRD) being positively significant, while the investment on labour and employment (LDLE) and food storage and warehousing (LDFSW) are both significantly negative. The relationship between the variables over the long term is implied by the short-run estimations and ECM. These three variables are cointegrated because the coefficient of the error-correcting method is both significant and negative (Chadha & Chadda, 2020b).

The stable long-term association between the variables must have an ECM that is between 0 and −1 in order to be statistically significant and substantial. The optimal ECM value, in this model, is −0.6934. Indicating that inclusive growth in India would deviate from social sector development at a rate of 69 per cent, or within a year, the ECM is 69.34 per cent, which illustrates the speed of correction towards long-run equilibrium.

A positive impact on inclusive growth in India is indicated by the component education, art, and culture (LDED). Increased education spending undoubtedly encourages inclusion in India. Quality education plays a pivotal part in any economic growth strategy. The rise in enrolment rates and decline in school dropouts show that education standards have improved, which is crucial for creating human capital and ensuring that all population segments have equitable access to opportunities (Hanushek, 2013).

Another key factor affecting inclusion is the money used to improve water supply and provide basic sanitation facilities (LDWSS). Healthy and productive people are more engaged in society's progress, which is improved by potable water

Table 41. Estimated Short-run Coefficients Using the ARDL Approach and ECM of Model 1.

Selected model: ARDL(1,0,1,1,1,1,1,1,1,1)			Dependent variable is LDIIG	
Variable	Coefficient	Std.Error	*t*-Statistic	Prob.
D(LDHFW)	−1.974205	1.035754	−1.906055	0.0831
D(LDWSS)	1.360873	0.884626	1.538360	0.1522
D(LDHUD)	−1.518068	0.724446	−2.095489	0.0601
D(LDWPC)	0.188413	1.364174	0.138115	0.8926
D(LDLE)*	**−4.007196**	**0.755739**	**−5.302352**	**0.0003**
D(LDSSW)	−1.348362	1.097311	−1.228787	0.2448
D(LDRD)*	**4.810384**	**1.012484**	**4.751070**	**0.0006**
D(LDFSW)*	**−2.916010**	**0.374467**	**−7.787098**	**0.0000**
ECM (−1)	−0.693411	0.150662	−1.239781	0.0000
R^2	0.894276	Mean dependent var		0.067030
Adjusted R^2	0.854000	S.D. dependent var		−1.274548
S.E. of regression	0.487004	AIC		1.642235
Sum squared resid	4.980625	SC		2.062594
Log likelihood	−15.63353	Hannan–Quinn criterion		1.776712
DW statistic	2.478961			

Source: Chadha and Chadda (2020b).

Note: *indicates significance of 5 per cent level and the bold values represent that these variables are significant to inclusive growth in the present model.

and basic sanitation. Only 30 per cent of the population could receive basic sanitation services and safe drinking water, despite the fact that costs for delivering clean water have been growing up until the Eighth Five Year Plan (Panchamukhi, 2000). So, in order to make it effective, sufficient monitoring must be done.

The increase in social security and welfare spending (LDSSW) would make India more inclusive. Between 1991 and 2015, the budget for social security and welfare climbed from Rs. 1,706.60 crores to Rs. 18,012.54 crores, while consumption rose from Rs. 1,435.53 crores to Rs. 22,107.44 crores, expanding at average rates of 12.25 per cent and 14.60 per cent, respectively. Chadha and Chadda (2016) has observed the slight increasing trend in allocations and spending for social security and welfare was found to have a greater coefficient of variation than those for labour and employment. Due to increased spending on social security and welfare, the findings show that there had been a significant decrease in poverty in India. Rao (2002) also mentioned that benefits from social security were provided to improve and expand people's capacities, adequately protect them from morbidity and mortality, and thereby elevate their quality of life (Rao, 2002).

An increase in spending on housing and urban development (LDHUD) has a weak correlation with inclusivity, according to the findings. The Indian government has introduced a number of housing development-related programmes. Nevertheless, because there was insufficient surveillance and cooperation from the government, the 'Housing for All' mission had been collapsing in India. Beneficiaries reported that despite verification, funds were not received by local entities to disburse to them (Sagar, 2018). Daramsot (2018) mentioned that in addition to the intended beneficiaries, there were a number of illegal recipients who received the benefits. To ensure that the advantages reach the underprivileged groups in society, authorities should work carefully.

In India, inclusive growth is negatively correlated with the variable expenditure on the welfare of underprivileged classes (LDWPC). The lack of real empowerment of marginalised groups, especially women, is one of the main causes of this delayed progress towards inclusivity. Segments of the population who are marginalised and underprivileged have not yet had access to all of the regulatory and legal resources needed to obtain access to healthcare and education. Similarly, despite having the skills and qualifications necessary for full-time employment, women have been denied their full involvement in decision-making at the political and home levels as a result of institutional and societal constraints (Zohir, 2011).

Thorat (2011) explained that due to widespread societal bias against the marginalised classes, the disadvantaged and marginalised groups were kept out of the redistribution or profit-sharing process. As a result, their ability to contribute to development was hindered, which reduces growth's capacity for inclusivity. To make progress more inclusive, attention should be paid not only to the underprivileged classes but also to other excluded groups. De-notified tribal groups, semi-peripatetic tribes, primitive tribal classes, differently abled individuals, widows, elderly people, those who had been relocated within their own country, those who were HIV/AIDS positive, and those who had consumed drugs or alcohol, needed greater attention. It would encourage inclusive growth to close this widening gap (Ponmuthusaravanan & Ravi, 2014).

In India, inclusive growth and expenditure on labour and employment (LDLE) are inversely correlated in the present study. The reason for this is that while these operations improved the infrastructure and increased the share of employment in the construction sector alone, they also reduced the amount of available productive jobs. Although the employment share in the manufacturing and service sectors shrank as a result of the reduction in the workforce in agriculture, employment growth increased in the construction sector.

Additionally, it has been observed that investment in rural development (LDRD) has a negative relationship with inclusive growth. This is due to the government's overwhelming preference for urban expansion and increased focus on capital-intensive industries, which results in the neglect of the rural economy (Chand et al., 2017).

Inclusion in India is found to be adversely correlated with expenditure on food storage and warehousing (LDFSW) of this model. The targeted public distribution system (TPDS) implementation encountered a number of problems, including the identification of households who qualified for assistance, problems with the procurement process relative to the production of food grains, a lack of storage capacity for these commodities, food subsidies, and grain leakage. This meant that people who were not eligible for the benefits were receiving unfair benefits while the eligible recipients were not receiving food supplies. Large-scale food grain leakages into and out of ration stores and into the open market occurred during transportation, which was the main issue with TPDS. These kinds of leaks and corruption impeded inclusive progress (Balani, 2014).

Increased spending on the welfare of underprivileged sections (LDWPC), food storage and warehousing (LDFSW), and housing and urban development (LDHUD) have not contributed to inclusive growth in India. Despite deviating from expectations, the sign coefficient illustrates the underlying nature of government-sponsored social schemes and programmes (Chadha & Chadda, 2020a). Hasnul (2016) observed that the inappropriate and ineffectual use of funds is the reason for the negative correlation between government spending and inclusiveness in India. This is true because there are numerous leaks and unethical practices, as well as a lack of awareness and visibility, which prevent the benefits from reaching the grass root levels. Therefore, growth is not inclusive. The decision-makers could develop an environment that is favourable to encouraging government spending in order to improve inclusive growth in India with the aid of laws and programmes (Chadha & Chadda, 2020b).

Model 2: Relationship Between Physical Components of the Social Sector and Inclusive Growth (Regression Analysis)

Studying the effects of various physical social sector components on India's inclusive growth composite index (LDIIG) is the second model. By using log differences of independent and dependent variables, this model has also been prepared. Natural log transformations are preferred (Gujarati, 2003).

SPSS has been used to run the regression estimations. The developed model is displayed below:

$$\ln Y^* = a + b_1 \ln(X^*) + U_t$$

$$\text{Here, } \ln Y^* = \ln(Y_{i,t} - Y_{i,t-1})$$

$$b_1 \ln(X^*) = b_1 \ln(X_{i,t} - X_{i,t-1})$$

ln is the natural logarithm.

Social Sector Components as Independent Variables.   The next step is to identify the independent variables under different social sector components so that the most significant variables affecting inclusive growth can find out. The variables have been identified based on a review of the vast literature available and due care has been taken to consider the relevant variables for the present model.

The variables that have been chosen to fulfil the objectives of the study are as follows:

- ➤ *Education, sports, art, and culture*:
  - Gross enrolment ratio (LDGER).
  - Pupil teacher ratio (LDPTR).
- ➤ *Medical and public health and family welfare*:
  - The number of beds available per 1,000 people (LDBED).
  - The number of doctors available per 1,000 people (LDDR).
  - The number of health centres available per 1,000 people (LDHC).
  - The percentage of people who recovered from an illness under the category of epidemiology out of the general population (LDPRE).
  - The proportion of vaccinated children in the target child population (LDCI).
- ➤ *Water supply and sanitation*:
  - Percentage of the population access to potable water (LDPPW).
  - Percentage of the population who have availability of toilets (LDPAT).
  - Percentage of the population served by sewage treatment (LDPST).
- ➤ *Housing and urban development:*
  - Percentage of population covered under Economically Weaker Section (EWS) and Low Income Group (LIG) housing scheme out of a targeted population (LDBH).
- ➤ *The welfare of underprivileged classes:*
  - Number of beneficiaries covered under different welfare schemes (LDBWS).
- ➤ *Labour and employment:*
  - Number of construction workers employed (LDCW).
- ➤ *Social security and welfare:*
  - Number of beneficiaries insured under employee state insurance scheme (LDBEN).
  - Number of beneficiaries covered under social security benefits (LDBSS).
- ➤ *Rural development:*
  - Percentage of the population's access to electricity in rural areas (LDPER).
  - Road constructed in rural areas out of total roads constructed (LDR).
  - Rural food consumption expenditure out of total expenditure (LDRF).
  - Rural literacy rate (LDRL).
  - Rural poverty (LDRP).
- ➤ *Food storage and warehousing:*
  - Food grains procured by Food Corporation of India (FCI) (lakhs tons) (LDPFG).

Deb (2017) studied the impact of social development on economic growth. For this purpose, the study constructed a multi-dimensional social development index of 29 states and union territories of India. The six main dimensions to construct the index were selected namely demographic dimension, health dimension, education dimension, basic amenities, economic dimension, and social dimension. Furthermore, these dimensions are represented by a sub-set of indicators like disparity ratio in literacy rates of underprivileged classes, contraceptive prevalence rate, literacy rate, infant mortality rate, households that live in the pucca house, percentage of institutional deliveries, pupil–teacher ratio, toilet facility, school attendance rate, unemployment rate, households which have access to safe drinking water, head-count rate, total fertility rate, households have electricity connection, monthly per capita expenditure, educational and employment deprivation of underprivileged classes, and percentage of undernourished children.

The model is shown as follows:

$$\text{LDIIG}_2{}^* = a + \sum_{i=1}^{k} \ln_e X_{it}{}^* + U_{2t}$$

Here, LDIIG_2 is the inclusive growth index; X_{it}, the components of social sector; a, the intercept; k, the number of independent variables; t, the time; and U_t the white noise disturbance term.

For this model also, backward multiple stepwise regression is deployed, showing the significant variables of this model. Table 42 highlights 10 variables entered for Model 2. Here, 'gross enrolment ratio' (LDGER), 'number of beds available per 1,000 population' (LDBED), 'Percentage of patients recovered under epidemiological diseases out of total population' (LDPRE), 'percentage of population access to potable water' (LDPPW), 'number of beneficiaries covered housing scheme under EWS and LIG' (LDBH), 'number of beneficiaries covered under different welfare schemes' (LDBWS), 'number of beneficiaries insured under insurance scheme' (LDBEN), 'rural food consumption' (LDRF), 'rural poverty' (LDRP), and 'food grains procured by FCI' (LDPFG), in the proposed model, contributed to India's inclusive growth.

The next table elaborates on the important components of the model. In the second model, several variables which constitute social sector components are used as a predictor. The backward regression method serially removes the variables one by one which does not contribute significantly to the model and comes with the final model.

Here, in Table 43, model 12th is the final model by retaining 10 variables to pursue further work. The correlation between the final components and inclusiveness is 0.944, that is, 99.4 per cent. R^2 explains the variability in inclusiveness in India. Here, the R^2 for the 10 significant variables is 0.892, that is, 89.2 per cent. Adjusted R^2 is accounted for the fitness of the model and in this model, Adjusted R^2 is 0.835, that is, 83.5 per cent. For the autocorrelation, DW is preferable which should be between 1.5 and 2.5 values and in the present model, DW statistic value is 2.497.

Table 44 reveals the ANOVA test of Model 2. The ANOVA test of Model 2 shows that the F-value of Model 1 is 10.635, indicating the significance of the model. The value of the F-statistic of model 12th has been increased and is greater than from the successive models as the insignificant variables keep on removing from the model shown in Table 42. The F-ratio of the resulting model is 15.663 with a significant p-value. So, this model has significantly improved the ability to predict the outcome.

Table 45 displays the parameters of the Model 2. Here in the table, it has been observed that step by step insignificant variables are removed from the selected model, and a model where all the parameters make a significant contribution to inclusiveness becomes apparent.

Table 42.   Variable Entered/Removed as Per Backward Elimination Method in Model 2.

Models	Variables Entered	Variables Removed	Method
1	LDGER, LDPTR, LDBED, LDDR, LDHC, LDCI, LDPPW, LDPAT, LDPST, LDBH, LDBWS, LDCW, LDBEN, LDPER, LDR, LDRL, LDRP, LDPFG, LDRF, LDPRE, LDBSS		Enter
2		LDBSS	Backward (criterion: probability of F-to-remove ≥ 0.100)
3		LDDR	Backward (criterion: probability of F-to-remove ≥ 0.100)
4		LDCW	Backward (criterion: probability of F-to-remove ≥ 0.100)
5		LDPER	Backward (criterion: probability of F-to-remove ≥ 0.100)
6		LDCI	Backward (criterion: probability of F-to-remove ≥ 0.100)
7		LDPAT	Backward (criterion: probability of F-to-remove ≥ 0.100)
8		LDRL	Backward (criterion: probability of F-to-remove ≥ 0.100)
9		LDPST	Backward (criterion: probability of F-to-remove ≥ 0.100)
10		LDPTR	Backward (criterion: probability of F-to-remove ≥ 0.100)
11		LDR	Backward (criterion: probability of F-to-remove ≥ 0.100)
12		LDHC	Backward (criterion: probability of F-to-remove ≥ 0.100)

Source: Author's calculation using IBM SPSS Statistics 21.

The 10 significant variables entered are shown together with their *b*-values and *p*-values. As per the results 'gross enrolment ratio' (LDGER) has the highest impact followed by rural food consumption expenditure' (LDRF); 'access to potable water' (LDPPW); 'beneficiaries receiving benefits under social security and welfare' (LDBEN); 'beneficiaries receiving benefits under marginalised classes' (LDBWS) and lastly 'patients recovered under epidemiological disease'

Table 43.   Summary of Model 2.

Model	R	R^2	Adjusted R^2	Std. Error of the Estimate	DW
1	0.983	0.965	0.875	0.4513	2.497
2	0.982	0.964	0.884	0.4339	
3	0.981	0.962	0.890	0.4228	
4	0.978	0.957	0.886	0.4300	
5	0.974	0.948	0.874	0.4519	
6	0.967	0.936	0.856	0.4830	
7	0.966	0.933	0.862	0.4731	
8	0.965	0.931	0.867	0.4642	
9	0.961	0.923	0.860	0.4775	
10	0.955	0.911	0.849	0.4953	
11	0.951	0.904	0.845	0.5011	
12	0.944	0.892	0.835	0.5180	

Source: Author's calculation using IBM SPSS Statistics 21.

Table 44.   ANOVA Test of Model 2.

Model		Sum of Squares	Df	Mean Square	F	Sig.
1	Regression	45.481	21	2.166	10.635	0.001
	Residual	1.629	8	0.204		
	Total	47.110	29			
2	Regression	45.416	20	2.271	12.064	0.000
	Residual	1.694	9	0.188		
	Total	47.110	29			
3	Regression	45.322	19	2.385	13.342	0.000
	Residual	1.788	10	0.179		
	Total	47.110	29			
4	Regression	45.076	18	2.504	13.542	0.000
	Residual	2.034	11	0.185		
	Total	47.110	29			
5	Regression	44.659	17	2.627	12.864	0.000
	Residual	2.451	12	0.204		
	Total	47.110	29			

Table 44. (*Continued*)

Model		Sum of Squares	Df	Mean Square	F	Sig.
6	Regression	44.077	16	2.755	11.810	0.000
	Residual	3.032	13	0.233		
	Total	47.110	29			
7	Regression	43.976	15	2.932	13.097	0.000
	Residual	3.134	14	0.224		
	Total	47.110	29			
8	Regression	43.877	14	3.134	14.541	0.000
	Residual	3.233	15	0.216		
	Total	47.110	29			
9	Regression	43.462	13	3.343	14.663	0.000
	Residual	3.648	16	0.228		
	Total	47.110	29			
10	Regression	42.939	12	3.578	14.586	0.000
	Residual	4.171	17	0.245		
	Total	47.110	29			
11	Regression	42.589	11	3.872	15.416	0.000
	Residual	4.521	18	0.251		
	Total	47.110	29			
12	Regression	42.013	10	4.201	15.663	0.000
	Residual	5.096	19	0.268		
	Total	47.110	29			

Source: Author's calculation using IBM SPSS Statistics 21.

(LDPRE). Variables like 'percentage of population covered under EWS and LIG housing scheme' (LDBH), 'food grains procured by FCI' (LDPFG), 'number of beds available per 1,000 population' (LDBED), and 'rural poverty' (LDRP) have negative beta values.

These beta values suggest that a 1 unit increase in 'patients recovered under epidemiological disease' (LDPRE), 'beneficiaries receiving benefits under marginalised classes' (LDBWS), 'beneficiaries receiving benefits under social security and welfare' (LDBEN), 'access to potable water' (LDPPW), 'gross enrolment ratio' (LDGER), and 'rural food consumption expenditure' (LDRF) will augment 0.32, 0.37, 0.42, 0.43, 0.55, and 0.89 units in inclusiveness, respectively. Variables like 'rural poverty' (LDRP); 'percentage of population covered under EWS

Table 45. Results of Stepwise Regression – Backward Elimination Method of Model 2.

Variables	Steps											
	1	2	3	4	5	6	7	8	9	10	11	12
Constant	-2.382	-2.793	-2.802	-3.190	-3.215	-1.998	-1.689	-1.779	-1.961	-2.042	-2.023	-2.033
	(0.090)	(0.017)	(0.013)	(0.004)	(0.005)	(0.007)	(0.001)	(0.000)	(0.000)	(0.000)	(0.000)	(0.000)
LDGER*	**0.686***	**0.748***	**0.797***	**0.769***	**0.748***	**0.629***	**0.601***	**0.621***	**0.630***	**0.617***	**0.579***	**0.546***
	(0.006)	**(0.001)**	**(0.000)**	**(0.000)**	**(0.000)**	**(0.000)**	**(0.000)**	**(0.000)**	**(0.000)**	**(0.000)**	**(0.000)**	**(0.000)**
LDPTR	0.193	0.238*	0.255*	0.256*	0.219*	0.166	0161	0.165	0.128	—	—	—
	(0.161)	(0.031)	(0.016)	(0.015)	(0.032)	(0.089)	(0.089)	(0.076)	(0.150)			
LDBED*	**-0.186**	**-0.183**	**-0.219***	**-0.206**	**-0.274***	**-0.218***	**-0.230***	**-0.232***	**-0.218***	**-0.236***	**-0.235***	**-0.240***
	(0.151)	**(0.139)**	**(0.049)**	**(0.061)**	**(0.011)**	**(0.033)**	**(0.021)**	**(0.017)**	**(0.025)**	**(0.019)**	**(0.020)**	**(0.020)**
LDDR	0.099	0.065	—	—	—	—	—	—	—	—	—	—
	(0.406)	(0.498)										
LDHC	-0.205	-0.236	-0.254	-0.275*	-0.247	-0.234	-0.203	-0.233*	-0.244*	0.193	-0.160	—
	(0.176)	(0.086)	(0.054)	(0.038)	(0.064)	(0.093)	(0.107)	(0.045)	(0.041)	(0.092)	(0.147	
LDPRE*	**-0.308***	**0.289***	**0.288***	**0.311***	**0.355***	**0.338***	**0.321***	**0.336***	**0.313***	**0.332***	**0.350***	**0.316***
	(0.019)	**(0.015)**	**(0.012)**	**(0.006)**	**(0.002)**	**(0.004)**	**(0.004)**	**(0.002)**	**(0.003)**	**(0.002)**	**(0.001)**	**(0.003)**
LDCI	-0.198	-0.283	-0.308	-0.302	-0.307	—	—	—	—	—	—	—
	(0.431)	(0.148)	(0.101)	(0.109)	(0.117)							
LDPPW*	**0.419***	**0.420***	**0.412***	**0.469***	**0.447***	**0.435***	**0.421***	**0.417***	**0.372***	**0.416***	**0.419***	**0.428***
	(0.005)	**(0.003)**	**(0.003)**	**(0.000)**	**(0.001)**	**(0.001)**	**(0.001)**	**(0.001)**	**(0.001)**	**(0.000)**	**(0.000)**	**(0.000)**
LDPAT	0.402	0.610	0.751	0.785*	0.909	0.186	—	—	—	—	—	—
	(0.562)	(0.280)	(0.148)	(0.000)	(0.096)	(0.521)						
LDPST	-0.355	-0.373	-0.440	-0.484	-0.537	-0.237	-0.134	-0.153	—	—	—	—
	(0.240)	(0.198)	(0.101)	(0.074)	(0.057)	(0.247)	(0.266)	(0.186)				

LDBH*	**−0.475***	**−0.493***	**−0.501***	**−0.523***	**−0.534***	**−0.504***	**−0.485***	**−0.483***	**−0.464***	**0.461***	**−0.464***	**−0.443***
	(0.001)	(0.000)	(0.000)	(0.000)	(0.000)	(0.000)	(0.000)	(0.000)	(0.000)	(0.000)	(0.000)	(0.000)
LDBWS*	**0.283**	**0.232**	**0.193**	**0.238***	**0.241***	**0.298***	**0.311***	**0.327***	**0.317***	**0.318***	**0.356***	**0.370***
	(0.104)	**(−0.085)**	(0.092)	(0.033)	(0.037)	(0.013)	(0.008)	(0.004)	(0.005)	(0.006)	(0.002)	(0.001)
LDCW	−0.079	−0.094	−0.105	—	—	—	—	—	—	—	—	—
	(0.451)	(0.338)	(0.268)									
LDBSS	−0.107	—	—	—	—	—	—	—	—	—	—	—
	(0.588)											
LDBEN*	**0.582***	**0.589***	**0.638***	**0.677***	**0.711***	**0.565***	**0.547***	**0.577***	**0.555***	**0.530***	**0.482***	**0.417***
	(0.010)	(0.006)	(0.001)	(0.001)	(0.001)	(0.001)	(0.001)	(0.000)	(0.000)	(0.000)	(0.001)	(0.000)
LDPER	0.147	0.179	0.149	0.156	—	—	—	—	—	—	—	—
	(0.290)	(0.149)	(0.177)	(0.162)								
LDR	0.293	0.339	0.381*	0.399*	0.376*	0.137	0.116	0.134	0.159	0.104	—	—
	(0.184)	(0.086)	(0.040)	(0.033)	(0.049)	(0.208)	(0.248)	(0.161)	(0.102)	(0.249)		
LDRL	−0.257	−0.348	−0.398	−0.366	−0.383	−0.133	−0.097	—	—	—	—	—
	(0.380)	(0.140)	(0.073)	(0.095)	(0.093)	(0.418)	(0.516)					
LDRF*	**1.070***	**1.008***	**1.007***	**0.984***	**0.974***	**−1.064***	**1.071***	**1.045***	**0.979***	**0.946***	**0.942***	**0.893***
	(0.000)	(0.000)	(0.000)	(0.000)	(0.000)	(0.000)	(0.000)	(0.000)	(0.000)	(0.000)	(0.000)	(0.000)
LDRP*	**−1.274***	**−1.280***	**−1.281***	**−1.307***	**−1.337***	**−1.282***	**−1.270***	**−1.270***	**−1.247***	**−1.275***	**−1.290***	**−1.300***
	(0.000)	(0.000)	(0.000)	(0.000)	(0.000)	(0.000)	(0.000)	(0.000)	(0.000)	(0.000)	(0.000)	(0.000)
LDPFG*	**−0.403**	**−0.480***	**−0.474***	**−0.540***	**−0.490***	**−0.355***	**−0.301***	**−0.332***	**−0.360***	**−0.355***	**−0.377***	**−0.393***
	(0.091)	(0.012)	(0.010)	(0.003)	(0.005)	(0.016)	(0.008)	(0.001)	(0.001)	(0.001)	(0.000)	(0.000)

Source: Author's calculation using IBM SPSS Statistics 21.

Notes: 1. Figures in parenthesis are *p*-values.

2. *signify that coefficient is significant at 5 per cent and the bold values represent that these variables are significant to inclusive growth in the present model.

and LIG housing scheme' (LDBH), 'food grains procured by FCI' (LDPFG), and 'number of beds available per 1,000 population' (LDBED) will cause a decline of 1.30, 0.44, 0.39, and 0.24 units in inclusiveness, respectively.

Thus, it can be stated that in terms of physical performance of the social sector, the most significant and positive contributions, are 'gross enrolment rate' (LDGER), 'number of patients recovered under epidemiological diseases' (LDPRE), 'access to have clean and potable water to the masses' (LDPAT), 'increased number of eligible beneficiaries of marginalised classes' (LDBWS), 'rising benefits of insurance scheme as social security' (LDBEN), and 'more expenditure incurred on food consumption by people of rural areas' (LDRF) would positively towards inclusive growth in India.

The variables that contribute negatively and significantly to inclusiveness in India are the 'number of beds available per 1,000 population' (LDBED), 'number of beneficiaries covered under housing scheme under EWS and LIG' (LDBH), 'growing rural poverty' (LDRP), and 'food procured by Government of India' (LDPFG).

Collinearity diagnosis helps obtain the tolerance level and the VIF. Table 46 depicts that all the variables entered in the model show a tolerance level of more than 0.10. VIF should be less than 5, and here, all variables indicate the VIF less than 5. The condition index of the variables is less than 15, as per the rule of thumb. This ensures that there is no multicollinearity in the model.

The regression model using the unstandardised coefficients can be an inference from Table 47. The model is:

Table 46.   Collinearity Statistics and Diagnostics of Entered Variables in Model 2.

Variables Entered	Collinearity Statistics		Collinearity Diagnostics	
	Tolerance Level	VIF	Eigen Value	Condition Index
LDGER	0.540	1.853	1.941	1.423
LDBED	0.632	1.582	1.422	1.662
LDPRE	0.685	1.459	1.009	1.974
LDPPW	0.623	1.606	0.767	2.264
LDBH	0.699	1.431	0.694	2.380
LDBWS	0.572	1.747	0.458	2.930
LDBEN	0.459	2.179	0.353	3.338
LDRF	0.538	1.860	0.172	4.784
LDRP	0.410	2.439	0.223	4.198
LDPFG	0.714	1.400	0.031	11.303

Source: Author's calculation using IBM SPSS Statistics 21.

Table 47.   Coefficients – Final Model 2.

Model	Unstandardised Coefficients		Standardised Coefficients	*t*-Value	Sig.
	Beta	**Std. Error**	**Beta**		
Constant	−2.033	0.396		−5.139	0.000
LDGER	26.663	5.014	0.546	5.318	0.000
LDBED	−2.498	0.987	−0.240	−2.532	0.020
LDPRE	9.883	2.840	0.316	3.463	0.003
LDPPW	130.248	29.121	0.428	4.473	0.000
LDBH	−0.709	0.145	−0.443	−4.906	0.000
LDBWS	5.131	1.384	0.370	3.707	0.001
LDBEN	4.557	1.218	0.417	3.740	0.001
LDRF	12.099	1.097	0.893	8.677	0.000
LDRP	−96.131	11.079	−1.300	−11.027	0.000
LDPFG	−2.097	0.477	−0.393	−4.396	0.000

Source: Author's calculation using IBM SPSS Statistics 21.

Inclusive growth's index $(LDIIG_2) = (− 0.2.033) + 26.663$ (LDGER) − 2.498 (LDBED) + 9.883 (LDPRE) + 130.248 (LDPPW) − 0.709 (LDBH) + 5.131 (LDBWS) + 4.557 (LDBEN) + 12.099 (LDRF) − 96.131 (LDRP) − 2.097 (LDPFG)

Inferences from Model 2. The first variable is the 'gross enrolment rate' (LDGER) which has a positive and significant relation with inclusive growth as shown in Table 47. The Government of India has made many attempts to provide and improve the quality of education for all diverse sections of the country. There had been significant growth in the number of students enrolled in various educational classes, including primary school, higher school, university education, skills training, and vocational and technical education. At the time of independence, it was observed that a small number of the population (14 per cent) was literate. Several efforts have been put in by the government to improve education which further leads to fulfilling the basic requirements after obtaining employment. For this purpose, the concept of universal education for all age groups has become significant as a fundamental contribution to nation-building and acceleration of economic development. The enrolment in all levels of education since independence had been substantially increased, which, evidently indicates the development of the country (Sachdeva, 2013).

Education plays a significant contribution to human development; an increased number of enrolments in the different levels of education have importantly resulted in the outcome of the reduction in poverty (Tilak, 2005).

The next variable is the 'number of hospitals beds available in India' (LDBED), indicating a negative relation with inclusive growth in India. Kalnad et al. (2017) explained that to meet the needs of the expanding population, India's current health infrastructure is insufficient. According to the Indian Government Health and Family Welfare Report (2017), the central and state governments had funded free medical care and basic medications at government hospitals under universal healthcare. However, these hospitals were still found to be understaffed and the number of hospital beds had not been quite enough for the Indian population. The ratio of hospital beds per 1,000 population has been 1.3 much lower than the guideline of 3.5 hospital beds to a 1,000 population in India. Despite adding one lakh hospital beds annually, it failed to achieve the requirement (Sharma, 2017).

'Increasing number of people recovered under different epidemiological diseases' (LDPRE) has become a positive and significant contributor to inclusive growth in India. Gupte et al. (2001) explained that there had been the eradication of diseases like smallpox, plague, poliomyelitis, measles, and diphtheria with the implementation of many government national programmes. Effective surveillance machinery is established for the diseases like leprosy, HIV/AIDS, tuberculosis, and malaria so that these become vehicles for an efficient disease surveillance system for the country in the future. The government introduced numerous health measures effectively and efficiently in the country, and as a result, the losses due to diseases like leprosy and polio were reduced significantly. However; infectious diseases like HIV/AIDS, tuberculosis, and malaria prevalence are still escalating.

The next variable is 'access to potable water' (LDPPW), which contributes positively to the model. As per the Department of Drinking Water Supply (DDWS), 70.5 per cent of rural inhabitants and 77 per cent of urban habitats are covered by the drinking water supply in India. The Indian government has been attempting to follow the novel modern legal mechanism to ensure that every village, town, and city in the country must have a potable water supply. The problem was insufficient water supply availability to different areas (Government of India, 2005). Noga and Wolbring (2012) stated that all the masses, especially those who suffered from social exclusion, must have access to potable water, sufficient in both quantity and quality even-handed access to water. Furthermore, as per the United Nations Special Report (2012), Millennium Development Goals (MDG) (2015) development agenda should be universal access to potable and clean water for the whole country. There must be an improvement in framing the methodology like monitoring inequalities related to age, religion, gender, disability, and social classes using the public facilities.

The variable 'number of beneficiaries receiving the benefits under the housing scheme of EWS and LIG' (LDBH) is contributing negatively towards inclusiveness in India. Menon (2009) confirmed that the trend of EWS and LIG shows a decreasing trend indicating that there had been a shortfall of houses under these schemes. The population living in urban slum areas is still increasing without any accommodation. The shortage of approximately 2.5 crore dwelling units under the EWS and LIG housing scheme was observed. Because of the growing migration of workers from rural to urban areas or from the agrarian economy to industrialisation, this deficit is still exhibiting an upward pattern. Hence, decreasing this shortfall would increase the availability of housing units which further contribute to more inclusiveness in India.

The next variable is the 'number of beneficiaries covered under welfare of marginalised classes' (LDBWS) indicates a positive relationship with inclusiveness.

> Government of India (2006) mentioned in the report of the National Confederation of Dalit Organisations (NACDOR) that SCs/STs were still facing social, economic, and political exclusion. It was cited that, in India, 37.8 percent of village SCs/STs students were not allowed to sit with other caste students in government schools. Furthermore, 27.6 percent and 25.7 percent of Indian village's barred SCs/STs from entering police stations and ration shops, respectively. Public Health workers in villages had declined to visit marginalized class houses and the number is 33 percent. In 14.4 percent of the villages, SCs/STs were not allowed to enter panchayat buildings and even more, 48.4 percent of the SCs/STs were denied access to water sources. In 25 percent of villages, SCs/STs had been paid lower wages than non-SCs/STs. They worked for long hours and had more delayed wages as compared to other castes. Dalits also suffered from verbal and physical abuse at their workplace. In addition to this, 64 percent and 50 percent SCs/STs had been restricted from entering Hindu temples and cremation grounds, and 73 percent of villages in India, did not permit SCs/STs to enter non-SCs/STs houses. (Pradhan, 2004)

Lal (2014) recommended that education will be an important parameter for the promotion of the economic interests of deprived sections and downtrodden sections of society. Among the school drop-outs, Dalits left the school because of the abusive behaviour and the negligible attitude towards them. With positive and equal participation and involvement, many existing financial and physical problems could have resorted. Hence, a systematic, accountable, and transparent approach has to be followed to have the desired output.

'Beneficiaries covered under social security and welfare' (LDBEN) positively contributed towards inclusive growth in India. Good social protection policies have always been consistent with the growth process. Both the central and state governments had initiated several social security and welfare programmes like the National Social Assistance Program, Employee State Insurance Programmes, and other social security schemes. These social security and pension schemes covered the significant support of the programmes to old-aged persons, widows, and employees. There has been a strong association between social security schemes and the protection of working conditions and rights at work for employees (Government of India, 2013). Srivastava (2013) highlighted that the government expenditure on major social security and welfare programmes had increased in the last decade. This study pointed out that the creation of more social protection schemes would lead to more inclusiveness and sustainability. Through the expansion of this approach, the generation of a long-term basis for equity and inclusiveness in India would be achieved.

'Rural food consumption expenditure' (LDRF) also acted as a significant variable for inclusive growth in India. Rural India has been a major consumer of goods and services as 55 per cent of the overall consumption came from rural India. The food consumption expenditure by the rural population has shown an increasing trend ensuring growth. Chakravarty (2017) mentioned that as per the current National Sample Survey Office (NSSO) survey report, the 40–50th percentile of rural India spent Rs. 659.1 per head per month on food as compared to the bottom 5 per cent who spent Rs. 315.84 per head per month. The urban richest (5 per cent) spend more on food compared to rural people. Rural consumption is positively associated with rural incomes. So, measures should be adopted to enhance a crop's minimum support price (MSP) is set at 1.5 times its production cost (Malviya, 2018).

'Rural poverty' (LDRP) is negatively related to inclusive growth in India. If there will be an increase in the poverty rate in rural areas then less will be inclusiveness in India. So, eradicating poverty in rural areas would result in more inclusive growth in India. Reducing chronic poverty is the main challenge and hence, to make growth inclusive, it is necessary to reduce poverty. Policies framed for reducing poverty should be in conjunction with growth-oriented policies, which will ensure broad-based per capita income growth and then the benefits of the growth would percolate to the downtrodden members of society (Thomas & Chittedi, 2015). Ghosh (2010) suggested that improved agricultural performance had been related to the reduction in rural poverty, affirming that the benefits of agricultural growth percolated the poor but at a marginal pace. Rural poverty could not be eliminated only by agricultural growth but increasing productive employment opportunities and escalation in wage rate also.

'Food grains procured by FCI' (LDPFG) also show a significant impact but are negatively related to inclusive growth in India. 'Food grain procurement is the product of output and procurement prices.' It had been observed that food grain outcome decreased by 6 per cent while procurement increased by 5 per cent in the year 2000–2001. Though food grain procurement had indicated an increasing trend this was not linked with the growth of food grain output. An increase in MSPs at a diminishing rate is one of the significant reasons for less growth. Though the output had been increasing as well as MSPs the scenario of an increase in other costs was observed. This continuous increase in the cost indicated low inclusiveness in India. The reduction in public investment along with the rising subsidies is also the reason responsible for low inclusiveness growth in India (Gaiha & Kulkarni, 2005).

The public distribution system (PDS) was set up by the government as an institutional mechanism. This system first procured grains and rice from the farmers, then this procured food was provided to another government mechanism, that is, fair price shops. The poor masses with the proper identification proof could buy this subsided food at a discounted price. As per the NSSO (2000) report, 11.3 per cent and 5.7 poor households accessed rice and wheat from the PDS system. The government claimed that only 29 per cent of wheat and rice are distributed via PDS (Bhalla, 2011).

There existed a two-way relationship between the social sector and inclusive growth. It is the social sector development that ensures human development via improving the quality of life of the people that helps to eradicate poverty, ultimately aiming for promoting inclusive growth and economic development. Therefore, to ensure that growth is inclusive, the development of the social sector must result in better health outcomes, universal access to education for children, skill development, more employment opportunities, and improved essential services like water, power, roads, sanitation, and housing (Ponmuthusaravanan & Ravi, 2014). The government has also promoted the Aadhaar-based direct benefit transfer (DBT channel to overcome the problem related to leakages). So, it leads to the opening of Jan Dhan bank accounts for the poor (31 crores). Under the Subsidised Accident Insurance Scheme, 13.4 crore people received; furthermore, under the life insurance scheme, 5.3 people got the amount. Also, 5.72 crores had obtained the benefits of farm insurance under various schemes in the last six years. In addition to it, the government also announced that there will be an increase in the proportion of social welfare expenditure schemes through Aadhaar-based DBT (*The Financial Express*, 2018).

Model 2: Relationship Between Significant (Obtained) Variables of the Social Sector and the Inclusive Growth (Auto Regressive Lag Model)

The next stage is to see the relationship between those variables which significantly contributed to the inclusive growth in India in Model 2. These variables were entered by employing backward multiple stepwise regression. The relationship between the physical variables significantly contributed, obtained via step-wise regression and inclusive growth in India in Model 2 has been examined. Because of annual frequency, only short lags might be plausible, so, for the robustness of the model, the indicators which significantly contributed to inclusiveness have been used to run ARDL (Kolawole, 2016).

Each of these series is converted into a log form. Heteroscedasticity is a problem that can be mitigated through log transformation. Anand et al. (2014) studied the role of growth and distribution in eradicating poverty and inequalities. For this purpose, the study examined the state-level panel data of India and used the four NSSO surveys of 1993–1994, 1999–2000, 2004–2005, and 2009–2010 to gauge the impact of social sector spending and financial and macro-economic conditions on inclusive growth.

Following is the model which is framed to gauge the relationship between inclusiveness and significant social sector variables:

$$LDIIG_2 = a + b_{21}\ LDGER + b_{22}\ LDBED + b_{23}\ LDPPW + b_{24}\ LDBH + b_{25}\ LDBWS + b_{26}\ LDBEN + b_{27}\ LDRF + b_{28}\ LDRP + b_{29}\ LDPFG + U_{2t}$$

Unit Root Tests. Firstly, a unit root test has been employed on these 10 extracted variables. These variables are integrated with different orders revealed in Table 48. The ADF and PP tests are used to decide the order of integration for

Table 48. Unit Root Test Results of Significant Variables of Model 2.

Variables	ADF			PP			Result of ADF and PP			Order of Integration
	At Level	At First Difference	At Second Difference	At Level	At First Difference	At Second Difference	At Level	At First Difference	At Second Difference	
LDIIG	−2.403 (0.150)	−5.370* (0.002)	—	−2.403 (0.150)	−12.234* (0.000)	—	Do not reject	Reject null hypothesis	—	I(1)
LDGER	−0.8706 (0.9936)	−4.572* (0.001)	—	0.7677 (0.991)	−4.592* (0.001)	—	Do not reject	Reject null hypothesis	—	I(1)
LDBED	−2.107 (0.2435)	−4.696* (0.000)	—	−2.105 (0.244)	−4.693* (0.000)	—	Do not reject	Reject null hypothesis	—	I(1)
LDPRE	−1.331 (0.600)	−2.565 (0.112)	−8.195* (0.000)	−0.965* (0.752)	−2.784 (0.072)	−8.009* (0.000)	Do not reject	Do not reject	Reject null hypothesis	I(2)
LDPPW	−3.280* (0.025)	—	—	−3.458* (0.016)	—	—	Reject null hypothesis	—	—	I(0)
LDBH	−2.675 (0.090)	−7.971* (0.000)	—	−2.605 (0.103)	−9.871* (0.000)	—	Do not reject	Reject null hypothesis	—	I(1)
LDBWS	0.6391 (0.988)	−5.187* (0.002)	—	−2.229 (0.180)	−5.318* (0.000)	—	Do not reject	Reject null hypothesis	—	I(1)
LDBEN	−1.996 (0.287)	−4.133* (0.004)	—	−1.753 (0.395)	−2.525* (0.037)	—	Do not reject	Reject null hypothesis	—	I(1)
LDRF	−2.208 (0.208)	−4.672* (0.000)	—	−1.239 (0.644)	−4.731* (0.000)	—	Do not reject	Reject null hypothesis	—	I(1)
LDRP	−3.598 (0.012)	—	—	−2.389 (0.153)	−6.101* (0.000)	—	Reject null hypothesis	Reject null hypothesis	—	I(1)
LDPFG	—	−6.742* (0.000)	—	—	−6.180* (0.000)	—	Reject null hypothesis	—	—	I(0)

Source: Author's calculation using E VIEWS 10.

Note: All these values show test statistics and the probability of test statistics is in parentheses.

the various variables. The variables LDIIG, LDGER, LDBED, LDBH, LDBWS, LDBEN, and LDRF are integrated at the order 1, that is, $I(1)$. LDRP is integrated at level, that is, $I(0)$ as per the ADF test but it is integrated at the first difference, that is, $I(1)$ as per the PP test. So, due to the robustness of the PP model, it is preferable. So, the variable LDRP is also integrated at $I(1)$. But LDPPW and LDPFG are integrated at the level, $I(0)$ both in ADF and PP tests. LDPRE is integrated at the second difference, that is, $I(2)$. So, the variable integrated at order two or $I(2)$, that is, LDPRE has been dropped from the model, considering the robustness of the results (Kumari, 2015). ARDL is a suitable technique if the variables are integrated at different orders.

Bound Testing Approach to the Cointegration/ARDL Model.   Like Model 1, in Model 2 also, variables are not integrated at the same order. It was already mentioned that if the variables are integrated with different orders, then an alternative cointegration technique called ARDL model is more suitable. This cointegration technique has been found to be the most effective in creating long-term relationships between independent and dependent variables when the variables are not integrated in the same order. The Wald test, Breusch–Godfrey serial correlation LM test, Breusch–Pagan–Godfrey heteroskedasticity test, JB normality test, Ramsey RESET test, and lag length selection criteria defined by VAR are the diagnostic tests that must be performed prior to using ARDL like Model 1 (Kolawole, 2016).

The empirical models for estimating used in the following respecifications aim to determine the kind, size, and direction of the relationship between inclusive growth and the various social sectoral components in India.

Therefore,

$$\text{LDIIG}_{2t} = f\,(\text{LDGER, LDBED, LDPPW, LDBH, LDBWS, LDBEN, LDRF,} \\ \text{LDRP, LDPFG})$$

$$\text{LDIIG}_{2t} = \beta_{20} + \beta_{21}\,\text{LDGER} + \beta_{22}\,\text{LDBED} + \beta_{23}\,\text{LDPPW} + \beta_{24}\,\text{LDBH} + \beta_{25} \\ \text{LDBWS} + \beta_{26}\,\text{LDBEN} + \beta_{27}\,\text{LDRF} + \beta_{28}\,\text{LDRP} + \beta_{29}\,\text{LDPFG} + \varepsilon_{2t}$$

By a priori expectation, $\beta_{21}, \ldots, \beta_{29} > 0$.

SC therefore chooses the selected model based on the ARDL (1,0,1,1,1,1,1,1,1,1) with a maximum latency of 1 as shown in Table 49.

Diagnostic Tests.   The Breusch–Godfrey serial correlation LM test, Wald test, JB normality test, heteroskedasticity test by Breusch–Pagan–Godfrey, and Ramsey RESET test must be performed first before using ARDL (Kolawole, 2016).

Wald Test (F-statistic).   The ARDL bound testing is performed on the Wald test (F-statistic). At the 95 per cent level, 2.365–3.513 was the pertinent critical value for the upper bound. There is no long-term association between the dependent variable and the independent variables of the model, according to this, if the F-statistic is between these levels (Pesaran et al., 1996). The asymptotic distribution of the ARDL bound test is non-standard, based on the Wald test. The null hypothesis of no cointegration between the variables is presented below:

Table 49. VAR Lag Order Selection Criteria of Model 2.

Sample: 1985–2016				Included observations: 30		
Lag	Log	LR	Final Prediction Error (FPE)	AIC	SC	Hannan–Quinn Criterion
0	−22.20974	NA*	0.603957*	2.300696	2.776843	2.446149
1	−21.55297	0.797511	0.626234	2.325212*	2.848578*	2.485210*
2	−19.81675	0.1984256	0.602839	2.272625	2.843570	2.447168

Source: Author's calculation using E VIEWS 10.

Note: *indicates lag order selected by the criterion.

Null hypothesis: $H_0 = C(1) = C(2) = C(3) = C(4) = C(5) = C(6) = C(7) = C(9) = C(10) = 0$

Alternate hypothesis: $H_1 = C(1) \neq C(2) \neq C(3) \neq C(4) \neq C(5) \neq C(6) \neq C(7) \neq C(9) \neq C(10) \neq 0$

    The computed *F*-statistic is 4.627 as shown in Table 50, indicating that there is the existence of a long-run association between the variables of the model. A long-run association between the variables has existed, according to the results of the *F*-bound test and also the model is well fitted. There is a rejection of the no cointegration hypothesis (Kolawole, 2016).

    Breusch–Godfrey Serial Correlation LM Test. The next diagnostic test is the Breusch–Godfrey serial correlation LM test which explains whether the residual is serially correlated or not, up to the specified order of lag (Kolawole, 2016).

    The *p*-value is 0.604 in Table 51 is more than 0.05 up to the predefined lag of 1, which was chosen by the VAR technique, hence the hypothesis could not be rejected. As a result, the current model lacks autocorrelation.

    Breusch–Pagan–Godfrey Test. Breusch–Pagan–Heteroskedasticity Godfrey's test results are presented in Table 52. The model's null hypothesis is that the variables have a homoscedastic distribution. The heteroskedasticity test's conclusion supported the notion that the model's residuals are not heteroscedastic. Given that the *p*-values are greater than 0.05, the model includes homoscedasticity (Kolawole, 2016).

Table 50. Wald Test of Model 2.

Test Statistic	Value	Df	Probability
F-statistic	4.626866	(9,21)	0.0055
χ^2	41.64180	9	0.0000

Source: Author's calculation.

Null hypothesis: $C(1) = C(2) = C(3) = C(4) = C(5) = C(6) = C(7) = C(9) = C(10) = 0$.

Table 51. Breusch–Godfrey Serial Correlation LM Test of Model 2.

F-statistic	0.277521	Prob. F(1,20)	50.6041
Obs*R^2	0.424271	Prob. $\chi^2(1)$	0.5148

Test equation:
Dependent variable:RESID
Method: Least squares
Included observation: 30
Presample missing value lagged residuals set to zero

Variable	Coefficient	Std. Error	t-Statistic(Prob.)
RESID-1	−0.179875	0.341446	−0.526803(0.6041)
R^2	0.013686	Mean dependent var	−2.96E−15
Adjusted R^2	−0.479471	S.D. dependent var	0.614472
S.E. of regression	0.747403	AIC	2.522699
Sum squared resid	11.17224	SC	3.035833
Log likelihood	−28.16848	Hannan–Quinn criterion	2.692866
F-statistic	0.027752	DW statistic	2.053349
Prob(F-statistic)	0.999999		

Source: Author's calculation using E VIEWS 10.

Ramsey RESET Test. Testing for specification flaws and model linearity is done by using the Ramsey RESET approach. It also checks the linearity of the model (E Views 10, 2017).

The test statistic was not significantly different from zero at the 5 per cent level, as indicated in Table 53, indicating the absence of specification error.

JB Test. The JB test assumes that the residuals are not normally distributed, which is the null hypothesis of the residuals (E Views 10, 2017).

The null hypothesis is rejected since the *p*-value is greater than the assumed level of significance, as shown in Fig. 3 by the values of the JB test and the *p*-value of 1.264 and 0.5315. The residuals, therefore, follow a normal distribution.

The proposed model is shown to be well-specified, normally distributed, has no heteroscedasticity, and is free from collinearity as per the results of diagnostic testing.

Inferences of ARDL Results. Table 54 represents the long-term relationship's estimated significant coefficients for 'accessibility of potable water' (**LDPPW**), 'beneficiaries of EWS and LIG who receive benefits of housing schemes' (**LDBH**), 'beneficiaries who receive benefits under schemes for welfare of marginalised sections' (**LDBWS**), 'rural food consumption expenditure' (**LDRF**), and 'rural poverty' (**LDRP**) but not significant for 'gross enrolment ratio' (**LDGER**);

Table 52.   Heteroskedasticity Test: Breusch–Pagan–Godfrey of Model 2.

F-statistic	1.152114	Prob. F(9,21)	0.3726
Obs*R^2	10.24704	Prob. $\chi^2(9)$	0.3309
Scaled explained SS	11.47271	Prob. $\chi^2(9)$	0.2447

Test equation:

Dependent variable:RESID∧2

Method:Least Squares

Included observation: 30

R^2	0.330550	Mean dependent var	0.365396
Adjusted R^2	0.043643	S.D. dependent var	0.820493
S.E. of regression	0.802389	AIC	2.653249
Sum squared resid	13.52038	SC	3.115826
Log likelihood	−31.12537	Hannan-Quinn criterion	2.804038
F-statistic	1.152114	DW statistic	2.249758
Prob(F-statistic)	0.372608		

Source: Author's calculation using E VIEWS 10.

'availability of number of beds per 1,000 population' (LDBED), 'beneficiaries under various insurance schemes' (LDBEN), and 'procurement of food grains' (LDPFG). Granger causality exists between the independent and dependent variables, at least in one direction, according to the long-run relationship.

Anand et al. (2014) claimed that if the gross domestic product (GDP) growth rate would increase, only then the objective of inclusiveness could be achieved. GDP growth would produce a larger base for total income and production which ultimately lead to rising the living standards of the Indian population by providing them with employment and other income-enhancing activities. Government

Table 53.   Ramsey RESET Test of Model 2.

Specification: LDIIG$_2$ C LDED-1 LDHFW-1 LDWSS-1 LDHUD-1 LDWPC-1 LDLE-1 LDSSW-1 LDRD-1 LDFSW-1

Omitted variables: Squares of fitted values

	Value	Df	Probability
t-Statistic	1.16123	20	0.2627
F-statistic	1.438322	(1,20)	0.2627
Likelihood ratio	5.72906	1	0.1212

Source: Author's calculation using E VIEWS 10.

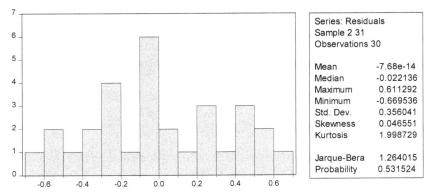

Fig. 3.   Normality Test of Model 2. *Source*: Author's own configuration using E VIEWS 10.

expenditure contributing to the social sector development is associated with promoting inclusive growth and eradicating poverty. Hence, escalating expenditure on the social sector by 1 per cent of GDP is directly linked with decreasing in the poverty rate by 0.5 per cent.

Estimated Long-run and Short-run Coefficients.   The next stage of ARDL is estimating the long-run coefficients of the model. The following formulation of the ARDL equation represents it as a general VAR model of order k in Z_t, where Z_t is a column vector:

$$
\begin{aligned}
\Delta(\text{LDIIG}_{2t}) =\ & \beta_{20} + \beta_{21}\,\text{LDGER}_{t-1} + \beta_{22}\,\text{LDBED}_{t-1} + \beta_{23}\,\text{LDPPW}_{t-1} \\
& + \beta_{24}\,\text{LDBH}_{t-1} + \beta_{25}\,\text{LDBWS}_{t-1} + \beta_{26}\,\text{LDBEN}_{t-1} + \beta_{27}\,\text{LDRF}_{t-1} \\
& + \beta_{28}\,\text{LDRP}_{t-1} + \beta_{29}\,\text{LDPFG}_{t-1} + \sum_{j=1}^{k}\beta_{21j}\,\Delta(\text{LDGER}_{t-1}) \\
& + \sum_{j=1}^{k}\beta_{22j}\,\Delta(\text{LDBED}_{t-1}) + \sum_{j=1}^{k}\beta_{23j}\,\Delta(\text{LDPPW}_{t-1}) \\
& + \sum_{j=1}^{k}\beta_{24j}\,\Delta(\text{LDBH}_{t-1}) + \sum_{j=1}^{k}\beta_{25j}\,\Delta(\text{LDBWS}_{t-1}) \\
& + \sum_{j=1}^{k}\beta_{26j}\,\Delta(\text{LDBEN}_{t-1}) + \sum_{j=1}^{k}\beta_{27j}\,\Delta(\text{LDRF}_{t-1}) \\
& + \sum_{j=1}^{k}\beta_{28j}\,\Delta(\text{LDRP}_{t-1}) + \sum_{j=1}^{k}\beta_{29j}\,\Delta(\text{LDPFG}_{t-1}) + \varepsilon_{2t}
\end{aligned}
$$

where Δ is the first difference operator, β_{20} is the drift component, and ε_{2t} is the white noise residual.

Table 54.   ARDL Estimates of Model 2.

Model dependent variable is LDIIG

Maximum lags: 1 (Automatic selection by Schwarz Information Criterion)

Selected model: ARDL(1,1,0,1,0,1,0,1,1,0)

Variable	Coefficient	Std. Error	t-Statistic	Prob.
C	−14.86382	88.69676	−1.675801	0.1160
LDIIG-1	0.037811	0.176383	02.14369	0.8334
LDGER-1	9.958947	7.650335	1.301766	0.2140
LDBED	−0.332691	1.346880	−0.249682	0.8065
LDPPW-1*	**108.8517**	**33.65250**	**3.262746**	**0.0057**
LDBH*	**−1.111690**	**0.258378**	**−4.302572**	**0.0007**
LDBWS*	**7.400084**	**1.900386**	**3.893991**	**0.0016**
LDBEN-1	−4.031416	1.483321	−2.717831	0.5995
LDRF-1*	**36.43373**	**18.29753**	**1.991183**	**0.0463**
LDRP-1*	**−6.665311**	**1.909585**	**−3.490451**	**0.0036**
LDPFG	1.492385	0.943139	1.582359	0.1359
R^2	0.941069	Mean dependent var		−1.697556
Adjusted R^2	0.877929	S.D. dependent var		1.466659
S.E. of regression	0.512431	AIC		1.805224
Sum squared resid	3.676192	SC		2.552529
Log likelihood	−11.07836	Hannan–Quinn criterion		2.044293
F-statistic	14.90446	DW statistic		2.340308
Prob(F-statistic)	0.000004			

Source: Author's calculation using E VIEWS 10.

Note: *indicates significance of 5 per cent level and the bold values represent that these variables are significant to inclusive growth in the present model.

The calculated long-run relationship's coefficients are significant and negative for 'number of beneficiaries covered under housing schemes' (LDBH) and 'number of beneficiaries under various insurance schemes' (LDBEN) with the inclusiveness while 'beneficiaries getting benefits under various welfare schemes for marginalised sections' (LDBWS) is positive and significant as shown in Table 55.

The educational indicators like literacy, enrolment, attendance, and drop-out rates were highly dependent on the social exclusion of disadvantaged and vulnerable groups. High enrolment rates, more literacy in India, and fewer drop-outs have not indicated inclusiveness in India. India's children belong to the marginalised sections and are required the right to free and equal education (Thorat & Dubey, 2013). Similarly, urban housing exclusions included families who were

Table 55.   Estimated Long-run Coefficients Using the ARDL Approach of Model 2.

Selected model: ARDL(1,1,0,1,0,1,0,1,1,0)			Dependent variable is LDIIG	
Regressor	**Coefficient**	**Std.Error**	***t*-Statistic**	**Prob**
C	−14.32228	88.69676	−1.597285	0.1325
LDGER	5.535197	7.860734	−0.704158	0.4929
LDBED	−0.324039	1.318164	−0.245826	0.8094
LDPPW	5.893488	8.306738	0.709483	0.4897
LDBH*	**−1.071188**	**0.272528**	**−3.930553**	**0.0015**
LDBWS*	**7.130473**	**2.151836**	**3.313669**	**0.0051**
LDBEN*	**−2.907502**	**1.004620**	**−2.894132**	**0.0118**
LDRF	33.88418	19.02872	1.780686	0.0967
LDRP	−0.122275	1.749336	−0.069898	0.9453
LDPFG	1.438012	0.942760	1.523532	0.1494

Source: Author's calculation using E VIEWS 10.

Note: *indicates significance of 5 per cent level and the bold values represent that these variables are significant to inclusive growth in the present model.

classified as LIG or EWS categories. There had been a shortage of houses as 3 million households were still homeless (Menon, 2009). Hence, poverty is closely related to social exclusion. There had been faulty designs of law and policy, the presence of institutional bias in the implementation of law and policy, discrimination by the state, and low budgetary allocations. Thus, inclusiveness is a collaborative process by ensuring equitable and fair access to every member of the country (Government of India, 2016a).

Generating an error correction model variant of the ARDL model stated below yields the function's short-run dynamic parameters:

$$\Delta(\text{LDIIG}_t) = \sum_{j=1}^{k}\beta_{21j}\ \Delta(\text{LDGER}_{t-1}) + \sum_{j=1}^{k}\beta_{22j}\ \Delta(\text{LDBED}_{t-1})$$

$$+\sum_{j=1}^{k}\beta_{23j}\ \Delta(\text{LDPPW}_{t-1}) + \sum_{j=1}^{k}\beta_{24j}\ \Delta(\text{LDBH}_{t-1})$$

$$+\sum_{j=1}^{k}\beta_{25j}\ \Delta(\text{LDBWS}_{t-1}) + \sum_{j=1}^{k}\beta_{26j}\ \Delta(\text{LDBEN}_{t-1})$$

$$+\sum_{j=1}^{k}\beta_{27j}\ \Delta(\text{LDRF}_{t-1}) + \sum_{j=1}^{k}\beta_{28j}\ \Delta(\text{LDRP}_{t-1})$$

$$+\sum_{j=1}^{k}\beta_{29j}\ \Delta(\text{LDPFG}_{t-1}) + \lambda\text{ECT}_{t-1} + \varepsilon_{2t}$$

Table 56.   Estimated Short-run Coefficients Using the ARDL Approach and ECM of Model 2.

Selected model: ARDL (1,0,1,1,1,1,1,1,1,1)		Dependent variable is LDIIG		
Variable	**Coefficient**	**Std. Error**	***t*-Statistic**	**Prob.**
D(LDGER)	4.214458	3.557166	1.184780	0.2558
D(LDPPW)*	**114.9680**	**14.47211**	**7.944106**	**0.0000**
D(LDBEN)	1.013978	0.690723	1.467995	0.1642
D(LDRF)*	**71.59911**	**7.730630**	**9.261742**	**0.0000**
D(LDRP)*	**−6.792210**	**0.713965**	**−9.513361**	**0.0000**
ECM (−1)	−0.137811	0.092167	−11.26005	0.0000
R^2	0.921965	Mean dependent var		0.067030
Adjusted R^2	0.905705	S.D. dependent var		1.274548
S.E. of regression	0.391375	AIC		1.138557
Sum squared resid	3.676192	SC		1.418797
Log likelihood	−11.07836	Hannan–Quinn criterion		1.228208
DW statistic	2.340308			

Source: Author's calculation using E VIEWS 10.

Note: *indicates significance of 5 per cent level and the bold values represent that these variables are significant to inclusive growth in the present model.

where λ is the speed of adjustment parameter and ECT is the residual obtained from the above equation.

The results of the estimated ECM in relation to the long-run projections for Model 2 are shown in Table 56. The short-run coefficients show the dynamic modification of each variable. The coefficient for short-run are 'accessibility of potable water' (LDPPW), 'rural food consumption expenditure' (LDRF), and 'rural poverty' (LDRP) are statistically significant at the 5 per cent level. 'Accessibility of potable water' (LDPPW) and 'rural food consumption expenditure' (LDRF) are positively significant; however, 'rural poverty' (LDRP) is negatively significant with the inclusiveness in India.

The error correction coefficient term has a value of −0.1378, which is negative and significant at the 5 per cent level. Long-term causality therefore exists between the independent variables and the dependent variable. It also guarantees cointegration, or the existence of a long-term relationship, between all the variables. After correction, there is a difference of around 13.78 per cent between the long-run equilibrium value and the dependent variable's actual value.

The government had implemented various schemes for generating better productive employment opportunities, facilitating good social infrastructure, and providing basic amenities like potable water, free electricity, construction of roads, sanitation and sewerage facility, housing and housing facilities, food at discounted prices, and access to education for the poor masses of India. In the budget 2018–2019, the government took the initiative and proclaimed several policies related to promoting agricultural and allied activities, rural infrastructure, and employment opportunities in rural areas. This includes channelising strategies to create employment opportunities in medium-, small- and micro-enterprises (MSMEs) and agro-based industries. Several social protection schemes like Ayushman Bharat and National Health Protection Schemes were proposed to cover 10 crore poor and deprived people. It covers secondary and tertiary care hospitalisation up to a maximum of 5 lakh rupees per family per year (Government of India, 2018a).

The inclusive growth strategy is an ongoing and never-ending process and it rarely leads to all good outcomes. The policies that promote equality of opportunities will lead to rapid long-run growth. The impact of the major social sector programmes in achieving inclusiveness is possible if there is wider coverage of the schemes, more evaluation of existing beneficiaries, monitoring of every scheme, and transparency must be there. This strategy must combine dynamic efficiency, growth, and social justice as criteria for the creation of a well-ordered society, that is, free and equal opportunities so benefits are equally shared with the least privileged members of society (Naqvi, 2015).

Dev (2016) advocated for increasing the percentage of expenditure that should be invested in the social sector. For the social sector's constituent parts, the delivery mechanisms must be upgraded. Specifically in the infrastructure, health, education, and agriculture sectors to promote inclusive growth, the role of states in dispersing funding is regarded as crucial. Only 25 per cent of the funds provided for the scheme's execution were actually utilised; however, the scheme's utilisation rates exceeded the amount of money allotted, at the end of the year. The underutilisation of funds in the social sector was revealed by excessive spending, the existence of leaks, and political interference (Rajaraman, 2001).

Some social sector components, including education, health, and employment, need to receive more focus, according to observations. In addition to decreasing socio-economic disparities that are pervasive in society, the government must concentrate on skill development, and closing gender gaps in employment, earnings, and education. By doing this, India's progress will be inclusive, resulting in a better society (Chadha & Chadda, 2020a, 2020b).

Chapter 8

Problems, Government Measures, and Policy Implications

Ever since independence, poverty alleviation has been India's top priority. Our social objective is to eliminate poverty and hunger and guarantee a decent level of living for the majority of people. All of the Five Year Plans have placed a strong emphasis on the significance of reducing poverty and fulfilling other basic requirements of all (Dev, 2000).

In the early years of independence, India envisaged a trickle-down approach to embark on the path of development and followed the inclusive growth strategy. Especially since the Sixth Five Year Plan, social sector development has taken precedence over other developed issues. It is also realised that to fulfil the objective of social justice, the government requires multiple efforts to achieve inclusiveness in all dimensions (Dev & Mooij, 2004). Although, since independence, many programmes and policies have been formulated, success lies again in their proper implementation. India aimed for inclusive growth so that everyone, from the top down to the bottom up, may participate in the process of development.

The expenditure incurred on social sector development helps in diluting poverty significantly, but the reduction in poverty does not necessarily imply a reduction in hunger, malnutrition, and deprivation. Poverty eradication programmes raise incomes, which may have significant effects on raising people's level of living. The strategy of inclusive growth should surpass the traditional aim of reducing poverty. It must include various interrelated components like equality of opportunity, economic mobility, access to essential facilities, empowerment of underprivileged classes, and generating productive employment opportunities. The principal development strategy in India has been inclusive growth, yet despite this, exclusion persists in the form of economic disparities, social discrimination, declining agricultural growth, lower human development, economic inequalities, gender imbalances, plummeting employment growth, etc. Whatever policies and programmes were adopted, these did not bear the desired fruits. Its achievements have, however, created new challenges. There are many stumbling blocks in accomplishing inclusive growth. Below are mentioned some of the prominent problems/impediments in the implementation of social sector development programmes/policies that would enable the achievement of the objectives of inclusive growth.

Social Sector Development and Inclusive Growth in India, 187–197
Copyright © 2023 by Ishu Chadda
Published under exclusive license by Emerald Publishing Limited
doi:10.1108/978-1-83753-186-820231009

Problems Impeding the Effective Implementation of Social Sector Development Programmes to Achieve Desired Objectives

1. *Education*: Education is a great leveller, but in India, education has been restrictive, particularly the quality of education. Although there has been significant improvement in the gross enrolment ratio at the elementary and secondary levels, the dropout rate has also recorded dismal scores. There had seen outstanding progress in the accessibility of preschools and elementary schools in rural areas. But problems like irregularity in attendance of children as well as of the teachers, pending tasks, and overdue funds to schools still prevailed. Many educational opportunities were provided by the government to promote enrolment in rural and backward areas. Even the graph of expenditure incurred on education has shown an increasing trend yet; the benefits have not percolated to the grass root level. With the increasing funds, utilisation of funds is very much important. India's mean years of schooling are significantly low compared to other developing countries. The growing gap in enrolment from elementary to higher secondary requires more attention. Scholarships are not delivered properly. The drop rate of marginalised classes is more than the average in schools followed by Other Backward Classes (OBCs) and girls. Scheduled Caste/Scheduled Tribes (SC/ST) students face many problems concerning inequalities. The main reasons for not enrolling children are lack of counselling to children, awareness about policies and programmes, presence of leakages, and corruption in the system.

2. *Employment*: The organised sector, which employs highly trained and educated labour and provides them with some level of job security and social security benefits, should be used to determine how many people are adding to the labour force.

> As per the NSSO Survey, only 3.07 crore persons are working in the organized formal sector and employment in this sector has declined by 27 lakhs in the last five years, as it was, to 3.34 crores in 2004–05. (Mathur, 2014)

Generating productive employment in the economy for the unemployed is considerable for inclusive growth. But the problem here is that to make employment provision inclusive, informal employment needs social and job security assurance. The growth of the unorganised employment sector has always been more compared to the organised employment sector. The employment-generating programmes have also been half-baked. Employment is lopsided.

3. *Housing development*: Sabke Liye Awas is one of the comprehensive programmes for providing houses for economically weaker sections (EWS) and lower income groups (LIG) in urban and rural areas. At the end of 2014–2015, it was targeted to achieve the construction of 3 lakh dwelling houses but 83,967 houses were constructed in urban India (Government of India, 2015).

Rural India is neglected in this also as there is still a shortage of 14.8 million houses in 2015 in rural areas (Government of India, 2017).

4. *Accessibility to potable drinking water and sanitation*: Initially, at the time of planning, the government implemented the water supply schemes in easily reachable urban areas. Hence, the hard-core rural areas were ignored. The Government of India commenced many programmes to provide safe drinking water to the rural population also, so as to facilitate the availability of water supply to remote villages. But still, there is no potable water for urban as well as rural areas. Drinking water is a basic necessity of life. Every person can be provided with this facility without much expenditure. Kumar and Das (2014) studied that India struggles to provide safe drinking water and sanitation facility. Seventy per cent of India's rural and slum populations are exposed to waterborne and vector-borne diseases due to a lack of basic sanitation facilities, unsafe water, and unhygienic condition.

5. *Health infrastructure*: All health parameters in India have shown substantial progressive improvement since independence, but still India lacks a significant healthcare infrastructure. India is already facing problems related to shortages of medical teachers, doctors, well-trained specialists, and super specialists in rural areas. Advanced and innovative approaches are urgently needed in India, particularly for rural health services. Investing in medical professionals could possibly result in better patient care (Deo, 2013). Malaria, polio, typhoid, smallpox, and chicken pox have been controlled but the public healthcare system in India has had critical challenges with new infections like dengue and chikungunya.

> In 2012, there were 14,277 clinically confirmed cases of chikungunya fever as it was 1985 cases in 2006. In 2012, as many as 24 Indian states were hit by dengue. It caused 37,070 confirmed cases of dengue. A total of 227 deaths were reported. (Palaniyandi, 2013)

The public expenditure of India on healthcare is very low and India's public healthcare system is very limited, compared with other Brazil, Russia, India, China, and South Africa (BRICS) countries. The private out-of-pocket expenditure on health is more, indicating the burden on poor and destitute families (Garg, 2018).

6. *The passive role of women in decision-making*: Numerous schemes had been launched by the government to empower women including financial support for dependent children and disabled people, attendance scholarships for girls, financial assistance to widows and destitute women, etc. On 4 April 2012, the Punjab Women Empowerment Package (PWEP) established the Women Development Department with the goal of improving the socio-economic position of women by providing them with better opportunities (*The Hindu*, 2016). Nevertheless, despite these efforts, disparities and deprivation of women prevent women to attain economic independence, social freedom, and political participation, especially in rural India. Women have limited family decision-making autonomy regardless of the numerous efforts

done by government. It would require concerted efforts both by the government and society (Baliyan, 2014). The goal of improving women's socioeconomic conditions can only be accomplished by pursuing actions and efforts to empower them. Without enough representation for women in politics, the empowerment of women will not be attainable. Women would increase the inclusiveness of the democratic development of the economy and society if they were given adequate representation in politics and allowed to influence the decision-making process (Chaturvedi, 2016).

7. *The welfare of marginalised class*: Government must introduce programmes related to marginalised classes to empower them. Emphasis must be on the empowerment of marginalised classes by making the governance process inclusive at the local level. Despite the Indian Constitution's removal of untouchability, social discrimination against Dalits is still very prevalent (Sangeeth, 2016). Regardless of various efforts, there were still 170–200 million SCs/STs in the lowest levels of the caste system, making up 17 per cent of India's population. Due to discrimination and abuse, their vulnerability is further exacerbated. The programmes and policies for the well-being of the marginalised class only serve a small portion of this class (Panda, 2016).

India lacks a long-term perspective in designing and implementing policies and programmes. Lack of perspective planning, convergence, proper supervision, and monitoring; lack of commitment; and more political interference are the core ingredients that hamper inclusive growth. Thus, there is a need to combine three factors, viz. positive government intervention to remove barriers related to discrimination issues, inclusive participation and support of the beneficiaries in the programmes, and effective monitoring of the programmes.

Government Measures Taken to Enhance Inclusive Growth

Economic growth, while significant, cannot be used as a means to an end. Programmes that encourage the equality of opportunities not only facilitate the poor but also ensure equal participation in the development process. Policies need to be accompanied by better laws, regulations, and strategies to promote the welfare of marginalised classes, empowerment of women, employment generation, agricultural and rural growth, and elimination of poverty to have greater inclusiveness. Poverty elimination and employment generation are the primary objectives to achieve inclusive growth. The agenda of the government is focussed on triggering growth in this manner so that there must be equal opportunities for the downtrodden society to make growth inclusive. Recent measures are taken by the government to enhance inclusive growth:

1. *Mahatma Gandhi National Rural Employment Guarantee Act (MGNREGA)*: The Maharashtra government introduced the Employment Guarantee Scheme in 1970 which was later launched as a nationwide Food for Work Programme in 1977 to generate employment and to utilise the surplus food grains for rural as well as urban development. The National Rural

Employment Programme (NREP) replaced the Food for Work Programme in 1980. Later, in 1989, the Rural Landless Employment Guarantee Program (RLEGP) and the NREP were combined to become the Jawahar Rozgar Yojana (JRY). In 1996, the Jawahar Gram Samridhi Yojana (JGSY) and Employment Assurance Scheme (EAS) partnered. In April 1999, the JGSY was amended and renamed Sampoorna Grameen Rojgar Yojana (SGRY, 2001). In 2005, MGNREGA was combined with the National Food for Work Programme and SGRY. MGNREGA's primary goal was to guarantee employment by requiring at least 100 days of guaranteed wage employment per calendar year. It is helpful to enhance the livelihood security of every rural household if the volunteer adult member of the household is prepared to do unskilled manual work (Government of India, 2005).

The government restructured the programme and make it transformed into an asset for sustainable employment opportunities for vulnerable and poor people.

During 2018–19, an additional Rs. 6000 crores had been invested in the rural employment scheme, MGNREGA. The allocation under MGNREGA had been increased from Rs. 37588 crores in 2014–15 to Rs. 61084 crores in 2018–19. A similar trend had been seen for the number of beneficiaries from 26.85 percent to 91.82 percent during the same period i.e. 2014–19. The payments were made to beneficiaries within 15 days. (*Business Today*, 2019)

2. *Direct Benefit Transfer Schemes*: This scheme ensures transparency as the money is directly transferred to the bank accounts of the beneficiaries. For the year 2019–2020, the total direct benefit transfer to the beneficiaries is Rs. 27,012 crores entailing 439 schemes under 55 ministries. The highest funds transferred were Rs. 214,092 crores in the year 2018–2019 followed by Rs. 170,292 crores in the year 2017–2018. This scheme ensured the expansion of direct benefits transferred to the deprived and deserving beneficiaries along with the removal of the leakages and middlemen (Government of India, 2019). The amount of Rs. 82 crores had been saved by plummeting leakages. The government also took the initiative to remove the fraudulent and fake existing beneficiaries and saved Rs. 13 crores by removing 2.75 crore duplicate and inactive ration cards (Sharma, 2018).
3. *Pradhan Mantri Jan Dhan Yojana (PMJDY)*: This Savings Deposit Bank Account Scheme was initiated by Prime Minister of India Narendra Modi on 15 August 2014. To integrate the poorest of the poor, a programme called financial inclusion was started by opening bank accounts for them. This programme covered every family throughout the nation, including both rural and urban ones. The validity of these accounts was of 12 months. The continuation of the account if only, the account holder would provide the officially valid document.

The benefits of having PMJDY Scheme include Interest on Deposit; accidental insurance cover of Rs. 1.00 lakh personal accident insurance cover provided by HDFC Ergo, no minimum balance requirement; Overdraft facility of Rs. 5000; Issuance of RuPay Debit Card; a life covers of Rs. 30000/ provided by LIC; easy transfer of money across India, access to have the benefit of Government schemes under Direct Benefit Transfer. (Government of India, 2014)

4. *Pradhan Mantri Suraksha Bima Yojana (PMSBY)*: PMSBY is a merged yojana by converging Aam Aadmi Bima Yojana (AMBI) with Pradhan Mantri Jeevan Jyoti Beema Yojana (PMJJBY). This scheme is for people who are in the age group 18–70 years. The applicant must have a bank account with an Aadhar card as a primary Know Your Customer (KYC). The coverage of Rs. 2 lakhs is provided in case of accidental death and full disability; if it is a partial disability, then the risk coverage is reduced to Rs. 1 lakh. A premium of Rs. 12 per annum is deducted in one instalment from the account on an auto-debit basis as this is an annual renewal life insurance policy (Government of India, 2015).

5. *Pradhan Mantri Ujjwala Yojana (PMUY)*: PMUY was commenced by the Prime Minister in 2016 intending to safeguard the health of children and women. In India, many households were deprived of liquefied petroleum gas (LPG) and coal, dung cakes, firewood, etc. used for cooking. So, the smoke inhaled by women and children caused harmful respiratory disorders and diseases. This scheme targeted the below-poverty-line families by providing them with Rs. 1,600 per connection for three years. This scheme also focussed on the empowerment of rural women as connections of LPG were issued in the name of women. In addition to this, employment would be generated and more business opportunities would also take place in India as manufacturers of gas stoves, cylinders, gas hoses, and regulators would be expanded (Government of India, 2016a).

6. *Mission Indradhanusha*: The main motive behind Mission Indradhanush was to achieve full immunisation coverage for pregnant women as well as children. Mission Indradhanusha was reinitiated in 2014 by retrieving the existing programme called Universal Immunisation Programme (UIP). This mission focussed on children up to the age of two years and pregnant mothers by identifying 201 districts across the country. This scheme continued till August 2017 and covered more than 68 lakh pregnant women and 2.53 crore children across the country. Later on, in October 2017, Intensified Mission Indradhanush (IMI) commenced covering those women and children who have been left behind under earlier missions, especially the remote areas.

The vaccination provides against diseases including diphtheria, pertussis, tetanus, polio, measles, tuberculosis, hepatitis B, meningitis, pneumonia, and Japanese encephalitis (JE). Newer vaccines named rotavirus; IPV, pneumococcal conjugate vaccine (PCV) and measles-rubella (MR) vaccine were also introduced. (Government of India, 2018)

7. *Samagra Shiksha Abhiyan*: Samagra Shiksha Abhiyaan is a comprehensive programme for preschool to senior secondary level students to ensure
inclusive and equitable quality education for all and equal opportunities
for schooling. The prime objectives of this scheme are to bridge social and
gender gaps in school education, guarantee minimum standards for school
provisions, support the vocationalisation of education, and strengthen
Teacher Education Institutions (TEIs). Three schemes named Sarva Shiksha Abhiyan (SSA), Rashtriya Madhyamik Shiksha Abhiyan (RMSA),
and Teacher Education (TE) were amalgamated to form this scheme.

> The main interventions proposed under this programmes con-
> sist of universal access to infrastructure and retention; Gender
> and Equity of Classes; Inclusive Education; Improving Quality
> of School Education; Digital Initiatives; Right To Education
> entitlements for books, textbooks, and uniforms; Access to Pre-
> school Education in remote areas; Promotion of Vocational
> Education; Sports and Physical Education; Reinforcing of
> Teacher Education and Training; Monitoring and Programme
> Management.

The integration of the above-mentioned interventions would enable effective
coverage that further leads to innovations in pedagogy, mentoring and monitoring, etc. This merged scheme would facilitate the State Council of Education
Research and Training (SCERT) to become the central agency for conduct and
monitoring to make the programme need-oriented and dynamic (Government of
India, 2018).

8. *Social Security Schemes*: Ministry of Labour and Employment initiated three
schemes, viz. Education Scheme, Health Scheme, and Revised Integrated
Housing Scheme for limestone and dolomite mine workers, beedi workers,
iron ore manganese workers, cine workers, chrome ore mine workers, and
mica mine workers. Under the Education Scheme, financial assistance of Rs.
250 to 15,000 per year is provided to workers for their wards. Health Scheme
grants many healthcare facilities and services to workers and their dependents
through 256 dispensaries and 12 hospitals across the country. A subsidy of
Rs. 150,000 is offered in three instalments to workers for the construction of
the new houses under the Revised Integrated Housing Scheme (Government
of India, 2018).
9. *Pradhan Mantri Mudra Yojana (PMMY)*: PMMY is a scheme initiated by
Mr Narendra Modi in 2015 to create a sustainable and inclusive environment
to develop a value-based entrepreneurial culture for comprehensive social and
economic development. The numbers of loans up to Rs. 10 lakhs, classified
as MUDRA loans, are granted by commercial banks, regional rural banks,
cooperative banks, small finance banks, and non-banking financial institutions to non-farm enterprises, small/micro-enterprises, and non-corporate
enterprises.

The borrower can apply online and approach any above-mentioned lending institutions. Three stages namely 'Shishu' (up to Rs. 50,000), 'Kishore' (Rs. 50,000 to Rs. 5 lakhs), and 'Tarun' (Rs. 5 lakhs to Rs. 10 lakhs) created by MUDRA based on loan requirement. These MUDRA stages represented the level of growth, and funding requirements of the borrowers and also suggest the reference position for the next step of development (Government of India, 2015). In the financial year, 2018–2019, loans sanctioned under PMMY were 59,870,318 with sanctioned amount of Rs. 321,722 crores, and the amount distributed was Rs. 311,811 crores (Government of India, 2018).

10. *Ayushman Bharat National Health Protection Mission*: Ayushman Bharat Mission or Pradhan Mantri Jan Arogya Yojana (PMJAY) is implemented throughout the country via a nodal agency called State Health Agency (SHA) for the poorest, deprived, and vulnerable people. Under this scheme, beneficiaries were allowed to have cashless benefits of Rs. 5 lakhs per family per year from public/private impanelled hospitals. This scheme, till now, covered 40 per cent of the population. This scheme provides healthcare services related to maternal and child health services and non-communicable diseases.

    The list of health care services includes the Pregnancy and Maternal health services; neonatal and infant health services; child health; chronic communicable diseases; non-communicable diseases; management of mental illness; dental care and geriatric care emergency medicine. (Government of India, 2018b)

11. *Pradhan Mantri Kisan Samman Nidhi Yojana*: This scheme is implemented to support the small and marginal farmers who have a total cultivated holding up to 2 hectares. Under this scheme, the farmers will receive Rs. 6,000 as financial assistance in three equal instalments every year to have the required inputs at the time of sowing. The instalments would be credited to the bank account of the farmers to ensure transparency. It also provides assurance to farmers (Government of India, 2019).

One of the main causes of all other related issues with the Indian economy is generally attributed to the underutilisation of potential resources as well as the underestimation of these resources' potentialities. To encourage economic development, it is necessary to accept both economic and social transformation concurrently as parallel dimensions. By ensuring social security benefits and boosting economic activity simultaneously, steady progress thus enables the achievement of two broader goals, namely creating employment and eliminating economic inequities. Income disparities are growing in tandem with real wage growth, which is being driven by a desire to reduce general poverty and this increased economic instability is a result of these rising disparities. The process of inclusivity and the continuation of pro-growth economic policies are the key components of the answer (Klasen, 2010).

Policy Implications

India is home to the richest of the world, at the same time sheltered the poorest of the world. Hunger, disease, and inequity would all be eliminated as a result of this development process. Development ought to be inclusive in order to accomplish this. It is essential to keep an eye on the efficient implementation of the entire policy framework that has been ingeniously designed by policymakers for promoting inclusive growth. The social sector development in India, which is a sustainable pathway to eradicate poverty, can be supported by the following recommendations and policy implications in light of the aforementioned discussion:

1. It has been noted that certain facets of the social sector, such as employment, health, and education, have received more focus. The government must concentrate on competencies, persistent gender gaps, promoting prospects for successful employment, and eradicating the inequities that are still ingrained in society. As a result, society would improve and India's economic progress would be inclusive. Prabhu (2005) asserted that in order to maintain equitable and long-term sustained prosperity in India, authorities need to take a broader perspective towards labour and employment. To promote the objective of eliminating poverty, it is important to understand how different aspects of protective and promotion policies for the social sector contribute to economic growth.

2. The majority of government policies aim to mainstream weaker groups, predominantly through a trickle-down strategy, but the key is not just in creating policies and practices for the underprivileged; rather, it is in ensuring that they are carried out properly. Since there are numerous middlemen in the path of every rupee, the government spends on helping the poor, little really ends up in their hands. The economic and social mobility of all societal groups can only be increased through the effective execution of government programmes and policies.

3. There is a lack of public awareness about programmes. People are not aware of the programmes. The delivery system needs to be streamlined to make them more responsive to the people. Wide publicity should be given through radio and television. As stated by Dhaked and Gupta (2016), strengthening information and communication is necessary. They also suggested increasing the amount of community participation, modifying the programme design, developing a community base with strong community participation, and social mobilisation through advocacy. For the social sector's sub-components, the delivery mechanisms must be upgraded. In order to make growth more equitable, the infrastructure, health, education, and agriculture sectors all depend on the role that states play in distributing funds. According to Rajaraman (2001), only 25 per cent of the funds provided for the scheme's implementation were actually used in the first six months. However, by the end of the year, utilisation rates had surpassed the amount of cash allotted. It was due to the wasteful utilisation, presence of leakages, and political intervention that indicated the underutilisation of funds in the social sector.

4. The present social sector programmes that the government has initiated on inclusivity must be made more effective. The gaps have to be found and eliminated to facilitate inclusive development in the future. The problems related to implementing schemes such as favouritism in the selection of beneficiaries, allocation of benefits without checking the needy, and the presence of leakages in process of disbursements to the target groups are frequently observed, which must be dodged.

5. There is a lack of principal role in planning by Gram Panchayat. Gram Panchayats start activities to use the funds without even planning the benefit from the works. Panchayat Raj Institutions (PRIs) need to be involved in the planning, implementation, and monitoring of developmental programmes. The responsibility towards vulnerable groups should be properly refined by both PRIs and delivery systems.

6. To provide the basic amenities to the rural people, there is a need to increase people participation, decentralisation of planning, extension of irrigation facilities, better-equipped facilities, and improvement in the techniques of cultivation. Several efforts have been put by the Government of India into programmes and projects for the development of rural households. The main focus of these schemes and programmes is to improve in quality of life in rural areas. Better implementation of rural programmes with proper follow-up mechanisms should be adopted so that the actual deprived sections of the population would select and receive the benefits provided to them.

7. People preferred to work on farms instead of working under MGNREGA because of more wages and facilities getting there. Females are more interested in MGNREGA because market wages for males are much higher. There were also delays in wage payments for up to three to four months in some villages. Parshad et al. (2013) also mentioned the same scenario of MGNREGA in the villages.

8. The Mid-day Meal Scheme has been shabbily implemented. Many complaints of the poor-quality meal, pilferage, lack of proper management and storage of food items, some used gunny bags and did not have proper doors for the store room.

9. Parents prefer to send their children to private schools. Despite the increase in SSA's infrastructure budget, there is a shortfall in the number of teachers, classrooms, drinking water facilities, kitchens, playgrounds, and complete boundary walls.

10. Nirmal Bharat Abhiyaan (NBA) had led to an enormous increase in sanitation facilities with social cohesion and harmony in rural areas. There is no regular cleaning staff to clean the streets. While in urban areas, the financial allocations for sanitation were not provided to households.

11. There is a shortage of human resources in public health institutions with shortfalls of even specialists, doctors, and staff nurses. Improved quality of services at all levels of facilities should be provided. There is a lack of basic facilities like cleanliness, electricity, potable water, etc.

12. Various measures should be adopted to reduce corruption with the need to enforce to create a better level of governance mechanism, proper management, and more awareness and overseeing of developmental programmes by forming committees and sub-committees. It is necessitating the fine-tuning of the mechanism to select targeting beneficiaries, so, it improvises the access to benefits provided by the government. Transparency and accountability must be ensured by proper follow-up to avoid corrupt practices and other shortcomings. More suitable actions must be implemented to address implementation and governance issues given the policy's high deployment.

Leaks in the funding process, malfeasance, inefficient management, unawareness, non-surveillance of developmental programmes, and flaws in the implementation of schemes like favouritism in the beneficiary selection, allocating schemes without taking into account the fundamental necessities, and a lack of follow-up are some of the most likely causes. A lot of care must be taken in the earmarking of funding so that any gaps may be identified and also immediately addressed, which will support inclusive development. Even while the rates of infant and maternal mortality have improved, progress in literacy, education, and health has been slow. It is believed that for growth to be inclusive and balanced, rural India must be developed. Numerous initiatives are carried out by the Indian government to reduce poverty and at the macro-level, these steps would be significant for the Indian economy to make growth inclusive (Chadha & Chadda, 2020a). No doubt, economic growth manifests equality in income redistribution but the slowdown of the Indian economy portrays no such evidence.

The growth that is inclusive and focussed on the social sector is mutually beneficial and interdependent. While the accomplishment of inclusive growth manifests in social sector development, social sector development drives the attainment of inclusive growth. The purpose of government programmes and policies is to incorporate the underprivileged group to participate in the growth process. Higher nutrition, better health, access to clean water and sanitation practices, as well as improved access to education and housing, could result from a rise in incomes. The best way to achieve inclusive growth is through the strengthening of human capacities and improved delivery of social services and economic services (Government of India, 2012a).

References

Acharya, N. (2013). The Friday briefing: Battle of the economists. *Wall Street Journal India.* http://blogs.wsj.com/indiarealtime/2013/07/26/the-friday-briefing-battle-of-the-economists

Acs, J. Z., & Audretsch, B. D. (1988). Testing the Schumpeterian hypothesis. *Eastern Economic Journal, 14*(2, April–June), 129–140.

Adi, S. M. (2004). Public expenditure on social sector in India. *Indian Journal of Regional Science, 36*(2), 31–44.

Aggarwal, R. K. (2011). Social sector expenditure in India and Punjab: Trends during pre-reforms (1980–1991) and post-reforms (1991–2011) periods. *Artha Vijnana, 53*(3, September), 262–284. https://doi.org/10.21648/arthavij/2011/v53/i3/117562

Aghion, P., & Bolton, P. (1997). A theory of trickle-down growth and development. *Review of Economic Studies, 64*(2, April), 151–172. https://doi.org/10.2307/2971707

Ahmad. (2005). Social Sector Expenditure on Education. In R. k. Sen (Eds.), *Social sector development in India* (pp. 214-231). Delhi: Deep and Deep Publications.

Aghion, P., & Howitt, P. (1998). *Endogenous growth theory* (pp. 11–48). The MIT Press.

Ahmad, F. M., & Bhakta, S. R. (2008). A study of education and health status of India. In *Economics of health and education.* Deep and Deep Publications.

Ahuja, L. H. (2007). *Advanced economic theory (microeconomic analysis)* (14th ed.). S Chand and Colo. Ltd.

Akhtar, S. M. (2008). Human development in India: A review. In *Social sector development in India.* Deep and Deep Publications.

Ali, I. (2007). *Pro-poor to inclusive growth: Asian prescriptions* [ERD Policy Brief No. 48]. Economics and Research Department, Asian Development Bank. https://www.adb.org/sites/default/files/publication/28367/erd-policy-brief-48.pdf

Ali, I., & Son, H. H. (2007). *Defining and measuring inclusive growth: Application to the Philippines* [ERD Working Paper Series 98]. Asian Development Bank. https://www.adb.org/sites/default/files/publication/156251/ewp-098.pdf

Ali, I., & Zhuang, J. (2007). *Inclusive growth towards a prosperous Asia: Policy implications* [ERD Working Paper No. 97]. Economics and Research Department, Asian Development Bank. https://www.adb.org/publications/inclusive-growth-towards-prosperous-asia-policy-implications

Alkire, S. (2002). Dimensions of human development. *World Development, 30*(2), 181–205. https://doi.org/10.1016/S0305-750X(01)00109-7

Anand, R., Mishra, S., & Peiris, S. J. (2013). Inclusive growth revisited: Measurement and determinants. *Economic Premise, 122.* https://openknowledge.worldbank.org/handle/10986/22618

Anand, R., Tulin, V., & Kumar, N. (2014). *India: Defining and explaining inclusive growth and poverty reduction* [IMF Working Paper]. *Asia and Pacific Department, 14*(63). https://doi.org/10.5089/9781484354230.001

Anand, S., & Sen, A. (2000). Human development and economic sustainability. *World Development, 28*(12), 2029–2049. https://doi.org/10.1016/S0305-750X(00)00071-1

Antony, G. M., & Laxmaiah, A. (2008). Human development, poverty, health, and nutrition situation in India. *Indian Journal of Medical Research, 128*(2), 198–205.

Antony, G. M., & Rao, K. V. (2007). A composite index to explain variations in poverty, health, nutritional status and standard of living: Use of multivariate statistical methods. *Public Health, 121*(8), 578–587. https://doi.org/10.1016/j.puhe.2006.10.018

Arndt, W. H. (1983). The trickle-down myth. *Economic Development and Cultural Change, 32*(1), 01–19.

Asian Development Bank. (2011). *Key indicators for Asia and the Pacific 2011: Framework of inclusive growth indicators*. Asian Development Bank.

Awofeso, N., & Rammohan, A. (2011). Decades of the integrated child development services program in India: Progress and problems. In K. Smigorski (Ed.), *Health management – Different approaches and solutions* (pp. 243–259). London: IntechOpen Limited.

Balani, S. (2014). *Functioning of the public distribution system: An analytical report* [Working Paper]. RePEcess: Wpaper:id:5628eSocialSciences

Baliyan, K. (2014). *Factors affecting participation of women in household decision making: Implication for family welfare and agriculture development.* https://www.indiastat.com/SOCIO_PDF/103/fulltext.pdf

Balkrishnan, R. (2013, July 25). A brief history of poverty counting in India. *The Hindu.* https://www.thehindu.com/opinion/op-ed/a-brief-history-of-poverty-counting-in-india/article4958447.ece

Banerjee, D. (2008). *Social sector in India.* http://www.icrier.org/page.asp?MenuID=24&SubCatId=177&SubSubCatId=330

Barik, A. (2015). Social sector expenditure and economic growth in India: An empirical analysis. In H. S. Rout & P. Mishra (Eds.), *Social sector in India: Issues and challenges* (pp. 82–95). UK: Cambridge Scholars Publishing.

Basantaray, A. K., & Barik, A. (2015). Dejected social sector development in India during the reform period: Trends, patterns, and determinants. In H. S. Rout & P. Mishra (Eds.), *Social sector in India: Issues and challenges* (pp. 60–81). UK: Cambridge Scholars Publishing.

Basole, A. (2018). *State of working India–2018.* Center for Sustainable Employment, Azim Premji University. https://cse.azimpremjiuniversity.edu.in/state-of-working-india/swi-2018/

Basu, A. (2005). Trends in the social sector in developing countries. In R. K. Sen (Eds.), *Social sector development in India* (pp. 26–35). Delhi: Deep and Deep Publications.

Becker, G. (1962). Investment in human capital – A theoretical analysis. *Journal of Political Economy, 70*, 4–44.

Bhagwati, J., & Panagariya, A. (2013). *Why growth matters: How economic growth in India reduced poverty and lessons for other developing countries.* Public Affairs.

Bhat, M. G. (2005). Second-generation economic reforms and social sector. In R. K. Sen (Eds.), *Social sector development in India* (pp. 106–118). Delhi: Deep and Deep Publications.

Bhat, S. K., Pratheeba, J., & Sundari, T. (2005). *Socio-economic determinants of infant mortality rate in the Indian States.* Social and Economic Change Monographs, No. 8 (pp. 209–227). Institute for Social and Economic Change. https://www.isec.ac.in/WP%20-%20205.pdf

Bhattacharya, P. (2013). *Everything you wanted to know about Sen – Bhagwati Debate.* http://www.livemint.com/Politics/zvxkjvP9KNfarGagLd5wmK/Everything-you-wanted-to-know-about-SenBhagwati-debate.html

Bhalla, S. S. (2011, April). Inclusion and growth in India – Some facts, some conclusions. LSE Research Online Documents on Economics 38366, London School of Economics and Political Science, LSE Library.

Biradar, R. R. (2008). Educational status among social groups in India: Emerging issues. In Thakur, A. K. & Salam, M. A. (Eds.) *Economics of health and education* (pp. 278–300). Delhi: Deep and Deep Publications.

Blaung, M., Layard, G., & Woodhall, M. (1969). *The causes of graduate unemployment in India.* Allen Lane.

Bolt, R. (2004). *Accelerating agricultural and rural development for inclusive growth: Policy implications for developing Asia* [ERD Policy Brief No. 29]. Asian Development Bank. https://www.adb.org/sites/default/files/publication/28437/erd-policy-brief-29.pdf

Brooks, C. (2008). *Introductory econometrics for finance* (2nd ed.). Cambridge University Press.

Burange, G. L., Karnik, N. N., & Ranadive, R. R. (2012). India's inclusive growth and development: An assessment. *Proceedings of International Journal of Academic, 1*(2), 71–92.

Burton, A., Monasch, R., Lautenbach, B., Gacic-Dobo, M., Neill, M., Karimov, R., Wolfson, L., Jones, G., & Birmingham, M. (2009). WHO and UNICEF estimates of national infant immunization coverage: Methods and processes .*Bulletin of the World Health Organization, 87*(7), 535–541. doi 10.2471/blt.08.053819.

Business Today. (2019, January 6). *Modi Government allots additional Rs. 6000 crores to MGNREGA; highest ever in a year.* https://www.businesstoday.in/top-story/government-allots-additional-rs-6000-crore-to-mgnrega-highest-ever-total-allocation-in-a-year/story/310445.html

Chadha, V., & Chadda, I. (2016, December 27–29). Effectiveness of social welfare programmes in India – The case of MGNREGA and social security measures. In *Proceedings of issues related to government spending priorities in India: 99th annual conference of the Indian Economic Association* (pp. 178–188). Department of Economics, Sri Venkateswara University.

Chadha, V., & Chadda, I. (2018). Policies and performance of social sector in India since independence: A critical evaluation. *International Journal of Social Science and Development Policy, 4*(2), 64–77.

Chadha, V., & Chadda, I. (2020a). Has social sector development catalyzed the inclusiveness of India's economic growth? *Indian Economic Journal, 68*(1), 61–81. ISSN: 0019-4662. https://doi.org/10.1177/0019466220959795

Chadha, V., & Chadda, I. (2020b). The imperative of social sector development for achieving the goal of inclusive growth in India: An analytical study. *Journal of Social and Economic Development, 22*(2, December), 355–378. ISSN: 0972-5792. https://doi.org/10.1007/s40847-020-00102-4

Chakraborthy, A. (2002). Issues in social indicators, composite indices, and inequality. *Economic and Political Weekly, 37*(13), 1199–1202.

Chand, R., Srivastava, S. K., & Singh, J. (2017). *Changing structure of the rural economy of India implications for employment and growth* [Discussion Paper]. National Institution for Transforming India, Niti Aayog.

Chandra, S. (2008). *Introduction to Agricultural Extension: Rural Development Programme.* Anmol Publications Pvt. http://nsdl.niscair.res.in/jspui/bitstream/123456789/501/1/PDF%20Rural%20 development%20programme.pdf

Chakravarty, M. (2017). *How India eats: The class structure of food consumption in India.* https://www.livemint.com/Opinion/cQbHitMzcHDaEnQVHLPtHP/How-India-Eats-The-class-structure-of-food-consumption-in-I.html

Chaturvedi, S. (2016). Empowerment of marginalized section and their participation. *The Whole Journal on Juristic Polity, 2*(3). http://juristicpolity.org/wp-content/uploads/2016/10/2.3-Empowerment-of-Marginalized-Section-and-their-Participation.pdf

Clarke, M. (2003). *Is economic growth desirable? A welfare economic analysis of the Thai experience* [Ph.D. thesis]. Centre for Strategic Economic Studies, Victoria University. https://vuir.vu.edu.au/232/

Commission on Growth and Development. (2008). *The growth report: Strategies for sustained growth and inclusive development.* World Bank. http://www.growthcommission.org/index.php.

Daramsot. (2018, December 28). Punjab was not paid Rs. 1663 crore of the post-matric scholarship scheme by the central government. *Punjab News Express.* https://punjabnewsexpress.com/punjab/punjab-was-not-paid-rs-1663-crore-of-the-post-matric-scholarship-scheme-by-the-central-government-84632.aspx.

Das, P. (2013). Bharat Nirman – A sustainable and durable rural infrastructure in India. *Abhinav, 2*(1), 63–70.

Dasgupta, P. (2013). Getting India wrong. *Issue of Prospect Management.* http://www. prospectmagazine.co.uk/magazine/partha-Dasgupta-Amartya-sen-review-gdp-wealth-development-economics-getting-India-wrong#.Ue.698PJ5px

Dash, M. K., & Bhatia, K. (2011). A demand of value-based higher education system in India: A comparative study. *Journal of Public Administration and Policy Research,* *3*(5), 156–173.

Das Simpreet, C., & Bhise, R. (2014). *Slum-free India: Myths and realities – A status report on Rajiv Awas Yojana.* National Desk – Youth for Unity and Voluntary Action (YUVA), New Delhi. https://ideas.repec.org/p/ess/wpaper/id10971.html

Datt, G. (1999). Has poverty declined since economic reforms? *Economic and Political Weekly* [Special article], *34*(50), 3516–3518.

Datt, G., & Ravillion, M. (2010). Shining for the poor too? *Economic and Political Weekly,* *45*, 55–60.

De, A., & Endow, T. (2008). *Public expenditure on education in India: Recent trends and outcomes* [Working Paper No. 18]. Research Consortium on Educational Outcomes and Poverty (RECOUP), DFID Supported Research Consortium. https://ceid.educ. cam.ac.uk/publications/WP18-ADfin.pdf

Deb, S. (2017). *Impact of economic growth on social development dimensions in India: A state-level analysis* [Working Paper]. Council for Social Development, CSD1, New Delhi. http://csdindia.org/wp-content/uploads/2017/10/Working-Paper-Impact-of-Economic-Growth-on-Social-Development-2017.pdf

Deo, M. G. (2013). Doctor population ratio for India – The reality. *Indian Journal of Medical Research,* *137*(4), 632–635.

Dev, S. M. (2000). Economic reforms, poverty, income distribution, and employment. *Economic and Political Weekly,* *35*(10), 823–835.

Dev, S. M. (2006). Policies and programmes for employment. *Economic and Political Weekly,* *41*(16), 1511–1516.

Dev, S. M. (2010). *Inclusive growth in India: Agriculture, poverty and human development.* Oxford University Press.

Dev, S. M. (2016). Increase social sector expenditure. *The Hindu,* February 3. https://www. thehindu.com/business/increase-social-sector-spending/article8184822.ece

Dev, S. M., & Mooij, J. (2002). Social sector expenditure in the 1990s: Analysis of central and state budgets. *Economic and Political Weekly,* *37*(9), 853–866.

Dev, S. M., & Mooij, J. (2004). *Patterns in social sector expenditures: Pre and post-reform period.* Centre for Economic and Social Studies.

Dev, S. M., & Ravi, C. (2007). Poverty and inequality: All-India and states, 1983–2005. *Economic and Political Weekly,* *42*(6), 509–521.

Dev, S. M., & Rao, P. P. (2002). *Poverty alleviation programmes in Andhra Pradesh – An assessment.* Sponsored by Planning Commission, Centre for Economic and Social Studies. http://164.100.161.239/reports/sereport/ser/stdy_pvrty.pdf

Devadasan, P., & Kalicharan, M. (2016). Social security measures for the Indian work-force – A legal intervention. *International Journal of Computational Research and Development,* *1*(1), 47–57. https://doi.org/10.5281/zenodo.159773

Dhaked, R., & Gupta, C. M. (2016). A critical review of malnutrition and its management. *International Journal of Medical and Health Research,* *2*(4), 43–47.

Dinopoulos, E. (2006). *Growth in open economics – Schumpeterian models.* http://bear. warrington.ufl.edu/dinopoulos/Research.html

Divakar, P. N. (2017). *The 2017 budget is taking SC/ST welfare backwards.* http://thewire.in/ rights/budget-2017-sc-st-welfare

Dogan, B., & Akyuz, M. (2017). Female labour force participation Rate and economic growth in the framework of Kuznets curve: Evidence from Turkey. *Review of Economics and Business,* *10*(1), 31–54.

Dollar, D., & Kraay, A. (2001). *Growth is good for the poor* [Policy Working Research Paper]. Development Research Group, World Bank. https://elibrary.worldbank.org/doi/abs/10.1596/1813-9450-2587

Dreze, J., & Sen, A. (1989). *Hunger and public action.* Clarendon Press.

Dreze, J., & Sen, A. (2013). *An uncertain glory: India and its contradictions.* Princeton University Press.

Dua, A. S. (2005). *Programmes for the control of leprosy, tuberculosis, and malaria. Burden of diseases in India* [NCHM Background Papers]. Ministry of Health & Family Welfare. https://mhpolicy.files.wordpress.com/2011/05/burden-of-disease-in-india-commission-on-macroeconomics-and-health.pdf

Ebner, A. (2000, June–July). *Schumpeterian theory and sources of economic development: Endogenous, evolutionary and entrepreneurial?* [Conference Paper]. Presented at the International Schumpeter Society Conference on Change, Development, and Transformation: Transdisciplinary perspectives on the innovation process, Manchester.

EViews. (2017). E Views 10 *User's guide II* (2nd ed.), Irvine CA: IHS. *Markit.* https://www3.nd.edu/~nmark/FinancialEconometrics/EViews10_Manuals/EViews%2010%20Users%20Guide%20II.pdf

Evenson, R. E., & Mohan, R. (1974). *The intensive agricultural districts program in India: A new evaluation* [Centre Discussion Paper 198]. Economic Growth Center, Yale University. https://elischolar.library.yale.edu/cgi/viewcontent.cgi?article=1205&context=egcenter-discussion-paper-series

Fan, S., Hazell, P. B. R., & Thorat, S. K. (2000). Government spending, growth, and poverty in rural India. *American Journal of Agricultural Economics, 82*(4), 1038–1051. https://doi.org/10.1111/0002-9092.00101

Farzana, A., Mukhopadhyay, A., & Sahoo, S. (2012). *Female labour force participation and child education in India: The effect of the national rural employment guarantee scheme* [IZA Discussion Paper 6593]. Institute of Labour Economics (IZA). https://www.iza.org/publications/dp/6593/female-labour-force-participation-and-child-education-in-india-the-effect-of-the-national-rural-employment-guarantee-scheme

Felipe, J. (2012). Inclusive growth: Why is it important for developing Asia? *Cadmus Journal, 1*(4), 36–59.

Femando, N. (2008). Rural development outcomes and drivers: An overview and some lessons. In *EARD special studies.* Asian Development Bank.

Field, A. (2005). Discovering statistics using SPSS (2nd ed.). Sage.

Fukuda-Parr, S. (2003). The human development paradigm: Operationalizing Sen's ideas on capabilities. *Feminist Economics, 9*(2–3), 301–317. https://doi.org/10.1080/1354570022000077980

Gaiha, R., & Kulkarni, V. S. (2005). Food grain surpluses, yields and prices in India. *Presentation at the Global forum on agricultural: Policy coherence for development goal of eradicating extreme poverty and hunger,* May 1, 2005, Paris, France.

Gale, T. (2008). Welfare state. In *International encyclopedia of the social sciences.* Wiley Online Library. http://www.encyclopedia.com/topic/Welfare_state.aspx

Galor, O. (2011). Inequality, human Capital formation, and the process of development. *SSRN Electronic Journal, Handbook of the economics of education.* North-Holland. https://doi.org/10.2139/ssrn.2003661

Galor, O., & Moav, O. (2004). From physical to human capital accumulation: Inequality and the process of development. *Review of Economic Studies, 71*(4, October), 1001–1026. https://doi.org/10.1111/0034-6527.00312

Gangopadhyay, D., Mukhopadhyay, A. K., & Singh, P. (2009). Rural development: A strategy for poverty alleviation in India. *India Science and Technology.* http://www.ssrn.com/abstract=1473041/

Garg, S. (2018). *Healthcare policy in India – Challenges and remedies.* https://www.iima.ac.in/c/document_library/get_file?uuid=f4758624-d359-4608-82e7-abb73ad2f51f&groupId=52123

Gaur, A. K. (2006). Economic growth, population theory, and physiology – The bearing of long-term processes on the making of economic policy. *American Economic Review, 83*(I-3), 369–395.

Ghosh, D., & Dinda, S. (2017). Health infrastructure and economic development in India. In R. Das (Ed.), *Social, health, and environmental infrastructures for economic growth* (pp. 99-119). IGI Global. https://doi.org/10.4018/978-1-5225-2364-2.ch006

Ghosh, M. (2010). Inclusive growth and rural poverty in India: Policy implications for the eleventh plan. *International Journal of Agricultural Economics, 65*(3), 552–561.

Goswami, B., & Bezbaruah, M. P. (2011). Social sector expenditures and their impact on human development: The Indian experience. *Indian Journal of Human Development, 5*(2), 365–385. https://doi.org/10.1177/0973703020110204

Government of India. (various issues-a). *Annual reports.* Planning Commission.

Government of India. (various issues-b). *Economic survey.* Ministry of Finance.

Government of India. (various issues-c). *Outlays budget, 1.* Ministry of Finance.

Government of India. (various issues-d). *Plan documents.* Planning Commission.

Government of India. (various issues-e). *Programme evaluation studies.* Planning Commission.

Government of India. (various issues-f). *Annual reports.* Department of Health and Family Welfare.

Government of India. (various reports-a). *Electoral statistics pocketbook.* Elections Commission of India.

Government of India. (various reports-b). *Handbook on social welfare statistics.* Ministry of Social Justice and Empowerment.

Government of India. (various rounds-a). *NSSO reports on the employment and unemployment situation in India.* Ministry of Statistics & Programme Implementation.

Government of India (various rounds-b). *NSSO reports on employment and unemployment situations among social groups in India.* Ministry of Statistics & Programme Implementation.

Government of India. (1952). *The First Five-Year Plan.* Planning Commission. http://14.139.60.153/handle/123456789/1431

Government of India. (1961). *Third Five-Year Plan-Summary.* Planning Commission. http://14.139.60.153/handle/123456789/7215

Government of India (1963). *The Third Plan Mid-term Appraisal.* Planning Commission. http://14.139.60.153/handle/123456789/1790

Government of India. (1969). *Modernizing Indian agriculture – A report on the intensive agricultural programme (1960–68)* (Vol. 1). Ministry of Food, Agricultural, Community Development, and Cooperation.

Government of India (1971). *Fourth Five Year Plan 1969-74. Summary:* Ministry of Information and Broadcasting. http://14.139.60.153/handle/123456789/7275

Government of India. (1974). *Main Schemes of Non-Formal Education in the Fifth Five-Year Plan.* Ministry of Education Welfare and Education. http://14.139.60.153/handle/123456789/7291

Government of India (1976). *Annual Plan 1976-77.* Planning Commission. http://14.139.60.153/handle/123456789/9549

Government of India (1985). *The Seventh Five Year Plan 1985-90. Volume I. Perspective, Objectives, Strategy, Macro-Dimensions, and Resources.* New Delhi: Planning Commission. http://14.139.60.153/bitstream/123456789/484/3/Plan-SEVENTH%20FIVE%20YEAR%20PLAN%201985-90.%20VOL.%201.%20PERSPECTIVES%2C%20OBJECTIVES%2C%20STRATEGY%2C%20MACRO-DIMENSIONS%20AND%20RESOURCES.pdf

Government of India. (1991). Annual Report 1991-92. Planning Commission. http://14.139.60.153/handle/123456789/7630

Government of India (1993). Report of the Expert Group on Estimation of Proportion and Number of Poor, Planning Commission. http://planningcommission.nic.in/reports/publications/pub93_nopoors.pdf.

Government of India (1995). A Technical Note to The Eighth Plan of India (1992-97). Perspective Planning Division. http://14.139.60.153/handle/123456789/1790

Government of India (2000). Annual Report 1999-2000. Planning Commission. http://14.139.60.153/handle/123456789/8907

Government of India. (2001). *Census of India – Report on the post-enumeration survey.* Ministry of Human Affairs.

Government of India. (2002). *Eleventh five-year plan document.* Planning Commission.

Government of India (2005). Annual Report 2004-2005. Planning Commission. http://14.139.60.153/handle/123456789/2556

Government of India. (2006). *Twenty-point programme.* Ministry of Statistics and Programme Implementation.

Government of India. (2007). *Report of the working group on Panchayati Raj Institutions and rural governance.* Planning Commission and Ministry of Panchayati Raj.

Government of India. (2008a). *Poverty eradication in India by 2015.* Ministry of Rural Development.

Government of India. (2008b). *Eleventh five-year plan-social sector.* Oxford University Press.

Government of India. (2009). *Report of the expert group to review the methodology for estimation of poverty.* Planning Commission. http://www.indiaenvironmentportal.org.in/files/rep_pov.pdf

Government of India. (2010). *Performance evaluation of cooked midday meal scheme.* Planning Commission.

Government of India. (2011a). *Census of India – Report on the post-enumeration survey.* Ministry of Human Affairs.

Government of India. (2011b). *Indian human development report: Towards social inclusion.* Planning Commission.

Government of India. (2011c). *Health information of India.* Central Bureau of Health Intelligence. Ministry of Health and Family Welfare.

Government of India. (2012a). *Annual status of education report (Rural) (2011).* Ministry of Human Resource Development.

Government of India. (2012b). *Rajeev Awas Yojana – Module 1.* Ministry of Housing and Urban Development.

Government of India. (2013). *Twelfth five-year plan-social sector.* SAGE Publications India Pvt. Ltd.

Government of India. (2014). *Educational Statistics at a Glance.* Ministry of Human Resource Development, New Delhi. http://14.139.60.153/handle/123456789/13265

Government of India. (2015). *Key Indicators of the Labour Market.* Ministry of Labour and Employment, New Delhi. https://www.ilo.org/global/statistics-and-databases/research-and-databases/kilm/lang--en/index.htm

Government of India. (2016a). *MGNREGA 2005—The journey of a Decade.* Ministry of Rural Development, New Delhi. https://nrega.nic.in/Circular_Archive/archive/RTP2016_English.pdf

Government of India. (2016b). *Educational statistics at a glance.* Ministry of Human Resource Development, New Delhi. https://www.education.gov.in/sites/upload_files/mhrd/files/statistics-new/ESG2016.pdf

Government of India. (2017). *Key Indicators: Household Consumer Expenditure in India.* Ministry of Statistics & Programme Implementation, New Delhi. https://mospi.gov.in/98-consumption-surveys-and-levels-living

Government of India. (2018a). *Handbook on social welfare statistics*. Ministry of Social Justice and Empowerment, New Delhi. https://socialjustice.gov.in/writereaddata/UploadFile/HANDBOOKSocialWelfareStatistice2018.pdf

Government of India. (2018b). *National Health Mission-Immunization Hand*. Ministry of Health & Family Welfare. https://nhm.gov.in/index1.php?lang=1&level=2&sublink id=824&lid=220

Government of India. (2019). Operational Guidelines of *Pradhan Mantri Kisan Samman Nidhi Yojana* (PM-Kisan). Department of Agriculture & Farmers Welfare. https://agricoop.nic.in/sites/default/files/operational_GuidePM.pdf

Granger, C. W. J., & Newbold, P. (1974). Spurious regression in econometrics. *Journal of Econometrics, 2*(2), 111–120. https://doi.org/10.1016/0304-4076(74)90034-7

Guhun, S. (1995). Social sector in the union budget. *Economic and Political Weekly, 30*(18 and 19), 620.

Gujarati, D. N. (2003). *Basic econometrics*. McGraw-Hill.

Gupta, A. K. (2014). Inclusive growth policy: An analysis of the performance of Indian government during the eleventh five-year plan. *International Journal of Business, Management and Social Sciences, 3*(5), 13–22. https://mpra.ub.uni-muenchen.de/80029/

Gupta, S. C. (2013). *Fundamentals of statistics* (7th ed.). Himalaya Publishing House.

Gupte, M. D., Ramachandran, V., & Mutatkar, R. K. (2001). Epidemiological profile of India: Historical and contemporary perspectives. *Journal of Biosciences, 26*(4), 437–464. https://doi.org/10.1007/BF02704746

Hanushek, E. A. (2013). Economic growth in developing countries: The role of human capital. *Economics of Education Review, 37*, 204–212. https://doi.org/10.1016/j.econedurev.2013.04.005

Harbison, H. F., & Myers, C. A. (1964). *Education, manpower and economic growth*. Oxford and IBH Publishing Cooperation.

Hari, K. S. (2003). *Economic growth and human development: Empirical evidence from the Indian states*. http://www.econ.yale.edu/egcentre/research.httm

Harnawala, K. G., & Iyer, S. S. (2012). Globalization and social sector in India. *International Journal of Social Economics, 39*(1), 39–51.

Hasan, M. A. (2001). Role of human capital in economic development: Some myths and realities. In *ESCAP, development planning in a market economy*. United Nations Publications.

Hasnul, A. G. (2016). *The effects of government expenditure on economic growth: The case of Malaysia* [Paper No. 71254]. Munich Personal RepEC Archive (MPRA) (pp. 1–15). https://mpra.ub.uni-muenchen.de/71254/

Haq, M. (1995). *Reflections on human development*. Oxford University Press.

Haq, K. (2011). *The pioneer of the human development approach of economic growth*. Columbia University Press.

Hegde, G. N. (2000). Community development in India: An overview. Paper presented at Japan seminar on comparative study on planning process of community development: Component of people's participation, August 21–26, 2000, Ulaanbaatar, Mongolia.

Hicks, N., & Streeten, P. (1979). Indicators of development: The search for a basic needs yardstick. *World Development, 7*(6), 567–580. https://doi.org/10.1016/0305-750X(79)90093-7

Hicks, N. L. (1987). The economic and economic growth. In G. Psacharopouloulos (Ed.), *Economics of education research and studies* (pp. 101–106). Pregnant Press.

Hirway, I. (2011, October 24–25). Ideating for an inclusive growth framework. In *Consultation on conceptualizing inclusive growth*. United Nations Development Programme and Planning Commission.

Howitt, P. (2005). Health, human capital, and economic growth: A Schumpeterian perspective. In G. Lopez-Casasnovas, B. Rivera, & L. Currais (Eds.), *Health and economic growth: Findings and policy implications* (pp. 19–40). Cambridge, MA: The MIT Press.

Ianchovichina, E., & Lundstrom, S. (2009). *Inclusive growth analytics: Framework and application.* Economic Policy and Debt Department, the World Bank. http://www.wds.worldbank.org/external/default/WDScontentserver/IW3P/IB/2009/03/03/000158349_20090303083943/Rendered/PDF/WPS4851.pdf

International Institute for Population Sciences (IIPS), & ICF. (2017). National Family Health Survey (NFHS-4), 2015-16: India. Mumbai: IIPS.

International Labour Organization. (2018). *Employment intensive investment programme (EIIP).* International Labour Organization Publications. https://www.ilo.org/global/topics/employment-promotion/eiip/lang--en/index.htm

Jain, A., & Runa, P. (2014). Social sector and economic reforms (with special reference to public health). *International Research Journal of Social Sciences, 3*(4), 38–42.

Jha, P., & Acharya, N. (2011). Expenditure on the Rural Economy in India's Budgets since the 1950s. *Review of Agrarian Studies, 1,* 2.

Joshi, S. (2006). Impact of economic reforms on social sector expenditure in India. *Economic and Political Weekly, 41*(4), 358–365.

Kadekodi, G., & Kulkarni, K. (2006). *Status of health and medical care in India: A macro perspective.* CMDR Monograph Series No. 38. Centre for Multi-disciplinary Development Research, 2002.

Kainth, G. S. (2013). *Diagnostic analysis of midday meal scheme in Rural Punjab* [Research Report]. Guru Arjun Dev Institute of Development Studies.

Kakwani, N., & Pernia, E. (2000). What is pro-poor growth? *Asian Development Review, 18*(1), 1–16.

Kalnad, N., Bose, N., & Menon, H. (2017). *India's great healthcare challenge, also an opportunity.* https://www.hindustantimes.com/india-news/india-s-great-healthcare-challenge-and-opportunity/story-eB691Pj889x57TYo8MobaM.html

Kannan, K. P. (2007). *Informal economy and social security – Two major initiatives in India.* National Commission for Enterprises in the Unorganized Sector. http://nceuis.nic.in/PDFFiles/InformalEconomy.pdf

Kannan, K. P. (2007). Interrogating inclusive growth: Some reflections on exclusionary growth and prospects for inclusive development in India. *Journal of Labour Economics, 50*(1), 17–46.

Kapila, U. (2010). *Indian economy since independence.* Academic Foundation.

Karunaratne, G. (1976). The failure of the Community Development Programme in India. *Community Development Journal, 11*(2), 95–119. https://doi.org/10.1093/cdj/11.2.95

Kaul, K. (2015). *Swachh Bharat Abhiyan: Prospects and challenges.* Centre for Budget and Governance Accountability. http://www.cbgaindia.org/wp-content/uploads/2016/01/Swachh-Bharat-Abhiyan.pdf

Kaur, B., & Misra, S. (2003). Social sector expenditure and attainments: An analysis of Indian states. *RBI Bulletin, 24*(1 and 2), 105–143. https://www.rbi.org.in/Scripts/BS_ViewBulletin.aspx?Id=21472.

Kaur, H., Misra, S., & Suresh, A. K. (2013). Cyclicality of social sector expenditures: Evidence from Indian states. *Reserve Bank of India Occasional Papers, 34* (1 and 2), 1–36. https://rbidocs.rbi.org.in/rdocs/Content/PDFs/01EDE296E8C476DF4B5BA345D0DA9173C61B.PDF

Kaushik, K. K., Klein, K. K., & Arbenser, N. L. (2008). The relationship between health status and health care expenditure in developing hill economy: An economic approach. In A. K. Thakur & M. A. Salam (Eds.), *Economics of health and education* (pp. 32–46). Delhi: Deep and Deep Publications.

Khera, R. (2011). India's public distribution system: Utilisation and impact. *Journal of Development Studies, 47*(7), 1038–1060. https://doi.org/10.1080/00220388.2010.506917

Klasen, S. (2010). *Measuring and monitoring inclusive growth: Multiple definitions, open questions and some constructive proposals* [Working Paper Series 102018]. Asian Development Bank Sustainable Development. https://www.adb.org/sites/default/files/publication/27838/ewp-102018.pdf

Kolawole, B. O. (2016). Government spending and inclusive-growth relationship in Nigeria: An empirical investigation. *Zagreb International Review of Economics and Business, 19*(2), 33–56. https://doi.org/10.1515/zireb-2016-0007

Krishna, D., & Swaminathan, M. S. (1971). *The new agricultural strategy – The vehicle of the green revolution in India.* New Heights.

Krishnan, V. (2010). *Constructing an area-based socioeconomic index: A principal components analysis approach. Community.* Early Child Development Mapping Project. https://ecdmp.org/publications/constructing-an-area-based-socioeconomic-index-a-principal-components-analysis-approach/

Kumar, A., & Das, K. C. (2014). Drinking water and sanitation facility in India and its linkages with diarrhoea among children under five: Evidence from recent data. *International Journal of Humanities and Social Sciences Invention, 3*(4), 50–60.

Kumar, D., & Kumar, S. (2008). Education and health status of India. In R. Sen (Ed.), *Social sector development in India* (pp. 531–561). Delhi: Deep and Deep Publications.

Kumar, P., & Sharma, P. N. (2008). Progress of human development in India – Issues relating to education and health. In A. K. Thakur & M. A. Salam (Eds.), *Economics of health and education* (pp. 350–363). Delhi: Deep and Deep Publications.

Kumar, S. (2012). Recent reforms in education in India – Achievements and unfinished tasks. *International Journal of Social Sciences & Interdisciplinary Research, 1*(8), 82–94.

Kumari, D. (2015). Export-Led Growth in Select Asian Economies. Ph. D. Thesis, Punjab School of Economics, Guru Nanak Dev University, India. http://hdl.handle.net/10603/273931.

Kumari, P., & Yadav, S. (2008). Economics of education and health in Bihar. In A. K. Thakur & M. A. Salam (Eds.), *Economics of health and education* (pp. 491–505). Delhi: Deep and Deep Publications.

Kundu, A., & Varghese, K. (2010). *Regional Inequality and Inclusive growth in India under globalization: Identification of lagging states for strategic Intervention* [Oxfam Indian Working Papers, VI]. Institution of Human Development. http://www.ihdindia.org/IHD-Oxfamworkingpaper-PDF/I.%20Regional%20Inequality%20and%20Inclusive%20Growth%20in%20India%20under%20Globalization-Identification%20of%20Lagging%20States%20for%20Strategic%20Intervention.pdf

Kuroda, H. (2006). Investing in infrastructure: Key to economic growth. *ASCI Journal of Management, 35*(1 and 2), 1–6.

Lakshminarayanan, S. (2011). Role of government in public health: Current scenario in India and future scope. *Journal of Family and Community Medicine, 18*(1), 26–30. https://doi.org/10.4103/1319-1683.78635

Lal, M. (2014). *Education – The inclusive growth strategy for the economically and socially disadvantaged in society.* https://www.researchgate.net/publication/242197750_EducationThe_Inclusive_Growth_Strategy_for_theeconomically_and_socially_disadvantaged_in_the_Society

Lalvani, M. (2010). Bharat Nirman: A stocktaking exercise. *Economic and Political Weekly, 45*(17), 21–24.

Lange, O. (1942). The foundations of welfare economics. *Econometrica, 10*(3–4), 215–228. https://doi.org/10.2307/1905465

Lawania, K. V. (1992). *Rural development in India.* New Delhi: Ashish Publishing House.

Leech, N. L., Barrett, K. C., & Morgan, G. A. (2014). *SPSS for intermediate statistics: Use and interpretation.* Lawrence Erlbaum Associates Publishers.

Lipton, M., & Gaag, V. J. (1993). Including the poor. Washington, D.C: World Bank. https://openknowledge.worldbank.org/handle/10986/5977

Lucas, R. E. (1988). On the mechanics of economic development. *Journal of Monetary Economics, 21*(1), 3–16.

Madgavkar, A., Ellingrud, K., & Krishnan, M. (2016). The economic benefits of gender parity. In *Standard social innovation review*. McKinsey Global Institute. https://ssir.org/articles/entry/the_economic_benefits_of_gender_parity

Maheshwari, T. (2012, August–September). Social sector scenario of India after the economic reforms. *Socio-Economic Voices , 49*(4), 50–55.

Malhotra, N. K., John, H., Shaw, M., & Oppenheim, P. (2006). *Marketing research: An applied orientation*. Pearson Education.

Malone, C. C., & Johnson, S. E. (1971). The intensive agricultural development program in India. *Agricultural Economics Research, 23*(2), 25–35.

Malthus, T. (1798). *An essay on the principle of population*. Printed for J. Johnson in St. Paul's Church Yard, London.

Malviya, S. (2018). *Connectivity and well-being may get priority over food in rural India*. https://economictimes.indiatimes.com/news/economy/policy/connectivity-and-well-being-may-get-priority-over-food-in-bharat/articleshow/63493897.cms

Manap, N. M. A., & Ismail, N. W. (2019). Food security and economic growth. *International Journal of Modern Trends in Social Sciences, 2*(8), 108–118.

Mankad, P. (2013). *Rajiv Gandhi national drinking water mission – national rural drinking water program* [Presentation]. Ministry of Drinking Water and Sanitation, National Framework, New Delhi.

Marx, K. (1867). *Capital, I (English translation)*. Allen & Unwin, 1938.

Mathur, B. P. (2014). India's failed development new model rooted on cultural ethos. *Mainstream, LII*(5). https://www.mainstreamweekly.net/article5063.html

Mazumdar, K. (2001). Measuring human well-being of the countries: Achievement and improvement indices. In B. Ray (Ed.), *Welfare, choice and development, essays in honour of Professor Amartya Sen* (pp. 56–85). Kanishka Publishers.

Mello, L. D., & Dutz, M. A. (2012). *Promoting inclusive growth: Challenges and policies*. https://www.oecd-ilibrary.org/economics/promoting-inclusive-growth_9789264168305-en. OECD Publishing

Menon, P. M. (2009). Public private partnership in housing. In *NAREDCO conference*. Micro Housing Finance Corporation.

McKinley, T. (2010). *Inclusive growth criteria and indicators: An inclusive growth index for diagnosis of country progress* [Working Paper Series 102049]. Asian Development Bank Sustainable Development. https://www.adb.org/sites/default/files/publication/27678/wp102049.pdf

Meade, J. E. (1961). *A neo-classical theory of economic growth*. London: Allen & Unwin.

Mehrotra, S. (2005). Human capital or human development? Search for a knowledge paradigm for education and development. *Economic and Political Weekly, 40*(4), 300–306.

Mercy, W. J. (2007). *Social sector public outlay and social development – An inter state comparison* [Doctoral thesis]. University of Calicut. http://hdl.handle.net/10603/20501

Mojumdar, S. (2013). *National rural drinking water programme (NRDWP)* [Presentation]. Ministry of Drinking Water and Sanitation.

Mondal, P. (1993). *The integrated rural development programme*. http://www.yourarticle. http://library.com/sociology/integrated-rural-development-programme-irdp/31993

Mooij, J., & Dev, S. M. (2004). Social sector priorities: An analysis of budgets and expenditure in India in the 1990s. *Development Policy Review, 22*(1), 97–120. https://doi.org/10.1111/j.1467-8659.2004.00240.x

Morris, D. (1996). Professor offers a fresh approach to measuring the condition of the world's poor. Brown University. https://www.brown.edu/Administration/News_Bureau/1996-97/96-009i.html

Morris, D., & Alpin, B. M. M. (1982). *Measuring the condition of India's Poor*. Promilla & Co.

Mukhopadhaya, A., & Saha, N. (2005). *Poverty alleviation programmes in India*. The independent commission on development and health in India. VHAI.

Naidu, K. M., Rao, M. K. L., & Naidu, Mahesh. K. (2008). Education, health and human development: Need for secure linkages. In A. K. Thakur & M. A. Salam (Eds.), *Economics of health and education* (pp. 30–49). Delhi: Deep and Deep Publications.

Naqvi, S. N. H. (2015). *Economics of development: Toward inclusive growth*. Sage Publishing House.

Nath, A. (2011). India's progress toward achieving the millennium development goals. *Indian Journal of Community Medicine, 36*(2), 85–92. https://doi.org/10.4103/0970-0218.84118

Nayak, D. K., & Behera, N. R. (2014). Changing household size in India: An interstate comparison. *Transactions, 36*(1), 1–18.

Nayak, P. K., Chattopadhyay, S. K., Kumar, A. V., & Dhanya, V. (2010). Inclusive growth and regional dimension. *Reserve Bank of India Occasional Papers, 31*(3), 91–156.

Nayak, P., & Mishra, S. K. (2014). *A state level analysis of the status of social sector in India*. https://mpra.ub.uni-muenchen.de/id/eprint/58144.

Nayar, B. R. (1960). Community development programme – its political impact. *Economic Weekly*, September 17, 1401–1410.

Nkoro, E., & Uko, A. K. (2016). Autoregressive distributed lag (ARDL) cointegration technique: Application and interpretation. *Journal of Statistical and Econometric Methods, 5*(4), 3.

Noga, J., & Wolbring, G. (2012). The economic and social benefits and the barriers of providing people with disabilities accessible clean water and sanitation. *Sustainability, 4*(11), 3023–3041. https://doi.org/10.3390/su4113023

Nugent, J. B., & Yotopoulos, P. A. (1979). What has orthodox development economics learned from recent experience? *World Development, 7*(6), 541–554. https://doi.org/10.1016/0305-750X(79)90091-3

O'Brien, R. M. (2007). A caution regarding rules of thumb for variance inflation factors. *Quality and Quantity, 41*(5), 673–690. https://doi.org/10.1007/s11135-006-9018-6

Organization for Economic Cooperation and Development (OECD). (2001). *The wellbeing of Nations*. OECD.

Organization for Economic Cooperation and Development (OECD). (2006). *Promoting pro-poor growth: Key policy messages*. OECD.

Organization of Economic Cooperation and Development (OECD). (2008). *Handbook on constructing composite indicators methodology and user guide*. http://www.oecd.org/publishing/corrigenda. France.

Organization for Economic Cooperation and Development (OECD). (2009). *Promoting pro-poor growth: Employment and social protection*. OECD.

Organization for Economic Cooperation and Development (OECD). (2011). *Compendium of OECD wellbeing indicators*. OECD.

Organization for Economic Cooperation and Development (OECD). (2012). *India's sustaining high and inclusive growth*. Better Policies Series. OECD.

Organization for Economic Cooperation and Development (OECD). (2013). *Development co-operation report: Ending poverty*. OECD.

Pal, R., Gandhi, M., & Vidyapith, K. (2018). *Understanding MGNREGA: A scheme supporting economic development*. https://www.researchgate.net/publication/322796483_Understanding_MGNREGA_A_Scheme_Supporting_Economic_Development

Pal, S. P., & Pant, D. K. (1993). An alternative human development index. *Margin, 25*(2), Part II, 8–22.

Palanivel, T. (2011, October 24–25). Ideating for an inclusive growth framework In *Consultation on conceptualizing inclusive growth*. United Nations Development Programme and Planning Commission.

Palanivel, T., & Unal, F. G. (2010). *Inclusive growth and policies: The Asian experience* [Working Paper]. UNDP, New York.

Palaniyandi, M. (2013). *GIS for epidemic control in India*. http://www.geospatialworld.net

Palayi, A., & Priyaranjan, N. (2018, January). Affordable housing in India, RBI [Bulletin]. Reserve Bank of India. https://rbidocs.rbi.org.in/rdocs/Bulletin/PDFs/0SPGAC73E C4C3FD4BD4E392E767A5CC5D5B2.PDF

Panchamukhi, P. R. (2000). Social impact of economic reforms in India: A critical appraisal. *Economic and Political Weekly, 35*(10), 836–847.

Panda, R. K. (2016). *Socially exclusion and inequality: Opportunities in agenda 2030*. European Union, World Vision, and Welthungerhilfe. http:// www.sustainablede-velopment.un.org/content/documents/11145Social%20exclusion%20and%20 Inequality-Stud %20by%20GCAP%20India%20.pdf

Pande, R. (2003). Can mandate political representation increase policy influence for disadvantaged minorities? *American Economic Review, 93*(4), 1132–1151. https://doi.org/10.1257/000282803769206232

Pandey, T. M. (2011). Globalisation and social transformation in India: Theorising the transition. *International Journal of Sociology and Anthropology, 3*(8), 253–260.

Park, K. (1994). *Preventive and social medicine* (13th ed.). Banarsi Das Bharat Publishers.

Parshad, C. A. H., Sinha, K. N., & Khan, A. R. (2013). Performance of major social sector schemes: A sample survey report [Working Paper No. 3/2013-DEA]. New Delhi: Department of Economic Affairs. http://dea.gov.in/sites/default/files/Working%20 Paper%20No.%203-2013-DEA.pdf

Patel, A. (2010). Rural Development Projects and Programs. *Kurukshetra- A Journal on Rural Development, 58*(3), 09-15.

Pathak, C. (2005). Expansion of social sector and economic development. In R. K. Sen (Eds.), *Social sector development in India* (pp. 44–55). Delhi: Deep and Deep Publications.

Pattayat, S. S., & Rani, P. (2017). Social sector development and economic growth in Haryana. *Journal of Economics and Economic Educational Research, 18*(3), 1–13.

Pesaran, M. H., & Shin, Y. (1999). An autoregressive distributed lag modelling approach to cointegration analysis. In S. Strom (Ed.), *Econometrics and economic theory in the 20th century: The Ragnar Frisch centennial symposium* (pp. 371-413). Cambridge University Press.

Pesaran, M. H., Shin, Y., & Smith, R. J. (1996). *Testing for the existence of a long-run relationship* [Cambridge Working Papers in Economics]. Faculty of Economics, The University of Cambridge. http://www.econ.cam.ac.uk/cje/people/AllStaff/pesaran/ cwp512.pdf

Pesaran, M. H., Shin, Y., & Smith, R. J. (2001). Bounds testing approaches to the analysis of level relationships. *Journal of Applied Econometrics, 16*(3), 289–326. https://doi.org/10.1002/jae.616

Pigou, A. C. (1920). *The economics of welfare*. Macmillan.

Ponmuthusaravanan, P., & Ravi, G. (2014). Inclusive growth, poverty, and social sector development in India. *International Journal of Management and Development Studies, 3*(2), 1–8.

Prabhu, K. S. (1996). Social sector in economic development [Presentation]. Presented at the 79th annual conference of the Indian Economic Association at Jiwaji University, Gwalior.

Prabhu, K. S. (1997). *Social sector expenditures in India: Trends and implications* [Background Paper]. UNDP.

Prabhu, K. S. (2001). *Economic reforms and social sector development: A study of two Indian States*. SAGE.

Prabhu, K. S. (2005). Social sectors and economic development. In R. Sen (Ed.), *Social sector development in India* (pp. 3–25). Deep and Deep Publications.

Prabhu, K. S., & Chatterjee, S. (1993). *Social expenditure and human development: A study of Indian states* [Development Research Group, No. 6]. Reserve Bank of India.

Prabhu, K. S., & Kamdar, S. (2002). Economic growth and social attainment: The role of development strategy. In *Reforming India's social sector*. Social Science Press.

Pradhan, P. (2004). Social exclusion of the weaker sections: A Socio-Legal approach. *International Research Journal of Social Science & Humanities*, *1*(1), 62–65.

Pradhan, J. P., & Puttuswamaiah, S. (2005). *Trends and pattern of technology acquisition in Indian organized manufacturing: An interindustry exploration*. Institute of Development Research, Gujarat https://ideas.repec.org/p/ess/wpaper/id452.html

Psacharopoulos, G. (1994). Returns to investment in education: A global update *World Development*. *22*(9), 1325–1343. https://doi.org/10.1016/0305-750X(94)90007-8

Puri, V. K., & Mishra, S. K. (2013). *Indian economy – Its development experience* (31st ed.). Himalaya Publications.

Purohit, B. C. (2015). The efficiency of social sector expenditure in India. In H. S. Rout & P. Mishra (Eds.), *Social sector in India: Issues and challenges* (pp. 25–59). UK: Cambridge Scholars Publishing.

Radhakrishna, R., & Panda, M. (2006). *Macroeconomics of poverty reduction: India case study*. Indira Gandhi Institute of Development Research. http://oii.igidr.ac.in:8080/xmlui/handle/2275/180

Rai, P. (2017). Women's participation in electoral politics in India: Silent feminisation. *South Asia Research*, *37*(1), 58–77. https://doi.org/10.1177/0262728016675529

Rajaraman, I. (2001, May 10). Expenditure reform. *The Economic Times*. https://economictimes.indiatimes.com/expenditure-reform/articleshow/7322913.cms

Ramos, R. A., Ranieri, R., & Lammens, J. W. (2013). *Mapping inclusive growth, international policy center for inclusive growth* [Working Paper No. 105]. International Policy Centre for Inclusive Growth. https://ideas.repec.org/p/ipc/wpaper/105.html

Rani, S. A. (2008). Does a mother's participation in economic activity influence the nutrition and health status of children? In A. K. Thakur & M. A. Salam (Eds.), *Economics of health and education* (pp. 310–333). Delhi: Deep and Deep Publications.

Ranis, G., & Stewart, F. (2000). Strategies for success in human development. *Journal of Human Development*, *1*(I), 40–69.

Ranis, G., Stewart, F., & Ramirez, A. (2000). Economic growth and human development. *World Development*, *28*(2), 197–219. https://doi.org/10.1016/S0305-750X(99)00131-X

Ranjan, A. K. (2014). *A study on the status of integrated child development service (ICDS)*. http://www.countcurrent.org

Ranjan Padhi, S. R. (2016). Overcoming exclusion and marginalisation in education through inclusive approaches: Challenges and vision of Arunachal Pradesh in India. *International Journal of Social Science and Humanity*, *6*(4), 256–261. https://doi.org/10.7763/IJSSH.2016.V6.654

Rao, C. H. H. (1964). Intensive agricultural district program – An appraisal. *Economic Weekly*, November 28, 1887–1897.

Rao, V. K. R. V. (1964). *Education and economic development*. National Council of Educational Research and Training.

Rao, M. P. (2002). *Social security for the unorganized in India – An approach paper*. http://www.eldis.org/fulltext/raosocial.pdf

Rastogi, S. A. (2011). *Social welfare state: New dimensions of state*. http://www.lawyersclubindia.com/articles/Social-Welfare-State-New-Dimensions-Of-State--3706.asp#.UgIXENJQG3o

Rauniyar, G., & Kanbur, R. (2010). *Inclusive development – two papers on conceptualization, application, and the ADB perspective* [Working Paper No. WP 2010-01]. Department of Applied Economics and Management. Cornell University.

Ravallion, M., & Chen, S. (2003). Measuring pro-poor growth. *Economics Letters, 78*(1), 93–99. https://doi.org/10.1016/S0165-1765(02)00205-7

Rawat, D., Aggarwal, K., & Dev, M. (2008). Status of public health and its financing in India. In A. K. Thakur & M. A. Salam (Eds.), *Economics of health and education* (pp. 167–184). Delhi: Deep and Deep Publications.

Rath, N. (1985). Garibi Hatao: Can IRDP do it? *Economic and Political Weekly, 20*(6), 238–246.

Romer, P. M. (1986). Increasing returns and long-run growth. *Journal of Political Economy, 94*(5), 1002–1037. https://doi.org/10.1086/261420

Rosen, S. (1989). Human capital. In J. Eatwell, M. Milgate, & P. Newman (Eds.), *The new Palgrave Dictionary of Economics* (Vol. 2, pp. 681–693). Macmillan Press.

Roy, J. (2014). IRDP to NRLM: A brief review of Rural Development initiatives in India. *International Journal of Humanities and Social Science Invention, 3*(4), 05–08.

Rynn, J. (2001). *The power to create wealth: A system based theory of the rise and decline of the great powers in the 20th century*. University of New York. www.globalmakeover.com/sites/economicreconstruction.com/static/JonRynn/NeoclassicalGrowthTheory.pdf

Sachdeva, S. (2013). *Education scenario and needs in India: Building a perspective for 2025*. Planning Commission. http://gender.careinternationalwikis.org/_media/building_perspective_for_marginalised_final.pdf

Sadhu, A. N., & Mahajan, R. K. (1985). *Technological change and agricultural development in India*. Himalaya Publishing House.

Sagar, A. D., & Najam, A. (1998). The human development index: A critical review. *Ecological Economics, 25*(3), 249–264. https://doi.org/10.1016/S0921-8009(97)00168-7

Sagar, M. A. (2018). Housing for all. *Hindustan Times*, March, 21. https://www.hindu-stantimes.com/analysis/housing-for-all-can-only-be-a-reality-if-india-adopts-these-steps/story-kHXmCKHymxU6mRQuYi1WsL.html

Samra, S., Crowley, J., & Fawzi, M. C. S. (2011). Assessing equitable access to water through the Punjab rural water supply and sanitation project. *Health and Human Rights*. https://www.hhrjournal.org/2013/08/the-right-to-water-in-rural-punjab-assessing-equitable-access-to-water-through-the-punjab-rural-water-supply-and-sanitation-project/

Sangeeth, S. (2016). Inclusive development of marginalized population through social policy initiatives – Reflections to future development. *Paripex – Indian Journal of Research, 5*(3), 278–282.

Sanyal, S. (2014). *NREGA: Achievements so far*. http://www.sabrangp.comnews2014mner-gaAnnexe%201%20-%20RTI%201st%20Tranche.pdf

Sarma, J. S. (1981). *Growth and equity: Policies and implementation in Indian agriculture* [Research Reports 28]. International Food Policy Research Institute. https://ideas.repec.org/p/fpr/resrep/28.html

Sarma, S. A. E. (2005 April 2–8). Social sector allocations. *Economic and Political Weekly, 40*(14), 1413–1417.

Saxena, N. C., & Farrington, J. (2003). *Trends and prospects for poverty reduction in rural India: Context and options* [Working Paper 198]. Overseas Development Institute. https://cdn.odi.org/media/documents/2438.pdf

Schultz, T. W. (1961). Investment in human Capital. *American Economic Review, 51*(1), 1–17.

Schumpeter, J. A. (1934). *The theory of economic development: An inquiry into profits, Capital, credit, interest and the business cycle*. Transaction Publishing.

Schumpeter, J. A. (1942). *Capitalism, socialism, and democracy*. Harper & Brothers. http://www.ssrn.com/paper=1496200

Sekhar, C. C., Indrayan, A., & Gupta, S. M. (1991). Development of an index of need for health resources for the Indian states using factor analysis. *International Journal of Epidemiology, 20*(1), 246–250. https://doi.org/10.1093/ije/20.1.246

Sen, A. (1989). Development as capabilities expansion. *Journal of Development Planning, 19*, 41–58.

Sen, A. (1992). Radical needs and moderate reforms. In J. Dreze & A. Sen (Eds.), *Indian development: Selected regional perspectives* (pp. 1–32). Oxford University Press.

Sen, A. (1997). Editorial: Human capital and human capability. *World Development, 25*(12), 1959–1961. https://doi.org/10.1016/S0305-750X(97)10014-6

Sen, A. (2000). *Development as freedom*. Oxford University Press.

Shariff, A., Ghosh, K. P., & Mondal, K. S. (2002a). *Indian public expenditures on social sector and poverty alleviation programmes during the 1990s* [Working Paper 169]. National Council of Applied Economic Research, Human Development Division. Centre for Development Economics, Delhi School of Economics. http://www.cdedse.org/pdf/work169.pdf

Shariff, A., Ghosh, K. P., & Mondal, K. S. (2002b). State-Adjusted Public Expenditure on Social Sector and Poverty Alleviation Programmes. *Economic and Political Weekly, 37*(8), 713-720. https://www.jstor.org/stable/4411972

Sharma, A. D. (2014). Understanding the social sector, economic growth, social development, and economic development: Interrelationship and linkages. *Economic Affairs, 59*(4), 585–590. https://doi.org/10.5958/0976-4666.2014.00029.1

Sharma, S. (2017, August 29). India's public health system in CRISIS: Too many patients, not enough doctors. *Hindustan Times*. https://www.hindustantimes.com/india-news/india-s-public-health-system-in-crisis-too-many-patients-not-enough-doctors/story-UqDY52azmH9kYhCMg91jxI.html

Sharma, A. (2018). Saving from Direct Benefit Transfer pegged at Rs. 83000 crores. *The Economic Times*, May 23. https://economictimes.indiatimes.com/industry/banking/finance/banking/savings-from-direct-benefit-transfer-pegged-at-rs-83000-crore/articleshow/63423528.cms?from=mdr

Sharma, R. C., & Kumar, N. (1993). Regional disparities in the levels of socio-economic development in India. In R. S. Tripathi & R. P. Tewari (Eds.), *Regional disparities and development in India* (pp. 61–80). Ashish Publishing House.

Shivangi, S. (2017). *Impact of social security on economic growth in India*. Symbiosis Law School. http://crsgpp.nujs.edu/wp-content/uploads/2017/02/Article-10-Shilpa.pdf

Shukla, S. S., & Mishra, A. (2013). Employment generation and poverty alleviation in developing countries-challenges and opportunities special reference to India. *IOSR Journal of Business and Management, 11*(4), 18–23.

Singh, B. D. (1966). The role of agriculture in economic development. In J. G. Winant & R. E. Stoner (Eds.), *Economies of development with special reference to India* (pp. 30–71). Asia Publishing.

Smith, A. (1776). *An enquiry into the nature and causes of the wealth of Nations*. The Modern Library, 1937.

Smith, G. (2018). Step away from stepwise. *Journal of Big Data, 5*(1), 1–12. https://doi.org/10.1186/s40537-018-0143-6

Solow, R. M. (1956). A contribution to the theory of economic growth. *Quarterly Journal of Economics, 70*(1), 65–94. https://doi.org/10.2307/1884513

Srinivasan, A., & Verma, S. (1993). Human development: Concepts and international standards. In R. Dutt (Ed.), *Human development and economic growth* (pp. 42–48). Deep and Deep Publication.

Srivastava, R. (2013). A social protection floor for India, *Executive summary*, A Joint United Nations Study. International Labour Organization. https://www.ilo.org/wcmsp5/groups/public/---ed_protect/---soc_sec/documents/publication/wcms_230854.pdf

Sudhakar, S., & Mose, A. G. (2005). Budgetary Expenditure on the Social Sector. In R. K. Sen (Eds.) *Social sector development in India* (ed. pp. 66-98). Delhi: Deep and Deep Publications.

Sunkari, S. (2014). Poverty alleviation programmes of rural India: A comprehensive policy analysis. *Economic Affairs, 59*(4), 539.

Suryanarayana, M. H. (2013). *Inclusive growth: A sustainable perspective*. United Nations Development Programme. https://www.undp.org/sites/g/files/zskgke326/files/migration/in/inclusive-growth--a-sustainable-perspective.pdf

Sushmita. (2015). MGNREGA: A review. *International Journal of Arts, Humanities and Management Studies, 01*(7), 18–26.

Swan, T. W. (1956). Economic growth and capital accumulation. *Economic Record, 32*(2), 334–361. https://doi.org/10.1111/j.1475-4932.1956.tb00434.x

Taneja, M. L., & Myers, R. M. (2000). *Economic of development and planning* (9th ed.). Vishal Publication.

The Economic Times. (2016, July 3). *IRDAI asks insurance companies details of social sector business.* https://economictimes.indiatimes.com/news/irdai-asks-insurance-companies-details-of-social-sector-business/articleshow/53030045.cms.

The Financial Express. (2018, March 6). *More inclusive growth: Jump in CRISIL inclusion index is good news for the government.* https://www.financialexpress.com/opinion/more-inclusive-growth-jump-in-crisis-inclusion-index-is-good-news-for-government/1088564/

The Hindu. (2016, December 27). *Empowering women in Punjab.* https://www.thehindu.com/news/national/other-states/Empowering-women-in-Punjab/article16994306.ece.

Thirlwall, A. P. (2006). *Growth and development with special reference to developing countries* (8th ed.). Palgrave Macmillan.

Thomas, S., & Chittedi, K. R. (2015). Inclusiveness in poverty reduction in India: A great leap forward? *Journal of Stock & Forex Trading, 04*(1), 1–2.

Thorat, S. (2011, October 24–25). Conceptualizing inclusive growth and addressing exclusion. In *Consultation on conceptualizing inclusive growth*. United Nations Development Programme and Planning Commission. https://www.undp.org/india/publications/consultation-conceptualizing-inclusive-growth

Thorat, S., & Dubey, A. (2013). *How inclusive has growth been in India during 1993/94, 2009/10? Implications for XII plan strategy.* United Nations Development Programme. https://www.undp.org/india/publications/how-inclusive-has-growth-been-india-during-1993/94-2009/10-implications-xii-plan-strategy

Thorat, S., & Senapati, C. (2006). *Reservation policy in India: Dimensions and issues* [Working Paper Series, I, No. 2]. Indian Institute of Dalit Studies.

Tilak, J. B. G. (1995). Costs and Financing of Education in India: A Review of Issues, Problems, and Prospects, Thiruvananthapuram: Research Project on Strategies and Financing of Human Development, Centre for Development Studies.

Tilak, J. B. G. (1987a). *Economics of inequality in education*. SAGE/Institute of Economic Growth.

Tilak, J. B. G. (1987b). *Public subsidies in the education sector in India*. Presented at the World Bank Seminar.

Tilak, J. B. G. (2005). *Post-Elementary Education, Poverty, and Development in India*. Working Paper Series No. 6. Centre of African Studies. The University of Edinburgh. https://www.gov.uk/research-for-development-outputs/post-elementary-education-poverty-and-development-in-india-post-basic-education-and-training-working-paper-series-n-6

Tilak, J. B. G. (2007a). Post-elementary education, poverty, and development in India [Working Paper Series No. 6]. Centre of African Studies, University of Edinburgh

(*International Journal of Educational Development, 27*(4), 435–445. https://doi.org/10.1016/j.ijedudev.2006.09.018).

Tilak, J. B. G. (2007b). Inclusive growth and education: On the approach to the eleventh plan. *Economic and Political Weekly, 42*(38), 3872–3877.

Todaro, M. P., & Smith, S. C. (2003). *Economic development* (8th ed.). Pearson Education.

Tripathi, S. (2013). Is urban economic growth inclusive in India? *Margin, 7*(4), 507–539. https://doi.org/10.1177/0973801013500135

Trivedi, P. (2005). Social sector development and economic growth. In R. K. Sen (Eds.), *Social sector development in India* (pp. 56–67). Delhi: Deep and Deep Publications.

Tsujita, Y. (2005). *Economic reforms and social sector expenditure: A study of 15 Indian states 1980–81 and 1999–2000.* [Discussion Paper No. 31, pp. 20–23]. Institute of Development Economics.

Tulsidhar, V. B., & Sarma, J. V. (1993). *Public expenditure medical care at birth and infant mortality: A comparative study of states in India.* SAGE.

Uma, S. (2013). Midday meal scheme and primary education in India: Quality issues. *International Journal of Scientific and Research Publications, 3*(11), 1–3.

United Nations. (1995). *World summit for economic and social development.* Department of Economics and Social Affairs.

United Nations Development Programme (UNDP). (1990). *Human development report – Concept and measurement report.* Oxford University Press.

United Nations Development Programme (UNDP). (1995). *Human development report – Gender and human development.* Oxford University Press.

United Nations Development Programme (UNDP). (1997). *Human development report – Poverty eradication.* Oxford University Press.

United Nations Development Programme (UNDP). (1998). *Human development report – Consumption and sustainable development.* Oxford University Press.

United Nations Development Programme (UNDP). (2000). *Human development report – Human rights and development.* Oxford University Press.

United Nations Development Programme (UNDP). (2002). *Human development report – Deepening democracy in a fragmented World.* Oxford University Press.

United Nations Development Programme (UNDP). (2013). *Human development report – The rose of the south: Human progress in diverse world.* Oxford University Press.

United Nations Development Programme (UNDP). (2018). *Human development report – Human development indices and indicators: Statistical update.* Oxford University Press.

United Nations International Children's Education Fund. (2011a). *Integrated child development services (ICDS).* Social Policy, Planning, Monitoring, and Evaluation.

United Nations International Children's Education Fund. (2011b). *National rural health mission (NRHM).* Centre for Budget and Governance Accountability.

Varma, A. (2012). *Social sector.* http://www.pwc.com

Venkat, V. (2016, October 4). World Bank estimates show fall in India's poverty rate. *The Hindu.* https://www.thehindu.com/news/national/world-bank-estimates-show-fall-in-indias poverty-rate/article7727591.ece

Wadhwa, J. K. (2013). Growth of the public expenditures in India and its impact on the deficits. *IOSR Journal of Humanities and Social Science, 14*(4), 1–13. https://doi.org/10.9790/1959-1440113

World Bank. (2006). *India – inclusive growth and service delivery: Building on India's success* [Development Policy Review]. World Bank. https://documents.worldbank.org/en/publication/documents-reports/documentdetail/440311468011998205/india-inclusive-growth-and-service-delivery-building-on-indias-success

World Bank. (2008). *The growth report: Strategies for sustained growth and inclusive development.* World Bank. https://openknowledge.worldbank.org/handle/10986/6507.

World Health Organization. (2018). *Low-quality healthcare is increasing the burden of illness and health costs globally.* WHO. https://www.who.int/news-room/detail/05-09-2018-low-quality-healthcare-is-increasing-the-burden-of-illness-and-health-costs-globally

Water and Sanitation Program (WSP). (2011). *Flagship report economic impacts of inadequate sanitation in India.* World Bank. https://www.wsp.org/sites/wsp.org/files/publications/WSP-Flagship-Economic-Impacts-of-Inadequate-Sanitation-India.pdf

Xiao, D., Feng, X., & Shiqiang, Z. (2014). A simple and practical method of calculating the Gini coefficient. *Progress in Applied Mathematics, 8*(1), 29–33.

Yesudian, C. A. K. (2007). Poverty alleviation programmes in India: A social audit. *Indian Journal of Medical Research, 126*(4), 364–373.

Yotopoulos, P. A., & Nugent, J. B. (1976). *Economics of development empirical investigation.* Harper & Row Publishers.

Zhuang, J., & Ali, A. (2009). *Inequality and inclusive growth in developing Asia.* Asian Development Bank. https://www.adb.org/sites/default/files/publication/28302/inequality-inclusive-growth-developing-asia.pdf

Zohir, S. (2011, October 24–25). Ideating for an inclusive growth framework. In *Consultation on conceptualizing inclusive growth.* United Nations Development Programme and Planning Commission.

Index

Printed in the USA
CPSIA information can be obtained
at www.ICGtesting.com
JSHW011728210923
48932JS00003B/17